Contents

Scope and Sequence

		Social Studies Skills		Writing Skills
		Reading Strategies	Using Visuals	
Unit 1 Early Civilizations	Lesson 1	Preview	Use a timeline (Part 1)	Make a plan
	Lesson 2	Predict	Use a timeline (Part 2)	
Unit 2 The Classical World	Lesson 1	Visualize	Use a map key	Write a paragraph
	Lesson 2	Ask questions	Use a compass rose	
Unit 3 The Middle Ages	Lesson 1	Monitor comprehension	Read a map	Make an outline
	Lesson 2	Understand chronological order	Use a map scale	
Unit 4 The Renaissance	Lesson 1	Reread	Use physical maps	Write a first draft
	Lesson 2	Use selective attention	Use different types of maps	
Unit 5 Early United States	Lesson 1	Use what you know	Read a chart (Part 1)	Write a three-paragraph essay
	Lesson 2	Look for cause and effect	Read a chart (Part 2)	
Unit 6 A New Nation	Lesson 1	Compare and contrast	Read a graph (Part 1)	Revise a three-paragraph essay
	Lesson 2	Draw conclusions	Read a graph (Part 2)	
Unit 7 The Modern World	Lesson 1	Summarize	Use print resources	Edit and publish a three-paragraph essay
	Lesson 2	Understand fact and opinion	Use technology resources	

LONGMAN
SOCIAL STUDIES

TEACHER'S GUIDE

Longman Social Studies Teacher's Guide

Thanks to Charles Green for his contribution.

Pearson Education, 10 Bank Street, White Plains, NY 10606

Vice president, primary and secondary editorial: Ed Lamprich
Senior development editor: Virginia Bernard
Development editor: Deborah Maya Lazarus
Editorial coordinator: Johnnie Farmer
Editorial assistant: Emily Lippincott
Vice president, director of production and design: Rhea Banker
Production supervisor: Christine Edmonds
Associate managing editor: Jane Townsend
Vice president, marketing: Kate McLoughlin
Senior marketing manager: Don Wulbrecht
Senior manufacturing buyer: Nancy Flaggman
Cover design: Rhea Banker
Text design and composition: Quarasan
Text font: 11.5/15 Minion Regular

Credits

219 top, M. Jentoft-Nilsen/F. Hasler/D. Chesters/GSFC & T. Neilsen/NASA; bottom, David R. Frazier/Photolibrary, Inc.; 220, Drew-Brook-Cormack/Melissa Turk & The Artist Network; 221, DK Cartography; 224, Special Collections and Rare Books/Elmer L. Andersen Library/University of Minnesota; 226, Bojan Breceli/CORBIS; 227, John D. Dawson/ Dawson & Dawson, Ltd; 228, Courtesy of The Science Museum/Science and Society Picture Library, London/ Clive Streeter/Dorling Kindersley; 229, UNEP/Peter Arnold, Inc.; DK Cartography; 232, David Lees/CORBIS; 233, DK Cartography; 234, Adam Woolfitt/Robert Harding World Imagery; 235, Zeno Diemer/Deutsches Museum; 236, José Miralles/S.I. International; 237, Alan Oddie/PhotoEdit; 238, DK Cartography; 239, DK Cartography; 240, Scala/Art Resource, NY; 241, DK Cartography; 242, *Marco Polo with Kubilaj Khan in Peking* (detail), 1375/Ms. 2810/Bibliotheque Nationale, Paris; 243, CORBIS; 244, The Granger Collection, New York; 245, Corel Corporation; 246, DK Cartography; 247, DK Cartography; 248, *La Gioconda* (*Mona Lisa*)/Leonardo da Vinci (1452–1519)/Musée du Louvre, Paris, France/oil on wood, 30 1/4" x 21" (76.8 x 53.5 cm)/Lewandowski/LeMage/Art Resource, NY; 249, DK Cartography; 250, (detail) Charles & Josette Lenars/CORBIS; 251, Bettmann/CORBIS; 252, Michelangelo Buonarroti (Caprese 1475–Roma 1564, *The Libyan Sibyl*, Fresco, 1508–1512. Vatican Palace, Sistine Chapel; 253, Charles & Josette Lenars/CORBIS; 254, DK Cartography; 256, *The Mayflower in Plymouth Harbor*/William Formsby Halsall/Burstein Collection/CORBIS; 258, Hulton Archive Photos/Getty Images; 259, (detail) J.W. Orr/The Library of Congress; 260, *The Boston Tea Party*, 16 December 1773, colored engraving (detail), 19th century/The Granger Collection, New York; 261, *George Washington* (Vaughan portrait)/Gilbert Stuart, 1795, oil on canvas, 29" x 23 3/4"/Andrew W. Mellon Collection/© Board of Trustees/The National Gallery of Art, Washington, D.C.; 264, The Granger Collection, New York; 265, Historical Statistics of the United States; 266, Christie's Images/CORBIS; 267, Hulton Archive Photos/Getty Images; 268, *Ahead of the Storm*/Tim Cox, 1989/oil, 12" x 16"/Courtesy of Eagle Creek Enterprises; 269, United States Signal Corps; 270, Historical Statistics of the United States; 271, David K. Crow/PhotoEdit; 272, Hulton Archive Photos/Getty Images; 273, AEF/Serge Attal/Image Bank/Getty Images; 274, The Library of Congress; 275, UPI/CORBIS; 276, U.S. Air Force; 277, Mike Yamashita/Woodfin Camp & Associates; 278 top left, Myrleen Ferguson/PhotoEdit; 239 top middle, Pearson Longman; 239 top right, David K. Crow/PhotoEdit; 239 bottom left, Silver Burdett Ginn; 278 bottom middle, David Young-Wolff/PhotoEdit; 278 bottom right, Dorling Kindersley.

LONGMAN ON THE **WEB**

Longman.com offers online resources for teachers and students. Access our Companion Websites, our online catalog, and our local offices around the world.

Visit us at **longman.com**.

ISBN: 0-13-193028-1

Printed in the United States of America
4 5 6 7 8 9 10–CRK–09 08 07

Program Overview

Longman Social Studies is a program for English Language Learners (ELLs) and struggling readers who need to learn social studies concepts and vocabulary. It is designed for students at the beginning level of English proficiency. The program aims to help students learn key social studies vocabulary, understand geographical and historical terms and concepts, acquire and practice reading strategies, understand and use visuals, and develop essential academic language. Students will finish this course equipped with the vocabulary and skills needed to succeed in mainstream social studies classes.

The *Longman Social Studies* program integrates the following best practices for teaching English Language Learners.

- **Scaffolding** Point-of-use scaffolding is provided to make content material more meaningful to beginning students. Social studies content is scaffolded through the restatement of key concepts in simplified language, and the use of pictures, maps, charts, graphs, and graphic organizers.

- **Graphic Organizers** Graphic organizers provide a visual representation of information for strategies such as main idea and details, cause and effect, compare and contrast, and draw conclusions to help students easily grasp the skills and information they need to learn.

- **Academic Language** Understanding the academic language used in the classroom, in textbooks, and on standardized tests is vital to the success of English Language Learners. *Longman Social Studies* makes this academic language explicit through the teaching of social studies skills.

- **Social Studies Skills** Reading for content knowledge and understanding how to use visuals are important skills for students to master in order to succeed in content area classes. *Longman Social Studies* introduces and provides practice for a different reading strategy in each lesson. It also provides practice in using a wide range of visuals that students will encounter in mainstream social studies textbooks. Skills are introduced at the beginning of each lesson, practiced throughout the reading, and assessed at the end of each lesson and in the unit review.

Components

Longman Social Studies consists of a Student Book, a Workbook, and a Teacher's Guide.

Student Book

The Getting Started unit introduces students to social studies, including geographic terms, and to visuals such as maps and charts. The seven units that follow provide a broad overview of historical events from ancient to modern times.

Each unit consists of three parts: Lesson 1, Lesson 2, and a Unit Review. Each lesson includes key vocabulary, a reading strategy, a focus on using visuals, a content reading, and a review and practice section. Each unit ends with a writing skills strand.

To make social studies engaging and relevant, all content readings contain the following features:

- **Timelines** at the top of each reading spread. The timelines show dates of events in the reading, as well as dates of other world events.

- **More About It** boxes that extend students' knowledge with short paragraphs on interesting topics related to the reading.

- **Connect to Today** boxes that link a topic in the reading to modern times.

- **Elsewhere in the World** boxes that provide information about events in other parts of the world occurring at the same time as events in the reading.

- **Curriculum Connection** boxes that relate topics in the readings to other areas of the curriculum such as science, math, and art.

- **Language Tip** boxes that highlight grammar used in the reading so that students can practice it in context.

- **As You Read** boxes that encourage students to practice the lesson's reading strategy.
- **Profiles** that spotlight important people in history.
- **Primary Sources** that present authentic historical materials such as posters, diary excerpts, and speeches.
- **Before You Go On** questions that provide an on-going comprehension check at the end of each two-page reading passage. Students are asked two comprehension questions and a critical thinking question to promote discussion.

The Student Book also includes:

- a **Review and Practice** section after each lesson to check that students have learned the important elements of the lesson.
- a **Writing Skills** section at the end of each unit that takes students through the process of writing a short essay, from planning and outlining, to drafting, editing, and publishing.
- an **Understanding the Past Tense** section with explanations and exercises for practicing the past tense that can be taught at any time during the program.
- a **Glossary** that provides an extensive list of content vocabulary, definitions, and pronunciation for students' reference.

Workbook

The Workbook provides exercises and critical thinking activities to extend practice of key vocabulary, social studies skills, unit concepts, and the writing process. Workbook activities correspond to each section of the lesson and are indicated with a corresponding icon on the Student Book pages.

Teacher's Guide

The Teacher's Guide provides complete point-of-use instructions for each lesson in the Student Book. The instructions include guidelines for:

- addressing different learning modalities
- demonstrating concepts
- providing direct instruction
- teaching and modeling reading strategies

- using graphic organizers
- using visuals

The first page of each Teacher's Guide unit begins with an overview of the unit contents, reading strategies, featured visuals, learning objectives, and the writing component. The pages that follow provide direct instructional suggestions and procedures to present and teach key vocabulary, social studies skills, and content.

The Teacher's Guide uses a two-phase approach for teaching each reading section:

- **Preview Pages** using effective techniques for English Language Learners.
- **Teach Pages** using reading strategies, comprehension checks, and graphic organizers to help students understand, organize, and synthesize new concepts. Teachers can introduce the additional boxed material on the page whenever they feel it is appropriate. The answers to the Before You Go On questions are also in this section.

The Teacher's Guide provides the following additional support:

- **Working with Timelines** suggestions on how to use the timelines most effectively for students' practice and development.
- **Reaching All Students** activities that give specific instruction on adapting the content and reading strategies to auditory, visual, and/or kinesthetic learners.
- **Optional Activities** that enhance or extend the topic.
- **Website** prompts that direct students to links to interesting sites.

The Teacher's Guide also includes:

- a Scope and Sequence chart
- Student Book Answers
- Workbook Answer Key
- Tests
- Tests Answer Key

Optional Vocabulary Activities

The Student Book and Workbook contain a variety of exercises to help students practice the key vocabulary words that are introduced in each unit. However, reinforcing vocabulary with games and other activities is a fun way to help students learn. Here are some activities to adapt to your classroom. They can be used for practicing any content vocabulary from *Longman Social Studies*.

1. Grab and Run
Visual and kinesthetic learners
List the vocabulary words on index cards, one word per card, and attach them to the board, randomly or in columns and rows. Divide the class into two or three teams. The first member of each team runs to the board as you read a definition. The first one to find the correct word grabs it and returns to his or her seat. Then the next team members repeat the same process with your next definition. The team with the most captured words at the end of the game wins.

2. Word and Number Bingo
Visual and auditory learners
Give out blank bingo cards or tell students to make their own. Have students fill in numbers from 1 to 20 randomly on their cards. Write the vocabulary words on the board, assigning a number to each one. Have the definitions previously written on slips of paper, which you withdraw from a bag and read. Students will need to look for the correct word on the board and cover the corresponding number on their bingo cards. The usual rules for winning bingo apply.

3. What Are You?
Auditory learners
Write the vocabulary words on index cards and put them in a bag. Have a volunteer pick a card, look at it, and show it to you. Then students take turns asking the volunteer yes-no questions to ascertain the word. Questions should be in the form of, *Are you . . . ? Do you . . . ?* Students will only be able to ask ten questions. The student who guesses the target word becomes the next volunteer.

4. Pick a Task, Pick a Word
Visual, auditory, and kinesthetic learners
You will need two envelopes to prepare for this game. In one envelope, place all the vocabulary words on individual slips of paper. In the second envelope, write these four choices on individual slips: *define the word, pronounce the word, create a sentence,* and *spell the word.* Divide the class into two teams. One student from one of the teams comes to the front of the class and draws a piece of paper from the second envelope containing the four choices. If the student picked *pronounce the word, create a sentence,* or *define the word,* then he or she picks a word from the first envelope and does what was indicated by his/her choice. If the student picked *spell the word,* he or she picks a word from the first envelope and immediately passes the chosen slip of paper to you without looking at it. You say the word and the student must spell it. If the student does the task correctly without help from teammates, that team gets 3 points. If the team helps, it gets 1 point.

5. Tic-Tac-Toe
Visual and kinesthetic learners
Make a tic-tac-toe grid on the board with nine of the vocabulary words listed on it. Divide the class into two teams (X and O). The first team chooses a word from the grid and gives a sentence using that word. If the sentence is correct, that team can put its mark in that box. The first team to get three Xs or Os in a row is the winner. Tic-tac-toe can also be played at students' desks in pairs. Another variation is to have students give the definition instead of a sentence.

6. Memory Match
Visual and kinesthetic learners

Have pairs of students write each vocabulary word on one half of an index card and its definition on the other half. Cut the cards in half to make the game. Shuffle the cards and turn them over, arranging them randomly. Students take turns turning over two cards and reading what they say. If both cards are vocabulary words or definitions, the student reads them and turns them over again. If one card has a definition and the other card has a vocabulary word, the student decides if they match. If they match, the student keeps the cards. Whoever has the most matches at the end of the game is the winner.

7. Throw the Dice
Visual and kinesthetic learners

Write twelve vocabulary words on the board, numbering them from 1 to 12. Divide students into pairs or groups of three. Give each group a pair of dice. The first student rolls the dice and looks for the number on the board that he or she has rolled. The first time the student rolls that number, he or she pronounces the word next to that number. If the student happens to roll the same number again later on, he or she defines the word. If the student rolls that number a third time, he or she makes a sentence with that word. Students earn 1 point for pronouncing the word, 2 points for defining it, and 3 points for making a reasonable sentence. Set a time limit for the game. The student with the most points is the winner.

8. Word Association
Auditory, visual, and kinesthetic learners

Prepare a list of target vocabulary words. Then prepare a different list of words associated with the various vocabulary words. Make sure you have several related words for each vocabulary item. Write one of your target vocabulary words on the board. Select someone to be the scorekeeper. Tell students they are going to listen to a list of words that you will read slowly. When they hear a word that is associated with the vocabulary word on the board, they should immediately raise their hands. The first one to raise his or her hand gets a point, which the scorekeeper will record. Other students may challenge the one who raised a hand to explain the association. Quicken the pace of the game and repeat words to keep students interested and the game lively. A variation would be to have students silently write the words down instead of raising their hands.

9. Chart the Parts of Speech
Visual and kinesthetic learners

Have students make a chart in their notebooks with three column headings: *Noun, Verb,* and *Adjective.* At the end of one or more units, have students categorize their key vocabulary words under the correct part(s) of speech. Some words may fall into more than one category, or there may be related forms of the word that you want students to include.

10. Content Word Wall
Visual learners

Make a Word Wall of large-lettered words displayed on mural or poster paper. As students progress through the units, ask them what words they would like to place on the classroom Word Wall. Make the Word Wall interactive by incorporating those words into other listening, speaking, reading, and writing activities. Use them in dictated sentences, hangman games, crossword puzzles, bingo, categorizing, tic-tac-toe, chants, and word searches.

Introduction

Getting Started Overview

Content	Social Studies Skills	
	Reading Strategies	Using Visuals
• What Is Social Studies? • The Five Themes of Geography • Geographic Terms • Globes and Maps • Using Timelines, Charts, and Graphs • Using Primary Sources • Reading Social Studies	Introduction to Reading Strategies	Introduction to Maps, Timelines, Charts, and Graphs

Objectives

Vocabulary

- Develop new vocabulary related to social studies
- Use newly acquired vocabulary in context

Concepts

- Acquire knowledge of the scope of social studies and the themes of geography
- Acquire knowledge of the elements used in a social studies textbook

Reading Strategies

- Get an overview of the reading strategies used in this text

Using Visuals

- Understand the basics of how to read physical and political maps, timelines, charts, and graphs

What Is Social Studies?, pages 2–6

Teach this section page by page. Read the text and captions, or call on individual students to read them aloud. Use pictures, drawings on the board, maps, and mime to teach the meaning of any new words. Help students with pronunciation.

Have students read the page again silently. Alternatively, assign pairs or small groups and have students take turns reading aloud to each other. Ask comprehension and picture questions for each page. Depending on your students' abilities, you may want to ask more *Yes/No* questions than *Wh-* questions. If helpful, write all or part of the question and answer on the board. Alternatively, repeat the question and verbally model the type of response you expect. You may want to have the whole class repeat each answer for this first lesson. Hold up your book for the class to see as you ask questions.

Example questions for page 2: (pointing to the text; pointing to individual sentences) *What do we call history, geography, economics, and government? What do we learn when we study <u>social studies</u>? What is a society? Is there only one way to study a society?* (pointing to the picture of the market; pointing to the caption) *Is this a market? Is it crowded? Where is it? Are the people in India a society?*

Example questions for page 3: (pointing to the text) *What is <u>history</u> the study of? Who does history help us understand? What do we learn about? What facts can we learn? What else can we learn about?* (pointing to the picture) *What is this the ruins of? Where is it? What happened in August 1945? Can you see that the city is destroyed? What are the ruins today? Can you learn about the present from this?*

Example questions for page 4: *What is <u>geography</u> the study of? What's an example of a country? What's an example of an ocean? What can you look at to learn about a place? What can geography influence?* (pointing to the picture) *What kind of photo is this? What does it show?* (pointing to the Americas) *What is this?* (pointing to the Pacific) *Which ocean is this?* (pointing to the Atlantic) *Which ocean is this?*

Example questions for page 5: *When you study <u>economics</u>, do you study the way money is made and used? What else do you study? What are goods? What are services? What is trade?* (pointing to the picture) *What are these people doing? What kind of goods are they buying and selling? Is this trade? Is economics the study of trade?*

Example questions for page 6: *What is a <u>government</u>? What kind of government does the United States have? What does* democratic *mean?* (pointing to the picture) *What does this photo show? Are these people voting? Who are they electing? What kind of government do they have?*

Organize Information To help students consolidate the information on these five pages, do a word web after the reading. Write *Word Web* on the board. Say, *Let's make a word web about social studies. We'll do it together on the board. Copy it into your notebook.* Draw a circle on the board. Holding up your book and pointing to page 2, ask, *What is the title of this section?* In the circle, write the answer, *What Is Social Studies?* Pointing to page 3, ask, *What is one thing we study in social studies?* Draw a line and new circle and write the answer, *History.* Ask, *What is history the study of?*

Continue eliciting the subheadings and their definitions (the first sentence in each paragraph) and writing them on the board. The completed word web might look like this:

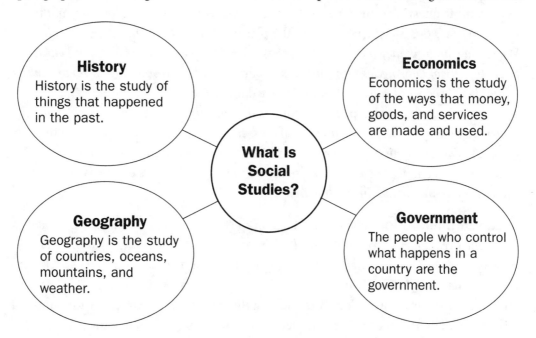

 Workbook pages 1–3 may now be assigned for homework or done in class. Make sure that students understand how to complete the pages by reading the directions with the class first. Elicit the first few answers for each exercise.

The Five Themes of Geography, pages 7–11

Teach Pages

Teach this section page by page. Read the text and captions, or call on individual students to read them aloud. Use pictures, drawings on the board, maps, and mime to teach the meaning of any new words. Help students with pronunciation.

Have students read the page again silently. Alternatively, assign pairs or small groups and have students take turns reading aloud to each other. Ask comprehension and picture questions for each page.

Example questions for page 7: (pointing to the text) *What can be a huge task? What can make the task easier? What is a theme? How many themes of geography are there? What's one theme? What question does <u>location</u> answer? What does location tell you?* (pointing to the picture) *What are these students locating?* Say, *Look at the map on page 15. Can you locate New Zealand? Point to its location.*

Example questions for page 8: *What are <u>regions</u>? What are two examples? What's their location? What are they near? What region are they in?* (pointing to the picture) *What does this picture show? What region is Thailand in?* Say, *Look at the world map on pages 22 and 23. Locate Thailand and Burma (also known as Myanmar). Raise your hand when you find them. Ask, What part of the world are they in? What region are they in?*

Example questions for page 9: *What does every area have? What can these features be? What do we call this theme? What is a <u>place</u>?* (pointing to the picture)

What does this photo show? What is Los Angeles? Are there many people in Los Angeles? Is the climate warm? Say, *The place Los Angeles has many people and a warm climate.*

   Example questions for page 10: *When can you learn about the geography of the world? What is this called?* (pointing to the picture) *Who do you think these people are? Where do you think they moved to? Why?* Say, *These people and their children helped make the city of Los Angeles.* <u>Movement</u> *is important.* Ask, *Did you move from one place to another? Where did you move from? Where did you move to?*

   Example questions for page 11: *What is this last theme? What will it help you understand? Why do people often make changes to their environment?* (pointing to the picture) *What does this photo show? Did people change the environment to make this? Is this an <u>interaction</u>? How does this interaction make people's lives better? What's an example of an interaction in our town/city?*

Organize Information   Write *Word Web* on the board. Say, *Let's make a word web about the five themes of geography. We'll do it together on the board. Copy it into your notebook.* Write *The Five Themes of Geography* and draw a circle around it. Ask, *What is one theme of geography? What does location tell you?* Draw a line and a new circle, and then write the answer. Continue eliciting the themes and their definitions and writing them on the board. The completed word web might look like this:

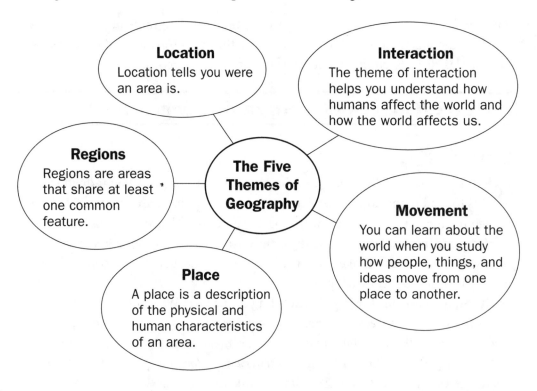

Workbook page 4 may now be assigned for homework or done in class. Make sure that students understand how to complete the page by reading the directions with the class first. Elicit the first few answers for each exercise.

Geographic Terms, pages 12–13

Teach Pages

Read the introduction and chart, or call on students to read them. Use pictures, drawings on the board, maps, and mime to teach the meaning of any new words. Give students specific examples of the features, either famous places (San Francisco Bay, the Grand Canyon, etc.) or places in your town/city. Help students with pronunciation. Point out that a *gulf* is very large, and a *bay* is smaller.

Have students read the pages again silently. Alternatively, assign pairs or small groups and have students take turns reading aloud to each other. Ask comprehension questions for each item such as, *What is a bay? What's an example of a bay? What's a deep valley with steep sides? What's an example of a valley?* Have students make a list of these geographic terms and their definitions in their notebooks. Have them title the page *Geographic Terms.* Model by beginning the list on the board.

Practice

Read the instructions, or call on a student to read them. Say, *Find as many geographic features as you can. Write down the terms for these features in your notebook.* Model by eliciting a few pictured terms and writing them on the board. Then have students work in pairs or small groups to complete their lists. When students have finished, call on different students to tell you the terms they found. Hold up your book and point to the feature, and then write it on the board. Have students add any features they missed to their list.

> **Answers**
> The illustration shows <u>all</u> the terms except for *continent, gulf,* and *hemisphere.* The large body of water could be either a sea or an ocean; the enclosed body of water is a bay.

 Workbook pages 5–6 may now be assigned for homework or done in class. Make sure that students understand how to complete the page by reading the directions with the class first. Go over the task on the page before students begin.

Globes and Maps, pages 14–15

Teach Pages

Read the text and captions, or call on students to read them. Help students understand and pronounce any new words, both in the text and on the map of Australia and New Zealand.

Have students read the page again silently. Alternatively, assign pairs or small groups and have students take turns reading aloud to each other. Ask comprehension and picture questions for each page. Ask, *What are the most common tools we use to study geography?* (pointing to the picture of the globe) *What's this?* (pointing to the picture of the map) *What's this? What is a map? What is a globe? What shape is a globe? What can it show? What can you see? Why is a globe harder to use than a map? What kind of drawing is a map? Why is it easier to use than a globe? Do maps show the correct size and shape of every feature? Is there just one type of map? What does each type of map have? What will you use as you study social studies? What are some features that mapmakers include to help us understand information?* (pointing to the map) *What countries are these?* (pointing to the key) *What's this? What kind of things does it show?* (pointing to the scale) *What's this? What does it show?* (pointing to the compass rose) *What's this? What do the letters mean?*

Draw a compass rose on the board. Elicit what the four main directions are and spell these out on the board. Then elicit or teach what the small points show and write these on the board. (northwest, northeast, southeast, southwest) Have students copy this into their notebooks.

Show students how to use a ruler or other straight object to align with the scale, and then apply it to the map. Ask, *How far is New Caledonia from Australia?* (about 1,000 miles)

Physical Maps, pages 16–19

Teach Pages

Read the introduction, or call on students to read it. Help students with any new words. Then have students read the introduction again silently. Review map terms and help students pronounce countries and oceans, etc. on the maps on pages 17 and 18–19.

Ask comprehension and picture questions such as, *What does a physical map show? What are some important physical features it shows? What does the key on a physical map show? What is elevation? How do mapmakers show elevation?* (pointing to the map of Africa) *What's this?* (pointing to the key) *What colors does the key use to show elevation? What color is the highest elevation? How many feet does the purple color show? What color is the lowest elevation? What is sea level? What color is most of Africa? What is that elevation?* (pointing to the Congo River) *This is the Congo. What does* R *stand for?* (pointing to Mt. Kilimanjaro) *Kilimanjaro is a mountain. What does* ft *mean?* Elicit as many of the geographical terms from the world map on pages 12–13 as possible. Ask questions such as, *Can you find a gulf? What's it called?* Point out that the bold words are names of continents.

Practice

Read the instructions, or call on a student to read them. Depending on the level of your students, have them work in pairs, in small groups, or as a class to answer the questions and write the answers in their notebooks. For pair or group practice, model by eliciting the first two answers and writing them on the board. Then when students have finished, elicit the rest of the answers.

Answers

1. The Kalahari Desert is a desert in southern Africa.
2. The Atlas Mountains are a mountain range in northwest Africa.
3. Kilimanjaro is the highest mountain in Africa.
4. Yes, this mountain is higher than 13,000 feet. (It's 19,341 feet.)
5. The Nile River is the long river in northeast Africa.
6. The Atlantic Ocean is west of Africa.
7. The Ahaggar Mountains and the Atlas Mountains are about 1,000 miles apart.

1. The seven continents are North America, South America, Africa, Europe, Asia, Australia, and Antarctica.
2. The world's oceans are the Pacific Ocean, the Atlantic Ocean, the Indian Ocean, the Arctic Ocean, and the Southern Ocean.
3. The largest mountain range in North America is the Rocky Mountains.
4. The Amazon River is a long river in South America.
5. Asia and South America have the highest mountains.
6. The elevation of these mountains is more than 13,000 feet (3,960 meters).
7. Antarctica is about 2,800 miles from Africa.

Political Maps, pages 20–23

Teach Pages

Read the introduction, or call on individual students to read it aloud. Help students with any new words. Then have students read the introduction again silently. Review map terms and help students pronounce the major names on the map of Africa.

Ask comprehension and picture questions such as, *What does a political map show? Why are there colors on the map? What's a capital? What's the capital of the United States? What do you need to look at to help you understand the map?* (pointing to the map of Africa) *What's this?* (pointing to the key) *What does the key use to show a national border? Look at the borders—which country looks the biggest?* (pointing to the key again) *What does a star with a circle around it show? What does a dot show?* Help students pronounce the names of major countries on the world map on pages 22–23.

Practice

Read the instructions aloud, or call on a student to read them. Have students work in pairs, in small groups, or as a class to answer the questions and write the answers in their notebooks. For pair or group practice, model by eliciting the first two answers and writing them on the board. Then when students have finished, elicit the rest of the answers.

Workbook pages 7–12 may now be assigned for homework or done in class. Make sure that students understand how to complete the pages by reading the directions with the class first. Go over the task on the page before students begin.

Using Timelines, Charts, and Graphs, pages 24–27

Teach Pages

Teach this section page by page. Read the text and timelines, charts, and graphs, or call on students to read them. Help students understand and pronounce any new words. Spell out year dates and large numbers on the board, and have students say them. Have students read the page again silently. Alternatively, assign pairs or small groups and have students take turns reading aloud to each other. Ask comprehension and picture questions for each page.

    Example questions for page 24: *What do you see when you study social studies? What do timelines show? What do charts use to help you compare a lot of things? What are graphs?* (pointing to the timeline, charts, and graphs on pages 25–27) *What's this? What are these?*

    Example questions for page 25: *How is each event listed in a timeline? What will a timeline help you do? How do you read the timeline? What are the years and events on this timeline?*

Before You Go On

Do these exercises as a class. Read or have a student read each question. Elicit the answer, write it on the board, and have students copy it into their notebooks.

Answers
1. Christopher Columbus was the first explorer to come to the Americas in 1492.
2. Hernán Cortés conquered the Aztecs in 1520.
3. Hernando de Soto explored southeastern America after Cabeza de Vaca.

Example questions for page 26: *What does a* <u>*chart*</u> *use to help you understand? How is the chart below divided?* (pointing to columns, and then rows, and then the title) *What are columns? What are rows? What are these? What's the title of this chart?* (pointing to the second chart) *What is this chart called? What does this kind of chart show? What happened first on the chart? What happened last?*

Example questions for page 27: *What are* <u>*graphs*</u>*? What can a graph show? What else? What are two types of graphs?* (pointing to the line graph) *What is this? What does it show? What is on the left side? Where are the years?* (pointing to the bar graph) *What is this? Does this graph show the same information as the line graph? What does it use instead of lines?*

Before You Go On

Do these exercises as a class. Read or have a student read each question. Elicit the answer, write it on the board, and have students copy it into their notebooks.

Answers
1. Asia had the most immigrants in 2004.
2. Two types of graphs are line graphs and bar graphs. They show information with numbers, lines, and bars.
3. The world population was 1 billion in 1800, 1.5 billion in 1900, and 6 billion in 2000.

Workbook pages 13–15 may now be assigned for homework or done in class. Make sure that students understand how to complete the pages by reading the directions with the class first. Go over the task on the page before students begin.

Using Primary Sources, page 28

Teach Page

Read the text and poster, or call on students to read it. Help them with any new words. Then have students read them again individually, or in pairs or small groups. Ask comprehension and picture questions such as, *What are* <u>*primary sources*</u>*? What are some examples of primary sources? What can you do when you read a primary source?*

Why? Are primary sources boring? When do you use them? What else can they help you do? What does interpret *mean? What questions will help you interpret a primary source? (pointing to the poster) What's this? When was it made? Who is Uncle Sam?*

Practice

Do this exercise as a class. Read or have a student read each question. Elicit the answer, write it on the board, and have students copy it into their notebooks.

> **Answers**
> **1.** I think the United States government is the author of the poster.
> **2.** Uncle Sam wants boys and girls to save their quarters. He wants them to buy war savings stamps to help win the war.
> **3.** The purpose of the poster is to sell war savings stamps.
> **4.** The audience is girls and boys.

Bring in the different examples of primary sources mentioned and show them to the class. Teach or elicit what it is, when it was written or made, and the author, audience, and purpose.

 Workbook page 16 may now be assigned for homework or done in class. Make sure that students understand how to complete the page by reading the directions with the class first. Go over the task on the page before students begin.

Reading Social Studies, page 29

Teach Page

Read the introduction and list of reading strategies, or call on individual students to read them. Explain any new words in the introduction. Help students with pronunciation of the strategy names, but don't explain them at this point. After going over the list, ask if students know any of these strategies. Elicit what they know and write it on the board.

Unit 1 Early Civilizations

Unit Overview

Lesson	Content	Social Studies Skills		Writing Skills
		Reading Strategies	Using Visuals	
1	• The Stone Age • The Ice Age • Early Farmers • The Bronze Age • Mesopotamia • The Phoenicians	Preview	Use a Timeline (Part 1)	Make a Plan
2	• Ancient Egypt • Ancient Nubia • Ancient China • Ancient Persia	Predict	Use a Timeline (Part 2)	

Objectives

Vocabulary
• Develop new vocabulary related to early ages and civilizations
• Use newly acquired vocabulary in context

Concepts
• Acquire knowledge of prehistory and the dawn of civilization
• Acquire knowledge of ancient civilizations

Reading Strategies
• Preview to understand what you will read
• Predict to consolidate information and extrapolate

Using Visuals
• Understand how to read and construct timelines

Writing Skills
• Practice making a plan

Unit Opener, pages 30–31

Preview Topic

Hold up your book and point to the unit title. Read it aloud or call on a student to read it. Say, and write on the board, *We live in a civilization. A civilization has cities, rules, and schools.* Say, *Many years ago, people didn't have these things. In this unit, we'll study about the way people lived before civilizations. Then we'll study how early civilizations started.* Point to the cave drawings and say, *People drew these pictures before there was writing.* Ask, helping with vocabulary as needed, *What can you see in the picture? How many people can you see? What are they doing? What are they holding?* Encourage students to make guesses. Don't correct their responses now; they are previewing.

Unit Contents

Read the headings on page 31 aloud. Say, *These are the people, places, and events we will learn about in this unit.* Help students pronounce the list of names. Say each name and have students repeat. Follow the same procedures with place names. Use a world map or globe to teach or elicit the locations of these places.

For key events, say, *These are the key, or most important, events we will learn about.* Read aloud the list of key events, or call on a student to read them. Elicit or teach any new words and help students pronounce them.

Get Ready

Read the instructions, or call on a student to read them. Ask students, *What do you need to name? What do you write about it?* Elicit or teach the names of civilizations your students might know about. Write them on the board. (Incan, Aztec, Egyptian, Chinese, Cambodian, etc.)

Since this is the first Get Ready, you may want to do this activity as a class. Point to each civilization on the board and ask, *Who knows about this civilization? Raise your hand.* Ask a student to tell what he or she knows about the civilization. Write this on the board.

Lesson ❶

Before You Read, pages 32–35

Vocabulary

The reading strategy <u>Previewing</u> will be formally presented later in this lesson. Get students used to the strategy (without naming it at this point). Hold up your book, point to the headings on page 32, and ask students, *What does this say?* Call on students to answer. Point to each picture and say, *Look at this picture.* Then ask simple picture questions such as (pointing at the picture of the hunters), *How many people can you see in this picture?* (pointing to the archaeologist) *Is this a man or a woman? What is she holding?* (pointing to the picture of glaciers) *Is this a warm place or a cold place? How do you know?* (pointing to the picture of corn crops on page 33) *What can you see in this picture? What kind of plants are these?* Encourage students to guess.

Read the captions, or call on individual students to read them aloud. Help students understand and pronounce any new words. Use pictures, props, and mime. Have students read the captions again silently. Ask picture and comprehension questions for each item to make sure students have understood. For example, ask (pointing to the hunters), *What are these men doing? What did they hunt?* (pointing to the archaeologist) *What kind of scientist is this woman? What do archaeologists do? What do they look for?* Say, *Look at page 39.* Ask (pointing to the tools), *What are these?* Say, *Look at page 66.* Ask (pointing to the pottery), *What is this?* (pointing to the glaciers) *What are these large areas of ice called? When did they cover much of the earth?* (pointing to the caption on page 33) *What did some early humans plant? What's an example of a crop? What did people use rivers for? What is irrigation? Is irrigation from rivers still used today to water crops?* (pointing to the picture of corn) *What plant is this? How is the corn getting water?*

Point out the key words in the box on page 33. Read them aloud and have students say them after you. Say, *These words are important in this lesson. Let's learn these words.* Have students close their books. Hold up your book so all students can see. Point to pictures illustrating the key words. Ask questions to elicit each key word such as, *What are these men? What is this woman? What are these large areas of ice called? What is water flowing to crops called? What is growing crops and raising animals called?* Encourage all students to answer together.

Practice

Read the instructions, or call on a student to read them aloud. Say, *First write the sentences in your notebook. Don't write the answers.* Model by writing sentence 1 on the board. Make sure students understand *farmer* in question 4. When most students have finished writing, say, *Now, let's choose the answer for number 1.* Model thinking aloud by asking the class, *Is* agriculture *the name of a scientist?* (no) *Is* hunter-gatherer *the name of a scientist?* (no) *Is* archaeologist *the name of a scientist?* (yes) *So the answer is* archaeologist. Fill in the answer on the board. Say, *Now choose the correct answers and write them in the sentences.*

When students have finished, have them compare their answers with a classmate. Check by calling on individual students to read their sentences aloud. Write the letters of the correct answers on the board.

Answers
1. c. archaeologist   3. a. Glaciers   5. a. irrigation
2. b. hunter-gatherers   4. b. Crops   6. c. Agriculture

 Workbook page 17 may now be assigned for homework or done in class. This workbook page provides practice in understanding and using the key words.

Content Reading Strategy: Preview Bring a magazine to class. Write *Preview* on the board. Ask, *Do you read magazines? What do you do before you read a story in a magazine?* Say, pointing at appropriate sections and writing key words on the board, *I* preview. *I read the headings. This is a heading. I look at the pictures. And I read the captions. This is a caption. Previewing helps me understand what I will read.*

Have students open their books to page 34. Read the headings aloud. Review the meaning of *strategy.* (a plan to help you do something) Then point to the text diagram at the bottom of the page. Elicit the parts of a page by pointing to each labeled section and asking, *What is this?* Read the introduction or call on individual students to read it aloud. Explain or elicit any new words. Have students reread it silently.

Ask comprehension questions such as, *What reading strategy will we practice? What does* preview *mean? How does this help you? What do you do when you preview? What questions do you ask yourself?* Have students turn to page 36. Say, *Let's preview this page. What's the heading? What are the vocabulary words? What do you see in the picture? What does the caption say?* Tell students they will practice previewing as they read this unit.

 Workbook page 18 may now be assigned for homework or done in class. Make sure that students understand how to complete the pages by reading the directions with the class first. Go over the task before students begin.

Using Visuals: Use a Timeline This textbook uses the increasingly common year demarcations B.C.E. and C.E. B.C.E. stands for *Before the Common Era* and is synonymous with B.C. (Before Christ) in usage. C.E. stands for *the Common Era* and is synonymous with A.D. (Anno Domini). The year 1000 C.E. is the same as the year A.D. 1000. While this system of dating is still historically linked to Christianity—the main Western method of dating—many historians and archaeologists now prefer the Common Era terms because they are seen as more inclusive of non-Christians, who make up two-thirds of the world population.

Have students read the heading on the top of page 35. Point to the timeline and ask, *What is this? Did we study timelines in Getting Started?* Hold up your book and point to the text. Ask, *What does a timeline show? How is each event listed? How do you read a timeline?*

To help students understand B.C.E. and C.E. years, draw a timeline on the board. Have students copy the timeline into their notebooks. The timeline might look like this:

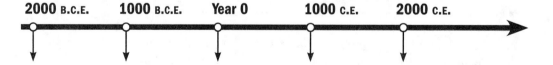

| 2000 B.C.E. | 1000 B.C.E. | Year 0 | 1000 C.E. | 2000 C.E. |

Write on the board: B.C.E. = *Before the Common Era* and C.E. = *the Common Era.* If students are familiar with A.D. and B.C., write these on the board also. Have students copy this into their notebooks. Pointing to B.C.E., ask, *What word does the letter* B *come from? How about* C *and* E? Pointing to C.E. on the timeline, ask, *What does* C.E. *mean?*

Say, *We live in the Common Era. What year is it now?* Write the year and c.e. on the board. Say, *This is (year) in the Common Era.* Ask, *Where do we write this year on the timeline?* Add this to the timeline and have students copy it into their notebooks. Say, *We read a timeline from left to right. What year is the beginning of the Common Era?* (year 0) *What year comes before year 0?* (year 1 b.c.e.) *What year comes before 1 b.c.e.? Where do we write the year 500 b.c.e.? How many years ago is 500 b.c.e.? Where do we write 750 b.c.e. on the timeline?* Write these numbers on the board and have students add them to their timelines.

Have students look at page 35. Read the information on the page, or call on individual students to read it aloud. Help students understand and pronounce any new words. Help students pronounce the numbers on the timeline.

As this is the first Using Visuals exercise, control this exercise. Have students study the timeline for a minute. Then read question 1 aloud. Elicit the answer and write it on the board. Have students copy it into their notebooks. Do the same for the other two questions.

Answers

1. "First crops grown" is the first event on the timeline.
2. In 4000 b.c.e. farming started in Europe.
3. There are 2,000 years between the first and second events.

Workbook pages 19–20 may now be assigned for homework or done in class. Make sure that students understand how to complete the pages by reading the directions with the class first. Go over the task before students begin.

Reading ❶

The Stone Age, page 36
The Ice Age, page 37

Preview Pages

To model the <u>Preview</u> strategy, write the word *Preview* on the board. Hold up your book and ask students, *What do you look at when you preview?* (headings, vocabulary, pictures, captions) Pointing, ask, *What is the heading on page 36? What's the vocabulary? What do you see in the picture? What's the caption?* Say, *Now let's preview page 37. What's the heading? What's the vocabulary? What do you see in the big picture? What's the caption?*

As You Read: Preview

Point to the box on page 36. Read it aloud, or call on a student to read it. Elicit or teach any new words. Ask the questions and call on students to answer.

Have the key words on the board before the students begin. Read the text and captions, or call on individual students to read them aloud. Use pictures, drawings, maps, and mime to teach the meaning of any new words. Help students with pronunciation. Ask if students found any key words. Ask for volunteers to read the sentences containing the key words. Ask what these words mean.

Understand Information Have students read the pages again silently. Alternatively, assign pairs or small groups and have students take turns reading aloud to each other.

Ask comprehension, picture, and thinking questions. For example, *When do archaeologists think that early humans lived? Where do they think they lived? Why is it called the Stone Age? What are tools? What are weapons? Why are early humans called hunter-gatherers? What did they learn how to make? Was fire important for early humans? How did they use fire?* (pointing at the picture on page 36) *What are these men hunting? Why are they hunting it? Are there still mammoths today?* (no, they are extinct, but elephants are similar, though smaller—mammoths were 11 feet high) (pointing to the picture on page 37) *What's the heading? How long did the Ice Age last? What was much of the earth covered with? What does* adapt *mean? What did early humans have to adapt to? What did they have to protect themselves from? What does* freezing *mean? When did the first humans come to North America from Asia? Why did they come? When did the Ice Age end? Who painted the hunting picture? Where did they paint it? Would you like to live in the Ice Age? Why or why not?*

Organize Information Draw a blank T-chart on the board. Tell students, *This is a T-chart. It looks like a T. A T-chart can help you learn and remember the information.* Ask, *What two ages did we study?* Write the response in the T-chart. Ask, *How long did the Stone Age last?* Encourage students to look at the first sentences on each page. Ask, *Why was it called the Stone Age?* Write these responses into the chart and have students copy them into their notebooks. Ask the same two questions about the Ice Age and write them on the board for students to copy. The chart might look like this:

The Stone Age	The Ice Age
It lasted from about 2,500,000 to 2,000,000 years ago.	It lasted from about 2,000,000 to 15,000 years ago.
Humans made tools and weapons from stone.	Glaciers covered much of the earth.

MORE ABOUT IT: Ice Age Homes

Read the text in the box on page 37, or call on individual students to read it aloud. Elicit or explain the meanings of any new words and help students pronounce them. Have students read the section again silently.

Ask questions such as, *What did people living during the Ice Age make homes out of? What did they use?* (pointing to the picture) *What's on the outside of the home?* (bones) *What animal do you think these bones are from?* (a mammoth) *What are these people wearing?* (animal skins) *Why did they make clothes from animal skins?* (to keep warm; they didn't have cotton)

Before You Go On

Have students read the first two questions. (The first two questions are informational; the third question is critical thinking.) Pair students and have them write the answers in their notebooks. Check the answers. Do the third question together as a class. Tell students that this is a thinking question. Write the answers on the board and have students copy them into their notebooks.

Answers
1. They hunted animals and gathered seeds, fruit, and plants for food.
2. It was important for keeping warm and for cooking.
3. Answers will vary. Possible answers: To tell a story about hunting. To teach others how to hunt.

Working with Timelines

Have students look at the timeline. Read the timeline aloud, and then call on students to read the entries. Help students understand and pronounce the years on the timeline and any new words. To review B.C.E. years, ask, *What does B.C.E. mean? Which year is earlier, 2,500,000 B.C.E. or 2,000,000 B.C.E.?* Ask comprehension and review questions such as, *When did the Stone Age begin? What happened in 2 million B.C.E.? When was the first use of fire? What happened in 10,000 B.C.E.?*

Assign pairs or small groups and have them make a list of the numbers on the timeline. Have them spell out each number. (two million five hundred thousand years before the common era, etc.) Model this on the board. When students have finished, check by asking students how to say each number.

Have students write the heading *Unit 1, Lesson 1 Timelines* on a new page in their notebooks. Then have them copy the Unit Events timeline. Students will add later timelines to this page. Model by writing the heading and beginning of the timeline on the board.

Choose World Events that your students will find interesting. Bring in pictures and maps to help teach these events.

Early Farmers, page 38
The Bronze Age, page 39

Hold up your book and ask students, *What do you look at when you preview?* (headings, vocabulary, pictures, captions) Have students silently preview the page. Then ask, *What do you see in the big picture on page 38? What do you see in the pictures on page 39? What are the topics on these pages? Why do you think so? What do you think bronze is?*

Teach Pages

Read the text and captions, or call on individual students to read them aloud. Use pictures, drawings, maps, and mime to teach the meaning of any new words. Help students with pronunciation. Ask if students found any key words. (crops, irrigation) Ask a student to read sentences containing the key words. Ask what these words mean.

Understand Information Have students read the pages again silently. Alternatively, assign pairs or small groups to take turns reading aloud to each other. Ask comprehension, picture, and thinking questions. For example, *When did early humans start farming? What did this control? Did they still move around to find food? What did they do instead? What crops did early farmers plant? What does* settle *mean? Why did people settle near large rivers? How did the farmers use water from the rivers? What did they make? What's a canal? Where were the first cities? When did people learn to make bronze? How did they make it? Which lasted longer, stone or bronze weapons and tools? What are some examples of bronze tools on this page? How do you use a razor? Were copper and tin easy to find in Europe? What did people have to do to find them? What did they begin to do with people in faraway places? What does* traded *mean? What does* goods *mean? What kind of goods did people trade? What did they trade these goods for?*

Organize Information Write the heading *Early Farmers* on the board and draw two boxes with an arrow between. Say, *Let's make a diagram about early farmers.* Fill in the second box, as below. Say, *In the Ice Age people moved around. Why did people begin to stay in one place? Can you find the answer in the text?* Write their responses in the first box of the diagram and have students copy it into their notebooks. Do a second diagram about the location of cities in the same manner. The diagrams might look like this:

Early Farmers

Early humans started farming in about 7000 B.C.E. This controlled their food source.	▶	People stayed in one place and stored crops from one season to the next.

Location of Cities

Because crops needed water to grow, people settled near large rivers.	▶	The first cities were near rivers.

Next, lead the students in making another diagram—a flowchart—about the growth of trade in the Bronze Age. Write the heading *The Bronze Age* on the board and draw four boxes with arrows between them. Fill in the <u>last</u> box, as below. To elicit each of the reasons in the chain from end to beginning, ask students, *Why did this happen?* Write responses on the board and have students copy the flowchart into their notebooks. The flowchart might look like this:

The Bronze Age

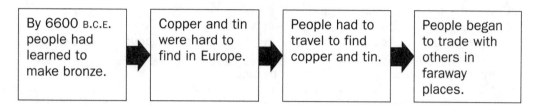

| By 6600 B.C.E. people had learned to make bronze. | → | Copper and tin were hard to find in Europe. | → | People had to travel to find copper and tin. | → | People began to trade with others in faraway places. |

CONNECT TO TODAY: Irrigation

Read the text in the box on page 38, or call on individual students to read it aloud. Elicit or explain the meanings of any new words and help students pronounce them. Have students read the section again silently. Alternatively, assign pairs or small groups and have students take turns reading aloud to each other.

Ask questions such as (pointing to the picture), *What is happening in the picture? How much fresh water goes to irrigating crops? What is the southwestern part of the United States like? What must farmers do? How much land needs water in California? How much water do farmers bring to the land? Where do you think the farmers get this water?* (from rivers and lakes) *Do farmers have to live near lakes and rivers now?* (no, they can bring water to their crops from far away)

Language Tip: Simple Past Tense

Read the text in the box on page 39, or call on a student to read it. Write the word *plant* on the board. Ask, *How do I make the simple past tense of* plant? Write → *planted* on the board. Have students copy this and the other examples in the box into their notebooks. Ask, *What are the three sounds* -ed *can be?* Elicit or teach that they are /id/, /d/, or /t/. Write these on the board. Then say and have students repeat the simple past tense forms of the verbs in the box. For each ask, *Which sound is* -ed *here?* (planted = /id/, needed = /id/, learned = /d/, lasted = /id/). (For examples of the /t/ sound, suggest *asked* or *laughed*.) Write the pronunciations on the board and have students copy them into their notebooks. Ask students to find other simple past tense verbs ending in -*ed* on these pages. (started, controlled, stayed, used, traded) Remind them that words ending in -*e* take -*d* only. Write the verbs on the board, elicit the pronunciation of -*ed*, and have students copy this into their notebooks.

Have students read the first two questions. (The first two questions are informational; the third question is critical thinking.) Pair students and have them write the answers in their notebooks. Check the answers. Do the third question together as a class. Explain the meaning of *ancient.* Tell students that this is a thinking question. Elicit answers from students and write them on the board. Have students copy them into their notebooks.

Answers

1. The first cities were near rivers.
2. Bronze was much harder, better, and lasted longer than stone.
3. Answers will vary. Possible answers: They had new kinds of goods in their lives, like baskets, cloth, spices, and bronze tools. They also began to make goods to trade. They met new people in faraway places.

Working with Timelines

Have students look at the timeline. Read the timeline aloud, and then call on students to read the entries. Help students understand and pronounce the years on the timeline and any new words. To review order of B.C.E. years, ask, *Which year is earlier, 6600 B.C.E. or 6000 B.C.E.?* Ask comprehension and review questions such as, *When did farming and settlement start in Mesopotamia? How did farming change how people lived? Where did people usually settle? Why? What happened in 6600 B.C.E.? What's special about bronze? When did people begin to trade? Why did they begin to trade? What did they begin to trade?* Have students copy the Unit Events timeline onto their Lesson 1 Timelines page. Model by beginning the timeline on the board.

Choose World Events that your students will find interesting. Bring in pictures and maps to help teach these events.

Mesopotamia, pages 40–41

Preview Pages

Hold up your book and ask students, *What do you look at when you preview?* (headings, vocabulary, pictures, captions) Have students silently preview the page. Then ask, *What do you see in the map on page 40? What do you see in the big picture on page 41? What is the topic of these pages? Why do you think so?*

Teach Pages

Read the text and captions, or call on individual students to read them aloud. Elicit or explain the meanings of any new words, and help students pronounce them. Be sure to show students the location of modern Syria and Iraq on a map or globe. Ask if students found any key words. (crops) Ask for volunteers to read the sentence containing this word. Ask what the word means.

Understand Information Have students read the pages again silently. Alternatively, assign pairs or small groups to take turns reading aloud to each other. Ask comprehension, picture, and thinking questions. For example, *Where was Mesopotamia? What color is Mesopotamia on the map? What does the word* mesopotamia *mean? Which two rivers was Mesopotamia between? What was the land between these rivers like? What does* fertile *mean? What did this allow people to do? Where was Sumer? What color is Sumer on the map? What did Sumerian farmers need? What are* products? *What did the Sumerians develop? What was the writing called? What did they write about? What were they the first people to do? What were the biggest and most important civilizations in Mesopotamia? What were the Babylonians like? What do warriors do? What does* conquered *mean? What was Babylonia a center for? Who was Hammurabi? What did he write? What was the capital of Assyria? What kind of city was it?* (pointing to the picture of an Assyrian palace on page 41) *Who lives in a palace? What are the people doing in the picture? Does Assyria look like a nice place to live?*

Organize Information Draw a large chart on the board (see below) and say, *Let's make a chart about Mesopotamia. What three civilizations in Mesopotamia did we read about?* Elicit the answers and write them as headings in the chart. In later lessons, you can help students learn how to condense information down to its key elements, but at this point just let them organize the information simply into a chart. Say, *Now let's copy the text about these places into the chart. What can we write about Mesopotamia?* Verbally elicit the text on Mesopotamia. Ask (pointing to the first sentence on page 41), *How can we make one sentence about Babylonia and one about Assyria?* Help students with this, and write these two sentences into the chart. Have students copy the chart into their notebooks and complete it individually, in pairs, or in groups. When students have finished, elicit the answers verbally. The chart might look like this:

Mesopotamia		
Mesopotamia was one of the first civilizations. It was where parts of Syria and Iraq are today. The word <u>mesopotamia</u> means "between two rivers." The land between the Tigris and the Euphrates rivers was very fertile, which allowed people to grow crops. The rivers also supplied fish, reeds to make boats, and clay for building.		
Sumer	**Babylonia**	**Assyria**
In southern Mesopotamia was a region called Sumer. Many Sumerians were farmers. They needed a way to record information about their products, so they developed a system of writing. The writing was called cuneiform. The Sumerians used cuneiform to write about how they lived. They were the first people to do this.	Babylonia was a big and important civilization in Mesopotamia. The Babylonians were warriors and they conquered many other lands. Babylonia was also a center for trade. Trading with and conquering other civilizations made the Babylonians rich. One great Babylonian ruler was Hammurabi. He wrote 282 rules for people to follow.	Assyria was a big and important civilization in Mesopotamia. Nineveh was the capital of Assyria. It was a city of great learning. It had a huge library.

MORE ABOUT IT: Invention of the Wheel

Have students look at the box on page 40. Practice <u>previewing</u>. Ask, *What's the heading? What do you see in the picture? What's the topic?* Read the text, or call on individual students to read it aloud. Elicit or explain the meanings of any new words and help students pronounce them. Have students read the section again silently. Alternatively, assign pairs or small groups and have students take turns reading aloud to each other.

Ask questions such as, *What do historians study? What do many historians believe? Where do wheels first appear? What were these wheels made of? What were they attached to? What were they pulled by? What did wheels make easier? Before wheels, how did people travel?* (they walked) *Before wheels, could people carry very big things?* (no) *How do we use wheels now?* (on cars, buses, bicycles, trucks, trains, airplanes, etc.)

MORE ABOUT IT: Battering Rams

Have students look at the box on page 41. Practice <u>previewing</u>. Ask, *What's the heading? What do you see in the picture? What's the topic?* Read the text, or call on individual students to read it aloud. Elicit or explain the meanings of any new words and help students pronounce them. Have students read the section again silently. Alternatively, assign pairs or small groups and have students take turns reading aloud to each other.

Ask questions such as, *Were the Assyrians good warriors? What did many ancient cities have? Why? When did the Assyrians develop battering rams? Why did they invent them? How did they make them? What did they do with them? What did this do to the walls?* (pointing to the picture) *What is this large piece of wood? What's at the end of it? How will the people get into the city?*

You may want to bring in a wooden model of an ancient battering ram to show students how it works. These can be ordered on the Internet.

Before You Go On

Have students read the first two questions. (The first two questions are informational; the third question is critical thinking.) Pair students and have them write the answers in their notebooks. Check the answers. Do the third question together as a class. Tell students that this is a thinking question. Write the answers on the board and have students copy them into their notebooks.

Answers

1. The invention of the wheel made it easier to carry goods from place to place. It also made traveling easier.
2. A battering ram is a large spear attached to a long beam. The Assyrians rammed this into a wall, loosened the stones, and destroyed the city walls of their enemies.
3. Answers will vary. Possible answers: The Assyrians wrote about how they lived. They had a huge library. Perhaps archaeologists found some of this writing.

Working with Timelines

Have students look at the timeline. Read the timeline aloud, and then call on students to read the entries. Help students understand and pronounce the years on the timeline and any new words. To review the order of B.C.E. years, ask, *Which year is later, 2500 B.C.E. or 4000 B.C.E.?*

Ask comprehension and review questions such as, *Where were Babylonia and Assyria? When did the Babylonian and Assyrian civilizations begin? How did the land and rivers help these civilizations develop? When was the wheel invented? What did Sumerian farmers invent? What happened in 3000 B.C.E.? When did the Assyrians invent the battering ram?* Have students copy the Unit Events timeline onto their Lesson 1 Timelines page. Model by beginning the timeline on the board.

Choose World Events that your students will find interesting. Bring in pictures and maps to help teach these events.

Primary Source, page 42

Preview Page

Ask students to preview this page, individually or in pairs. Point to the heading, *Cuneiform*. Help students pronounce this word. (kyoo-NAY-i-form) Then ask, *What's the topic of this page? Why do you think so? What do you think* cuneiform *means?*

Teach Page

Read the text, or call on individual students to read it aloud. Elicit or explain the meanings of any new words and help students pronounce the words. (flat, clay, facts, sheep, wedges, stood for)

Understand Information Have students read the pages again silently. Alternatively, assign pairs or small groups and have students take turns reading aloud to each other. Ask comprehension and picture questions such as, *When did the Sumerians create a system of writing? What did they write on? What is this writing called? What did the Sumerians use it for? What numbers do you see in the picture? What kind of facts did farmers use cuneiform to record?* (pointing to the picture of wedges) *What are these? What did they stand for?*

Have students work in pairs or small groups to write the answers to the questions in their notebooks. When students have finished, elicit the answers and write them on the board.

Answers

1. The Sumerians used cuneiform to write numbers. Farmers used cuneiform to record facts, such as how many sheep they had.

2.

Optional Activity

This activity will help students further explore and relate to cuneiform numbers.
Dictate five or six other numbers between 1 and 31 and have students write
them in cuneiform. Call on students to write them on the board as a check.
Then have students write their names along with the month and day of their
birthdays in cuneiform on a small piece of paper. Model by writing an example
birthday on the board. Show how you use space to separate the month and day
numbers. When students have finished, assign an even number of groups of
three to six students. Have each group exchange their birth dates with another
group. Have the groups translate the cuneiform into regular numbers. Then
have groups check with each other that their translations were correct.

The Phoenicians, page 43

Preview Page

Have students <u>preview</u> this page individually or in pairs. Point to the heading, *The
Phoenicians*. Help students pronounce this word. (foh-NEE-shuhnz) Then ask,
What's the topic of this page? Why do you think so?

Teach Page

Read the text and captions, or call on individual students to read them aloud. Elicit
or explain the meanings of any new words, and help students pronounce them.
(Lebanon, explorers, monsters, scary, creatures, so that, would, afraid, compete, basis,
busy, port) Be sure to show students the location of Lebanon on a map or globe.

Understand Information Have students read the pages again silently.
Alternatively, assign pairs or small groups and have students take turns reading aloud
to each other. Ask comprehension, picture, and thinking questions such as, *Where
did the Phoenicians live? When were they great sea traders and explorers?* (pointing to
the picture of a port) *What is this? What kind of things are the Phoenicians trading?
What did they tell stories about? What are monsters? What are some monster stories we
know today? Why did the Phoenicians tell these stories? What does* compete *mean? Why
do you think they didn't want other people to compete with them? What was important
to the Phoenicians? What is the basis of the English language?*

Organize Information Draw a chart on the board labeled *The Phoenicians*. Say,
Let's make a chart about the Phoenicians. Write subheadings into the chart as you say,
*Let's write about where they lived, about their trading and exploring, about the stories
they told, and about their writing.* Elicit the answers for the first two items and write
them into the chart. Have students copy the chart into their notebooks and complete
it individually, in pairs, or in groups. When students have finished, elicit the answers
verbally. The chart might look like this:

The Phoenicians	
Where:	The Phoenicians lived where the country of Lebanon is today.
Trading and exploring:	From 1200 to 600 B.C.E., the Phoenicians were great sea traders and explorers.
Stories:	They told stories about sea monsters so other people would be afraid and would not want to compete with them for trade.
Writing:	Writing was important to the Phoenicians. The Phoenician alphabet is the basis of many languages, including English.

REACHING ALL STUDENTS: Auditory and Visual Learners

This activity will help students further explore and relate to the Phoenician alphabet. Bring in a large chart or individual handouts showing the Phoenician alphabet, pronunciation of letter names, and their English equivalents. (These are available on the Internet.) Ask, *Which letters sound like their names in English?* Go through the chart with the class, helping students pronounce the names of the Phoenician letters and eliciting the pronunciation of their English equivalents. Then ask, *Which letters look the most like English letters?* Write student responses on the board. Write a few simple, short English words on the board for the students to write in Phoenician. Then have students write their names in Phoenician. You may want to do this as a group activity, with groups exchanging their Phoenician names on slips of paper, translating them back into English, and then checking that their translations were correct.

MORE ABOUT IT: Purple Dye

Have students look at the box on page 43. Practice <u>previewing</u>. Ask, *What's the heading? What do you think* dye *is?* Read the text, or call on individual students to read it aloud. Elicit or explain the meanings of any new words and help students pronounce them. Have students read the section again silently. Alternatively, assign pairs or small groups and have students take turns reading aloud to each other.

Ask questions such as, *What does the word* Phoenician *mean? Why did the Greeks call them this? What did they make the dye from? Whose favorite color was it? Why is this? Did other people wear purple? Why not? What do you see in the picture?* (a man holding a sea snail) *Can you see the color purple anywhere in the classroom?*

You may want to download or bring in pictures of kings and queens wearing purple in different periods. Discuss how the influence of the Phoenicians lasted such a long time.

Have students read the first two questions. (The first two questions are informational; the third question is critical thinking.) Pair students and have them write the answers in their notebooks. Check the answers. Do the third question together as a class. Tell students that this is a thinking question. Write the answers on the board and have students copy them into their notebooks.

Answers

1. The Phoenicians told stories about sea monsters so other people would be afraid and would not want to compete with them.
2. They made the dye from tiny sea snails.
3. Answers will vary. Possible answer: They wrote names, dates, stories, history.

Working with Timelines

Have students look at the timeline. Read the timeline aloud, and then call on students to read the entries. Help students understand and pronounce the years on the timeline and any new words. To review order of B.C.E. years, ask, *Which year is later, 3000 B.C.E. or 1200 B.C.E.?* Ask comprehension and review questions such as, *When did the Sumerians create cuneiform? What did they write on? What did they write about? What happened in 1200 B.C.E.? Where did it develop? What facts do you know about the Phoenicians?*

Have students copy the Unit Events timeline onto their Lesson 1 Timelines page. Model by beginning the timeline on the board.

Say, *Now I'm going to ask you questions about all the timelines in this lesson. Read your timelines again to yourself.* Ask, *What was the earliest event? When was it? What happened? What was the next event in time?* Elicit the events chronologically. Point out that students may need to look at several timelines to give you the next event in time. To review and consolidate knowledge, you may want to write this timeline on the board as you elicit it. Then have students copy the complete new timeline into their notebooks.

Choose World Events that your students will find interesting. Bring in pictures and maps to help teach these events.

Go to www.longmanusa.com/socialstudies for links to interesting websites about early civilizations.

Review and Practice, pages 44–45

Vocabulary

If your students need additional help in reviewing this vocabulary, see the Optional Vocabulary Activities (pages vii–viii) to choose an appropriate activity. Have students work individually to complete this exercise. Suggest that they copy all the sentences into their notebooks before they begin writing the answers. Check by calling on individual students to read their sentences aloud. Write the correct answers on the board. Have students correct their work, if needed.

Answers

1. glaciers   **3.** hunter-gatherers   **5.** crops

2. irrigation   **4.** agriculture   **6.** archaeologist

Check Your Understanding

Depending upon the language level and abilities of your students, have them work individually, in pairs, or in small groups to answer the questions. Let students look back at the text, as needed. Then have students share their answers with the whole class. Write the answers on the board. Have students correct or add to their answers, if needed.

Answers

1. Early humans settled near rivers because crops needed water to grow. The farmers used water from the river to irrigate their crops.

2. The discovery of bronze was important because it was much harder, better, and lasted longer than stone. People could make better tools and weapons.

3. Trade between different areas developed because copper and tin were hard to find in Europe. People had to travel to find them. They traded goods for copper and tin.

4. The Sumerians developed writing because they needed a way to record information about their products.

Apply Social Studies Skills

Content Reading Strategy: Preview Read the questions aloud, and then assign pairs to ask each other the questions and answer them. Elicit the answers. Write them on the board.

Using Visuals: Use a Timeline Read the heading. Tell students, *You learned a lot using the timelines in this lesson. Now you will practice making your own timeline.* Read the instructions and information on the chart, or call on individual students to read it aloud. Help students understand and pronounce any new words.

Draw a timeline on the board and label it *Ancient Cities*. Explain that "present-day location" means the country where the city (or ruins of the city) is today. Some countries (Iraq and Pakistan) were not known by those names thousands of years ago. Explain that "date founded" means when the city was originally built. Ask, *What's the earliest date on the timeline?* Elicit and write this date on the timeline. Ask, *What city was founded there? What is the present-day location?* Write this information on the timeline.

Have students work in pairs or small groups to complete their timelines. When students are finished, assign several students cities to write on the timeline on the board. The timeline might look like this:

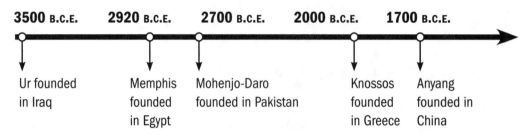

Ancient Cities

3500 B.C.E.	2920 B.C.E.	2700 B.C.E.	2000 B.C.E.	1700 B.C.E.
Ur founded in Iraq	Memphis founded in Egypt	Mohenjo-Daro founded in Pakistan	Knossos founded in Greece	Anyang founded in China

Elicit the answer for the first question and write it on the board as a model. Then assign pairs to ask and answer the questions. Have them write their answers in their notebooks. Check by eliciting the answers and writing them on the board. Have students correct or add to their answers, if needed. Tell students, *Look at the chart in your textbook and the timeline in your notebook. Which is easier to understand? Did the timeline help you answer the questions?*

Answers
1. The title of the timeline is "Ancient Cities."
2. There are 580 years between the founding of the cities of Ur and Memphis.
3. Mohenjo-Daro was founded in 2700 B.C.E.
4. This timeline covers 1,800 years.
5. The present-day location of the city of Ur is in Iraq.

Discuss

Read the discussion question. Have students discuss the question as a class. Encourage them to offer reasons or examples for their opinions. Some inventions today might include computers, calculators, digital cameras, cell phones.

Workbook pages 21–22 may now be assigned for homework or done in class. These pages provide extra practice in the same categories as the Review and Practice pages in the textbook. Students should already be familiar with these types of exercises.

Evaluation

Self-Assessment Questions

Write the following questions on the board, and have students respond in their notebooks. Then have them share their responses in small groups.
1. How can I use previewing to help me in reading?
2. How can timelines help me to understand historical events?
3. What was difficult for me in this lesson?
4. What was easy for me in this lesson?
5. What was most enjoyable to learn?

Lesson ❷

Before You Read, pages 46–49

Have students <u>preview</u> these pages individually or in pairs. Then ask, *What's the topic of this lesson? Why do you think so?*

Vocabulary

Read the captions, or call on individual students to read them aloud. Help students understand and pronounce any new words. Have students read the captions again silently. Ask picture and comprehension questions for each item to make sure students have understood. For example (pointing to the picture of the pyramids), *What are these? Who built them? How long did they take to build? Are they still there today? They're very old—what's another way to say that?*

Point out the key words in the box on page 47. Read them aloud and have students say them after you. Say, *These words are important in this lesson. These words will help you understand the lesson.* Have students close their books. Hold up your book so all students can see. Point to pictures illustrating the key words at random. For each, ask questions to elicit the key words, such as, *What are these?* (pyramids) *Who is this man?* (a pharaoh) *What does this painting show?* (levels of society) *What are the different levels called?* (classes) *Why did many cities build walls?* (to stop invaders) Encourage all students to answer together.

Practice

Read the instructions, or call on a student to read them aloud. Say, *First write the sentences in your notebook. Then choose the correct answers and write them in the sentences.* Make sure students understand the meaning of *separate* in question 1. When students have finished, have them compare their answers with a classmate. Check by calling on individual students to read their sentences aloud. Write the letters of the correct answers on the board.

Answers		
1. b. classes	**3.** c. society	**5.** c. ancient
2. a. invaders	**4.** b. Pyramids	**6.** a. ruler

 Workbook page 23 may now be assigned for homework or done in class. This workbook page provides practice in understanding and using the key words.

Social Studies Skills

 Content Reading Strategy: Predict Write *Predict* on the board. Tell students, *When we predict, we guess what will happen next. This makes a text more interesting to read.* To model the exercise to come, have students look at the picture of the battering ram on page 41. Ask, *What do you think will happen next? What will happen*

after that? What will happen then? Write student responses into a flowchart (like the one on page 48) on the board.

Have students look at the picture on page 48. Elicit and teach vocabulary that students will need. (elephant, warriors, bow and arrow, spear, etc.) Read the information and instructions, or call on individual students to read them aloud. Help students pronounce any new words. Have students reread it silently. Elicit several different predictions from students as to what will happen first. Assign pairs and have them work together to make their predictions. Circulate to help and encourage students. Remind them they can use words or pictures. To check, call on several different pairs to tell or show their predictions to the class.

 Workbook pages 24–25 may now be assigned for homework or done in class. Make sure that students understand how to complete the pages by reading the directions with the class first. Go over the task before students begin.

Using Visuals: Use a Timeline Have students read the heading on the top of the page. Ask, *What visual will you practice using in this lesson?* Read, or call on individual students to read, the instructions and the labels below. Help students understand and pronounce any new words. Have students reread silently.

Draw the timeline on the board and have students copy it into their notebooks. Elicit the first date on the timeline and write this on the board. Then have students complete the timeline in pairs or small groups. Check by eliciting the events in chronological order and writing them into the timeline on the board. The timeline might look like this:

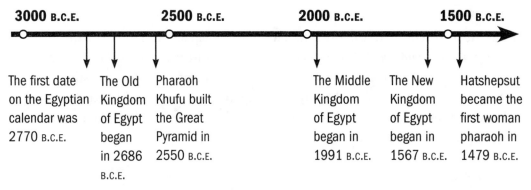

3000 B.C.E.			2500 B.C.E.	2000 B.C.E.		1500 B.C.E.
The first date on the Egyptian calendar was 2770 B.C.E.	The Old Kingdom of Egypt began in 2686 B.C.E.	Pharaoh Khufu built the Great Pyramid in 2550 B.C.E.		The Middle Kingdom of Egypt began in 1991 B.C.E.	The New Kingdom of Egypt began in 1567 B.C.E.	Hatshepsut became the first woman pharaoh in 1479 B.C.E.

 Workbook page 26 may now be assigned for homework or done in class. Make sure that students understand how to complete the page by reading the directions with the class first. Go over the task before students begin.

Reading ❷

Ancient Egypt, pages 50–51

Preview Pages

Have students <u>preview</u> these pages individually or in pairs. Then ask, *What's the topic of these pages? Why do you think so?*

Teach Pages

Have the key words on the board before the students begin. Read the text and captions, or call on individual students to read them aloud. Elicit or explain the meanings of any new words, and help students pronounce them. Ask if students found any key words. (ancient, class, society, rulers) Ask for volunteers to read sentences containing the key words. Ask what the key words mean.

Understand Information Have students read the pages again silently. Alternatively, assign pairs or small groups to take turns reading aloud to each other. Ask comprehension, picture, and thinking questions. For example, *How long did the ancient Egyptian civilization last? What are kingdoms? What were the three kingdoms of Egypt? What did the Egyptians study? Did the Egyptians like art? Do you like the Egyptian art in this book?* (Encourage students to look back at the art on previous pages.) *What did Egyptian artists make? Do any of these carvings and paintings still exist? What did the Egyptians write with? What do we call these?* (pointing to the picture of hieroglyphics on page 51) *What are these? Where are they? What kind of society was Egypt? What class groups did it have? What did most upper-class Egyptians own? What was the lowest class? What were the rulers of Egypt called? What did people believe about the pharaohs? Did the Egyptians have more than one god? What did they believe happened after death?*

Organize Information Draw a chart on the board labeled *The Egyptians*. Say, *Let's make a chart about the Egyptians.* Write subheadings into the chart as you say, *Let's write about when they lived, the three periods, what they studied, their art, their writing, their society, their rulers, and their gods.* Elicit the answers for the first two items and write them into the chart. Have students copy the chart into their notebooks and complete it in pairs or small groups. When students have finished, elicit the answers verbally. The chart might look like this:

The Egyptians	
When:	The ancient Egyptian civilization lasted from 3100 B.C.E. to 332 B.C.E.
Periods:	There were three main time periods we call kingdoms: the Old Kingdom, the Middle Kingdom, and the New Kingdom.
Studied:	The Egyptians studied mathematics and science. They learned about medicine.
Art:	They loved art. Egyptian artists made many paintings and carvings. They still exist today.
Writing:	The Egyptians wrote with pictures. We call this writing "hieroglyphics."
Society:	Egypt was a class society. Egypt had upper-class, middle-class, and lower-class groups. Most upper-class Egyptians owned slaves. Slaves were the lowest class.
Rulers:	The rulers of Egypt were called pharaohs. The people believed the pharaohs had god-like powers.
Gods:	The Egyptians had many gods. They believed that there was life after death.

MATH CONNECTION: Egyptian Calendar

Have students look at the box on page 50. Practice <u>previewing</u>. Ask, *What's the heading? What do you see in the picture? What do you think the topic is?* Read the text, or call on individual students to read it aloud. Elicit or explain the meanings of any new words, and help students pronounce them. Have students read the section again silently. Alternatively, assign pairs or small groups and have students take turns reading aloud to each other.

Ask questions such as, *What did the ancient Egyptians change? How did they do this? Do we use a 365-day calendar? When did their year begin? What two things happened every year at this time? What did the Egyptians use this calendar for?*

As You Read: Predict

Point to the text in the box on page 51. Read it aloud, or call on a student to read it. Elicit or teach any new words. Have students talk about this in pairs, and then elicit their responses. Possible answer: *They will probably be built near the Nile River because they need water for irrigation.*

ELSEWHERE IN THE WORLD: Stonehenge

Have students look at the box on page 51. Practice <u>previewing</u>. Ask, *What's the heading? What do you see in the picture? What do you think the topic is?* Read the text, or call on individual students to read it aloud. Elicit or explain the meanings of any new words and help students pronounce them. Have students read the text again silently. Alternatively, assign pairs or small groups and have students take turns reading aloud to each other.

Ask questions such as, *What did people in England build from 3500 to 1900 B.C.E.? How many years is that? What did they do? What color are the blocks? How much did some blocks weigh? What do we call this monument? What do people think it may have been?*

Bring in photos of Stonehenge, or help students find websites with photos. Discuss with the students how they think the blocks were moved.

Optional Activity

Help students navigate the Internet to find one of the several websites that will translate their names into hieroglyphics. Alternatively, translate your students' first names into hieroglyphics on the Internet, print these out, and bring them to class.

Have students read the first two questions. Pair students and have them write the answers in their notebooks. Check the answers. Do the third question together as a class. Tell students that this is a thinking question. Write the answers on the board and have students copy them into their notebooks.

Answers
1. They studied mathematics and science. They learned about medicine and they loved art.
2. Egyptian artists made many paintings and carvings of daily life. They still exist today. The Egyptians wrote with pictures called hieroglyphics. They used a calendar to record much of their history.
3. Answers will vary. Possible answers: I can see several birds, a bird with a fish, several people sitting or standing, a bowl of water or oil, a flower.

Working with Timelines

Have students look at the timeline. Read the timeline aloud, and then call on students to read the entries. Help students understand and pronounce the years on the timeline and any new words. Ask comprehension and review questions such as, *When did the Egyptian civilization begin? When did the Old Kingdom begin? When did the Middle Kingdom begin? When did the New Kingdom begin?* Have students write the heading *Unit 1, Lesson 2 Timelines* on a new page in their notebooks. Then have them copy the Unit Events timeline.

Ancient Egypt (continued), page 52
Ancient Nubia, page 53

Preview Pages

Have students preview these pages individually or in pairs. Then ask, *What are the topics on these pages? Why do you think so?*

Teach Pages

Read the text and captions, or call on individual students to read them aloud. Elicit or explain the meanings of any new words, and help students pronounce them. Have students close their books after reading the first paragraph on page 53. Ask students, *What is the reading strategy in this lesson?* Ask, *What do you do when you predict?* (think about what's going to happen next) Say, *Egypt ruled Nubia for 1,000 years. What do you think is going to happen to Nubia after that?* Elicit several guesses. Remind students, *Predicting makes reading more interesting.* Have them open their books and continue with the reading.

Ask if students found any key words. (pyramids, ancient, invaded [related to invader]) Ask for volunteers to read sentences containing these words. Ask what these words mean.

Understand Information Have students read pages 52–53 again silently. Alternatively, assign pairs or small groups to take turns reading aloud to each other. Ask comprehension, picture, and thinking questions such as (pointing to the picture of the mummy), *What is this? What did Egyptians do to the bodies of dead people? What does* preserved *mean? What are the preserved bodies called? What's a sarcophagus? What's a coffin? Where did the Egyptians bury the pharaoh? What's a tomb? Where were some tombs? Who did Egyptians build the largest pyramid for? How old was he when he became a pharaoh? What year was that? Where was ancient Nubia? What did Nubia and Egypt do? What are archers? Were Nubia's archers good? How long did Egypt rule Nubia? What was Kerma? How did the people bury their kings? What are mounds? Where did they place the king's body? What surrounded the beds? What happened around 700 B.C.E.? What happened after the Egyptians left? What did the Nubians do? What did they do in Meroe?*

Organize Information Draw a chart on the board labeled *The Nubians*. Say, *Let's make a chart about the Nubians.* Write subheadings into the chart. Elicit the answers for the first two items and write them into the chart. Have students copy the chart into their notebooks and complete it in pairs or small groups. When students have finished, elicit the answers verbally. The chart might look like this:

The Nubians	
Where:	Ancient Nubia was the land south of Egypt.
Trade:	Nubia and Egypt traded goods with each other.
Archers:	Nubia's archers were very skilled.
Mounds:	In the Nubian city of Kerma, people buried their kings in mounds.
Rulers:	Egypt ruled Nubia for about 1,000 years.
Independence:	Around 700 B.C.E., the Nubians gained their independence from Egypt.

MORE ABOUT IT: Mummies

Have students look at the box on page 52. Practice <u>previewing</u>. Ask, *What's the heading? What do you see in the picture? What do you think the topic is?* Read the text, or call on individual students to read it aloud. Elicit or explain the meanings of any new words, and help students pronounce them. Have students read the section again silently. Alternatively, assign pairs or small groups and have students take turns reading aloud to each other.

Ask questions such as, *How long did it take to make a mummy? What did the Egyptians remove first? Then what did they do to the body? What did they do next? What happened next?* (pointing to the bandages in the picture) *What are these? Where was a mummy finally put? What other things were mummified?*

(continued)

Bring in photos of the sarcophaguses and other artifacts from Tutankhamen's tomb, or help students find websites with photos. Discuss with students the Egyptian belief in life after death and that it was one reason pharaohs were buried in this manner.

REACHING ALL STUDENTS: Visual Learners

Say, *Let's draw a picture of how pharaohs were buried. Drawing pictures can help us understand.* Have students reread the text on page 52. On the board, write *A Pharaoh's Mummy* and draw a simple prone mummy or stick figure. Have students copy this into their notebooks. Ask, *Where was the mummy put?* Draw three or four coffins around the mummy. Ask, *What were these coffins called?* Label them *sarcophaguses.* Continue asking questions, drawing, and labeling to complete the picture with a tomb and pyramid. Have students draw each additional detail into their notebooks as you draw it on the board.

PROFILE: Hatshepsut

Have students look at the box on page 52. Practice <u>previewing</u>. Ask, *What's the heading? What do you see in the picture? What do you think the topic is?* Read the text, or call on individual students to read it aloud. Elicit or explain the meanings of any new words, and help students pronounce them. Have students read the section again silently. Alternatively, assign pairs or small groups and have students take turns reading aloud to each other.

Ask questions such as (pointing to the picture of Hatshepsut), *Who is this woman? Whose wife was she? What happened in 1479 B.C.E.? Who was going to be pharaoh? Who became a pharaoh instead? Why? Why is Hatshepsut famous? How long was she pharaoh? Did Egypt have wars while Hatshepsut was pharaoh? What did she send to other countries? What did the ships bring back? Was Hatshepsut a great builder? What did she do? Do any of these temples exist today? How old is it? Do you think Hatsheput was a good pharaoh?*

Language Tip: Possessive Nouns

Read the text in the box on page 53, or ask a student to read it to the class. Write *Possessive Nouns* on the board and have students copy it into their notebooks. Explain that *Nubia* and *the king* are possessive nouns. The *archers* belong to Nubia, and the *body* belongs to the king. Write another example on the board, such as *The book belongs to Luz = Luz's book.* Say, *Now write a sentence about something that belongs to someone in our class. Use a possessive noun.* When students have finished, elicit several of their sentences.

Have students read the first question only. Make sure students understand the word *prepare*. Pair students to write the question and answer it in their notebooks. Check answers. Do the second and third questions together as a class. Tell students question 2 is a thinking question. For question 3 say, *You need to predict*. Write the answers on the board and have students copy them into their notebooks.

Answers
1. It took about three months to prepare a mummy.
2. The Egyptians and Assyrians conquered the Nubians.
3. Answers may vary. Possible answers: They moved again./They stayed in Meroe./ They were conquered again. [Note: You may want to point out that an African kingdom conquered Meroe, but we don't really know what happened to the Nubians after that.]

Working with Timelines

Have students look at the timeline. Read the timeline aloud, and then call on students to read the entries. Help students understand and pronounce the years on the timeline and any new words. Ask comprehension and review questions such as, *When did King Khufu become pharaoh? What did the Egyptians build for him? When did Hatshepsut become pharaoh? Why did she become pharaoh? When did Nubia gain independence from Egypt? How long before this did Egypt rule Nubia?* Have students copy the Unit Events timeline onto their Lesson 2 Timelines page.

Ancient China, pages 54–55

Preview Pages

Have students preview these pages individually or in pairs. Then ask, *What's the topic of these pages? Why do you think so?*

Teach Pages

Read the text and captions, or call on individual students to read them aloud. Elicit or explain the meanings of any new words, and help students pronounce them. Ask if students found any key words. (ancient, ruler [and verb forms *rules, ruled*], invaders) Ask for volunteers to read a couple of sentences containing these words. Ask what the key words mean.

Understand Information Have students read the pages again silently. Alternatively, assign pairs or small groups to take turns reading aloud to each other. Ask comprehension and picture questions. For example, *What was the largest empire in Asia? What happened when a Chinese ruler died? What is it called when one family rules for many years? What was the longest dynasty in Chinese history? When did the Zhou dynasty rule China? About how many years is that? What's an emperor? What was the Chinese emperor called? Which dynasty ruled China next? Who was Shi Huangdi?*

What did he build? Why did he build it? How long is the Great Wall? (pointing to the picture of the Great Wall of China on page 54) *What do you think the towers were for?* (soldiers) (pointing to the picture of the terra-cotta statues on page 55) *What are these? What are they made of? What important things did the Chinese invent? What did they use for trade? What are coins? Do we use coins for trade today? Whose teachings did many Chinese follow? What did Confucius and Lao Tzu believe? Does anybody follow these teachings today?*

Ask, *What is the reading strategy in this lesson?* Ask, *What do you do when you predict?* (think about what's going to happen next) Say, *Shi Huangdi built the Great Wall of China to keep his kingdom safe from invaders. Do you think it worked? Do you think China still uses it to keep out invaders?* Elicit several guesses.

Language Tip: Comparatives and Superlatives

Read the text in the box on page 54, or ask a student to read it to the class. Write *Comparatives* and *Superlatives* on the board. Ask, pointing to the example words, *Which words are comparatives? Which are superlatives?* Write these words under the appropriate heading. Have students copy this into their notebooks. Have students find and read aloud the sentences in the text containing these examples. Remind students, writing on the board, *With short words like these, we don't use* more *or* most*. We don't say* more large *or* most large*. Instead of* more*, we add* -er*. Instead of* most*, we add* -est*. For a word ending in* -e*, we can just add an* -r*.

Elicit some other short adjectives whose comparatives and superlatives are formed with *-er* and *-est*. (old, tall, great, hard, fast, etc.) Write these on the board, and then have students copy them into their notebooks and write the comparative and superlative forms. Check by eliciting the spelling of each and writing them on the board.

Organize Information Introduce students to a paragraph's main idea and details. Draw a box on the board and label it *Main Idea*. Have students reread the first paragraph on page 55. Then say, *There are four sentences here. One tells the main idea, the most important idea. Which sentence is that?* When students have successfully identified it, write it in the box. Say, *Often the first sentence in a paragraph will tell the main idea.* Draw three more boxes and label each *Detail*. Ask, *What are the details?* Write the responses on the board. The chart might look like this:

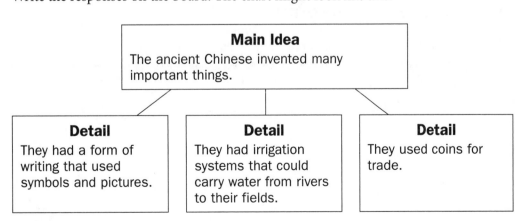

Main Idea
The ancient Chinese invented many important things.

Detail
They had a form of writing that used symbols and pictures.

Detail
They had irrigation systems that could carry water from rivers to their fields.

Detail
They used coins for trade.

Have students reread the second paragraph on page 55. Ask, *What is the main idea?* Write this on the board in a *Main Idea* box. Then draw lines to three more boxes labeled *Detail*. Have students work individually or in pairs to complete the charts in their notebooks. When students have finished, elicit the information and write it on the board. The chart might look like this:

Main Idea
Many Chinese followed the teachings of Confucius and Lao Tzu.

Detail
They were famous teachers who believed that all people are important and should be kind to each other.

Detail
They also taught that people should live in peace with nature.

Detail
Many people still follow these teachings today.

CONNECT TO TODAY: Acupuncture

Have students look at the box on page 55. Practice <u>previewing</u>. Ask, *What's the heading? What do you see in the picture? What do you think acupuncture is?* Read the text or call on individual students to read it aloud. Elicit or explain the meanings of any new words, and help students pronounce them. Have students read the selection again silently, or aloud in pairs or small groups. Ask comprehension questions such as, *What is acupuncture? When did it begin? What is it used for? What happens in acupuncture? How long do the needles stay in? Where is acupuncture practiced today? Would you like to try acupuncture?*

Before You Go On

Have students read the first two questions. Pair students and have them write the answers in their notebooks. Check the answers. Do the third question together as a class. Tell students that this is a thinking question. Write the answers on the board, and have students copy them into their notebooks.

Answers
1. The Zhou dynasty ruled China for 824 years (from 1045 to 221 B.C.E.).
2. The ancient Chinese used coins to buy things.
3. Answers will vary. Possible answers: They taught that all people are important and should be kind to each other. They also taught that people should live in peace with nature. These are good ideas. They are good for society, and they make life better.

Working with Timelines

Read the timeline aloud, and then call on students to read the entries. Help students understand and pronounce the years on the timeline and any new words.

Ask comprehension and review questions such as, *What happened in 1045 B.C.E. in China? What's a dynasty? What do you know about the Zhou dynasty? Which dynasty ruled China after the Zhou dynasty? When did the Qin emperor begin the Great Wall? Why did he build it? How long is it? When was Confucius born? What did he teach?* Have students copy the Unit Events timeline onto the Lesson 2 Timelines page.

Ancient Persia, pages 56–57

Preview Pages

Have students <u>preview</u> these pages individually or in pairs. Then ask, *What's the topic of these pages? Why do you think so?*

Teach Pages

Read the text and captions, or call on individual students to read them aloud. Elicit or explain the meanings of any new words, and help students pronounce them. After the sentence ending "united the Persians and Medes into one kingdom," have students close their books. Ask, *What is the reading strategy in this lesson?* Ask, *What do you think will happen to Persia now that it's united?* Elicit several guesses. Then continue the reading.

Ask if students found any key words. (ancient) Ask for volunteers to read a sentence containing this word. Ask what the word means.

Understand Information Have students read the pages again silently. Alternatively, assign pairs or small groups to take turns reading aloud to each other. Ask comprehension, picture, and thinking questions. For example, *Where was Persia located? What two peoples lived there? Who ruled? Were the Medes good warriors? Who defeated the Medes in 551 B.C.E.? What did he do then? What does* united *mean? What did a Persian king named Darius do? What happened to the Persian Empire?* (pointing to the map on page 56) *What places did Persia rule over? Did the Persians worship just one god? Who was the most important god? What was he the god of? What did the Persians build? Where did the Persians worship the gods? What does* worship *mean?* (pointing to the picture of the wall carving on page 56) *What did Persians carve these walls with? What does* carved *mean? What's this?* (pointing to the picture of Persepolis today on page 57) *What does this picture show? What do you think these buildings were?*

Organize Information Lead the students in making a flowchart about the Persian Empire. Write the heading *The Persian Empire* on the board and draw four boxes with arrows between them. Write *The Medes ruled the Persians* in the first box. To elicit each event in the growth of the Persian Empire, ask students, *What happened next?*

Write the responses on the board and have students copy them into their notebooks. The flowchart might look like this:

The Persian Empire

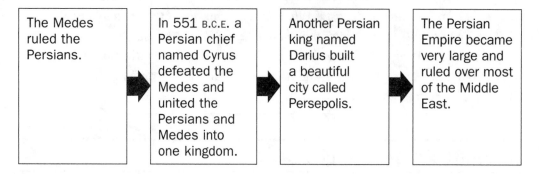

| The Medes ruled the Persians. | In 551 B.C.E. a Persian chief named Cyrus defeated the Medes and united the Persians and Medes into one kingdom. | Another Persian king named Darius built a beautiful city called Persepolis. | The Persian Empire became very large and ruled over most of the Middle East. |

MORE ABOUT IT: Persian Cats

Have students look at the box on page 57. Practice <u>previewing</u>. Ask, *What's the heading?* (pointing to the picture) *What animal do you think this is?* Bring in a picture of a Persian cat to show the class before the reading. Ask questions to elicit information about the traits of this type of cat, including length of hair.

Read the text, or call on individual students to read it aloud. Elicit or explain the meanings of any new words, and help students pronounce them. Have students read the selection again silently, or aloud in pairs or small groups. Ask comprehension questions such as, *What do some historians believe? What did the cats' long hair protect them from? Who were Persian cats the pets of? What was believed about the cats?*

Before You Go On

Have students read the first two questions. Make sure students understand the word *originally*. Pair students and have them write the answers in their notebooks. Check the answers. Do the third question together as a class. Tell students that this is a thinking question. Write the answers on the board, and have students copy them into their notebooks.

Answers
1. The Medes originally ruled ancient Persia.
2. A Persian king named Darius built the ancient city of Persepolis.
3. Answers will vary. Possible answers: They were proud of their history. They wanted to teach their children about important events.

Working with Timelines

Read the timeline aloud, and then call on students to read the entries. Help students understand and pronounce the years on the timeline and any new words. Ask comprehension and review questions such as, *When did Cyrus unite the Medes and Persians? Who were the Medes and Persians? Who was Cyrus? What did Cyrus*

(continued)

make Persia into? What did Darius do in 522 B.C.E.? Who was Darius? What did the Persian Empire finally rule over? Have students copy the Unit Events timeline onto their Lesson 2 Timelines page.

Go to www.longmanusa.com/socialstudies for links to interesting websites about ancient China and Persia.

Review and Practice, pages 58–59

Vocabulary

If your students need additional help in reviewing this vocabulary, see the Optional Vocabulary Activities (pages vii–viii) to choose an appropriate activity.

Have students work individually to complete this exercise. Suggest that they copy all the sentences into their notebooks before they begin writing the answers. Check by calling on individual students to read their sentences aloud. Write the correct key word on the board. Have students correct their answers, if needed.

Answers
1. society
2. ancient
3. invaders
4. ruler
5. classes
6. pyramids

Check Your Understanding

Depending upon the language level and abilities of your students, have them work individually, in pairs, or in small groups to answer the questions. Let students look back at the text, as needed. Then have students share their answers with the whole class. Write the answers on the board. Have students correct or add to their answers, if needed.

Answers
1. The classes in ancient Egyptian society were upper, middle, and lower class.
2. Ancient Egyptians buried their kings in tombs inside the pyramids.
3. The Persian civilization was located where Iran is now.
4. (The Qin emperor) Shi Huangdi built the Great Wall of China.

Apply Social Studies Skills

Content Reading Strategy: Predict Review the reading strategy. Ask students, *What do we do when we predict? How does this make reading more interesting?* Read the instructions and choices, or call on a student to read them aloud. Have students work with a classmate to choose one. Then ask students who chose the first prediction to raise their hands. Ask why they chose it. Do the same for the second prediction. Have the class vote on the best prediction. Have students write this in their notebooks.

Using Visuals: Use a Timeline Read the heading. Tell students, *This timeline will show you some new information.* Read the instructions, or call on individual students to read them aloud. Have students work in pairs to find the answers to the questions and write them in their notebooks. Tell students, *Look at the question. Then look at the timeline to find the answer.* Check by eliciting the answers and writing them on the board. Then go through the timeline with the students chronologically. Teach any new words and how to pronounce them. Ask students what they think of Tutankhamen's golden sarcophagus.

Answers
- Mummification began in Egypt
- Sphinx built and Thutmose I became pharaoh
- Tutankhamen became pharaoh

Discuss

Read the discussion question. Then assign small groups to discuss the question. Circulate to help and comment on student's responses. Allow time for students to share their answers with the class.

 Workbook pages 27–28 may now be assigned for homework or done in class. These pages provide extra practice in the same categories as the Review and Practice pages in the textbook. Students should already be familiar with these types of exercises.

Evaluation

Self-Assessment Questions

Write the following questions on the board. Have students respond in their notebooks. Then have them share their responses in small groups.
1. How can I use predicting to help me in reading?
2. How can timelines help me to understand information?
3. What was difficult for me in this lesson?
4. What was easy for me in this lesson?
5. What was most enjoyable to learn?

Unit Review, pages 60–61

Vocabulary

Read the instructions, or call on a student to read them aloud. Model by eliciting the answer for question 1 and writing it on the board. Have students work individually, with a classmate, or in small groups, depending on how much support they need. After they have finished, check answers together as a class, writing the answers on the board.

Answers

1. ancient	4. glaciers	7. classes	10. society
2. crops	5. pyramids	8. irrigation	11. agriculture
3. archaeologist	6. hunter-gatherers	9. ruler	12. invaders

Timeline Check

Read the instructions, or call on a student to read them aloud. Have students write the sentences (not the answers yet) in their notebooks. Then model by having students find the first event on the Unit 1 timeline. Elicit the year, and write this on the board. Suggest that students find the dates for all the events, and then put the events in order. Have students work with a partner or in small groups. After they have finished, check answers together as a class, writing the numbers on the board.

Answers

3	The Sumerians invented the wheel.
2	The first farmers settled near large rivers.
6	The Chinese built the Great Wall of China.
1	The earliest humans lived in the Stone Age.
4	Egyptian kings called pharaohs ruled Egypt.
5	Hammurabi wrote rules for his people.

Apply Social Studies Skills

Using Visuals: Use a Timeline Read the instructions aloud, or call on a student to read them. Have students reread the instructions. Model by drawing a timeline on the board about the life of a fictitious student. Include typical life events to teach vocabulary and concepts students can use. (born, started school, moved to the United States, started school in Los Angeles, joined a sports team, visited San Francisco, etc.) Have students work individually to complete their timelines. Circulate to help with vocabulary. Check by calling on students to share their timelines with the class.

Extension Project

Help students find information on the Internet or in the library, or bring in materials about Knossos for students to work with. Depending on your resources and student ability, have students work in pairs, in small groups, or as a class to find out more about this ancient city. Have pairs or groups discuss why people like to visit Knossos. (to see the ancient ruins, to learn about early Greek civilization) Elicit the students' opinions, write them on the board, and have students copy them into their notebooks.

Read More About It

Bring at least one of the suggested books to class. Show the cover and some of the inside pages to students as a <u>preview</u>. Ask students to <u>predict</u> what the book is about. Read an excerpt aloud to the class. Then ask several comprehension questions. Read the excerpt again before calling on students to answer. Encourage students to find this or another suggested book in their school library or local bookstore.

Workbook pages 29–30 may now be assigned for homework or done in class. These pages provide extra practice in the same categories as the Unit Review pages in the textbook. Students should already be familiar with these types of exercises.

Writing Skills, pages 62–63

Make a Plan

Preview

Have students <u>preview</u> these two pages individually or in pairs. Then ask, *Who do you think you will be writing about?*

Present the Model

Read the information on page 62 aloud, or call on students to read it. Help students understand and pronounce any new words (paragraph, plan, organize). Have students read the page again silently. Then ask comprehension questions such as, *What do you do before writing a paragraph? What does a plan help you do? How can you make a plan?* (pointing to the word web on page 62) *What's this? What's the topic? What are some details?* (pointing to the paragraph) *What's the beginning of the paragraph? What are the middle sentences? What's the end?*

Say, *Copy the model paragraph into your notebooks. Draw arrows to show the beginning, middle, and end.* Model (and facilitate checking the next section) by writing the paragraph on the board and labeling it. Then say, *Underline the information from the word web in this paragraph.* Model by eliciting and underlining the first two pieces of information from the word web. Have students work individually or in pairs to underline. Then check by eliciting the answers and underlining them on the board.

Practice

Since this is the first Writing Skills practice, do it as a class. Read, or call on students to read, the information on the word web about Confucius. Elicit the meanings of recently learned words to make sure students understand.

Ask students, *What's a good beginning to our paragraph about Confucius?* Encourage students to look back at the model paragraph. Elicit a full sentence, helping with structure, as needed. Write the correct student response on the board, and have students copy it into their notebooks. Continue by asking *What's a good middle? What's a good end?* The paragraph might look like this:

> *Confucius was born in 551 B.C.E. He was a Chinese teacher and thinker. He lived in a time of war. He believed people should be kind, and wanted to bring peace to China. He died in 479 B.C.E.*

After students have finished copying the paragraph into their notebooks, have them label it with *beginning, middle,* and *end.* To check, elicit this and write it on the board.

 Workbook pages 31–32 may now be assigned for homework or done in class. These pages provide additional writing practice.

Unit 2 — The Classical World

Unit Overview

Lesson	Content	Social Studies Skills		Writing Skills
		Reading Strategies	Using Visuals	
1	• The End of Egypt • Early Greek Cities • Greek Life • Sparta • Macedonia	Visualize	Use a Map Key	Write a Paragraph
2	• The Beginning of Rome • Life after Caesar • The Fall of the Roman Empire • The Byzantine Empire • The Muslim Empire	Ask Questions	Use a Compass Rose	

Objectives

Vocabulary
• Develop new vocabulary related to the classical world
• Use newly acquired vocabulary in context

Concepts
• Acquire knowledge of the Golden Age of Greece
• Acquire knowledge of the Roman Empire

Reading Strategies
• Visualize to understand and remember what you read
• Ask questions to help understand what you read
• Practice previously learned strategies

Using Visuals
• Understand how to use a map key and compass rose

Writing Skills
• Practice writing a paragraph

Unit Opener, pages 64–65

Preview Topic

Hold up your book and point to the unit title. Read it aloud or call on a student to read it. Say, and write on the board, *In this unit, we'll study the classical world. The great civilizations of Greece and Rome are called "classical." Many things in our society today come from the Greek and Roman civilizations.* Point out Greece and Rome on a map or globe. Point to the photo of the Roman frieze and say, *This is a Roman wall carving. It shows some of the people of Rome.* Ask, helping with vocabulary as needed, *How many people can you see? What are they wearing? What do they have on their heads? What do they have on their feet? How many children can you see?* Encourage students to make guesses. Don't correct their responses now; they are just previewing.

Unit Contents

Read the headings on page 65 aloud. Say, *These are the people, places, and events we will learn about in this unit.* Help students pronounce the list of names. Say each name and have students repeat. Ask if students recognize any names. Ask what they know about them. Write that information on the board. Follow the same procedures with place names. Use a world map or globe to teach or elicit the locations of these places.

For key events, say, *These are the key, or most important, events we will learn about.* Read aloud the list of key events, or call on a student to read them. Elicit or teach any new words and help students pronounce them. Have students copy the key events into their notebooks.

Get Ready

Say, *Before we start this unit, let's review some dates from Unit 1.* Read the instructions, or call on a student to read them. Ask students, *What do you need to do first? What do you write on the timeline?* Draw the timeline on the board as a model while students copy it into their notebooks. Review page 25 about timelines, if necessary. Have students look back at the Unit 1 Unit Events timeline to find the answers. Elicit the caption for the first date (7000 B.C.E.) on page 38 and write it on the board. Have students work in pairs or small groups to find the information and write it on their timelines. Check by eliciting the captions and writing them on the board. The timeline might look like this:

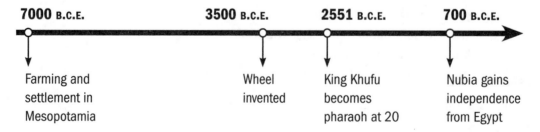

7000 B.C.E.	3500 B.C.E.	2551 B.C.E.	700 B.C.E.
Farming and settlement in Mesopotamia	Wheel invented	King Khufu becomes pharaoh at 20	Nubia gains independence from Egypt

Lesson 1

Before You Read, pages 66–69

Vocabulary

Read the captions, or call on students to read them aloud. Help students understand and pronounce any new words. Use pictures, props, and mime. Have students read the captions again silently. Ask picture and comprehension questions for each item to make sure students have understood. For example, ask (pointing to the sculpture), *What's this? Who made it? What did they use to make it? Do you think he's a soldier?*

Point out the key words in the box on page 67. Read them aloud and have students say them after you. Say, *These words are important in this lesson. Let's learn these words.* Have students close their books. Hold up your book so all students can see. Point to pictures illustrating the key words. Ask questions to elicit each key word. Encourage all students to answer together.

Practice

Read the instructions, or call on a student to read them aloud. Make sure students understand the words *feast* in question 1 and *structure* in question 6. Model by writing sentence 1 on the board, and then elicit the answer. Have students work individually to fill in the blanks. When students have finished, have them compare their answers with a classmate. Check by calling on students to read their sentences aloud. Write the letters of the correct answers on the board.

> **Answers**
> **1.** c. festival   **3.** c. amphitheater   **5.** b. pottery
> **2.** a. sculptures   **4.** b. drama   **6.** a. monument

 Workbook page 33 may now be assigned.

Social Studies Skills

 Content Reading Strategy: Visualize Write *Visualize* on the board. Tell students, *When we <u>visualize</u>, we think of pictures in our mind while we read.* Tell students to close their eyes. Tell them to imagine pictures as they listen to you read. Read the second paragraph about King Tutankhamen on page 70. Pause a few seconds after each sentence. Have students open their eyes. Ask, *What did you see? What words helped you see that?*

Read the information at the top of page 68, or call on students to read it aloud. Have students reread it silently. Ask comprehension and picture questions. Write the new words *papyrus* and *reeds* on the board and teach them before students begin the reading.

Read the paragraph aloud. Pause after each sentence and ask, *Did you visualize? Did you see a picture in your mind?* Have students read the paragraph once more silently. Say, *Visualize as you read. Stop for a few seconds after each sentence. Visualize a picture in your mind.*

Workbook page 34 may now be assigned.

Using Visuals: Use a Map Key Have students read the heading on the top of the page. Ask, *What visual did you practice using in Unit 1?* (timelines) *What visual will you practice using in this lesson?* Point to the map key and ask, *What is this?* Read the introduction, or call on a student to read it aloud. Help students understand and pronounce any new words. Help students pronounce the place names on the map, including *Mt./Mount* (= mountain). Then have them reread silently. Ask comprehension questions. Have students study the map. Then assign pairs. Say, *Ask and answer the questions, and then write the answers in your notebook.* When students have finished, elicit the answers, and write them on the board.

Answers

1. The name of the mountain on the map is Mt. (Mount) Olympus.
2. The Aegean Sea and the Mediterranean Sea are near Greece.
3. Answers will vary. Possible answer: Three cities are Delphi, Corinth, and Olympia.

 Workbook pages 35–36 may now be assigned.

Reading ❶

The End of Egypt, pages 70–71

Preview Pages

Have students preview these pages and predict the topic.

Teach Pages

Have the key words on the board before the students begin. Read the text and captions, or call on students to read them. Use pictures, drawings, maps, and mime to teach the meaning of new words. Help students with pronunciation.

Understand Information Have students reread the pages. Ask comprehension, picture, and thinking questions. For example, *When did the New Kingdom of Egypt begin? Who was it ruled by until then? What did the Egyptian princes do? Whose mask do you see? What do you think it's made of? What do you think of it?*

Write the word *visualize* on the board. Ask, *What do you do when you visualize? Visualize as you read. Stop for a few seconds after each sentence. Visualize a picture in your mind.*

 As You Read: Visualize

Read the text in the box on page 71, or call on a student to read it. Elicit or teach any new words. Ask the question and call on volunteers to answer. Encourage students to reconstruct the scene.

Organize Information Say, *Let's do a word web about King Tutankhamen.* Have students look back at the word webs on pages 62–63 as a review. Ask, *Who's the subject of our word web? What was he? When was he a pharaoh? When did he become the ruler of Egypt? When did he die? What was he buried with?* Write the responses into the word web and have students copy them into their notebooks. The word web might look like this:

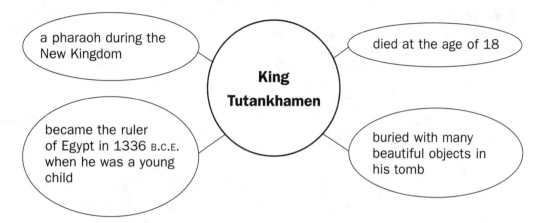

a pharaoh during the New Kingdom

King Tutankhamen

died at the age of 18

became the ruler of Egypt in 1336 B.C.E. when he was a young child

buried with many beautiful objects in his tomb

Then say, *Let's do a word web about Cleopatra.* Depending on student ability, do the word web as a class, or assign small groups to complete it. The word web might look like this:

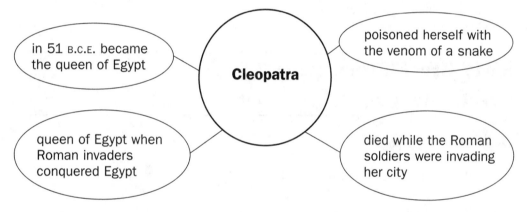

in 51 B.C.E. became the queen of Egypt

Cleopatra

poisoned herself with the venom of a snake

queen of Egypt when Roman invaders conquered Egypt

died while the Roman soldiers were invading her city

MORE ABOUT IT: Tutankhamen's Curse

Have students look at the box on page 70. Practice <u>previewing</u>. Ask, *What's the heading? What do you see in the picture? What do you think a curse is?* Read the text, or call on students to read it. Elicit or explain the meanings of any new words, and help students pronounce them. Have students read the section again silently. Alternatively, assign pairs or small groups and have students take turns reading aloud to each other. Ask questions such as, *Who were Howard Carter and Lord Carnarvon? What did they do? What did they find?*

Have students look at websites showing the discovery of King Tut's tomb. Alternatively, bring in photos to pass around. Discuss why Egyptians might have written curses in a mummy's tomb. (to protect the treasures from grave robbers) Discuss how mummy movies are based on the curses found in tombs.

Have students read the first two questions. Make sure students understand the word *cultures*. Pair students and have them write the answers in their notebooks. Check the answers. Do the third question together as a class. Write the answers on the board, and have students copy them into their notebooks.

Answers

1. Cleopatra poisoned herself with the venom of a snake.
2. Roman invaders conquered Egypt.
3. Answers will vary. Possible answers: We read about them. We study their history. We look at their art. We visit the country.

Working with Timelines

Read the timeline entries, or call on students to read them. Ask comprehension and review questions such as, *When did the New Kingdom begin? What did Egyptian princes do in 1567 B.C.E.? What happened in 1336 B.C.E.?* Have students write the heading *Unit 2, Lesson 1 Timelines* on a new page in their notebooks. Then have them copy the Unit Events timeline. Students will add more timelines to this page later in the lesson.

Choose World Events that your students will find interesting. Bring in pictures and maps to help teach these events.

Early Greek Cities, page 72
Greek Life, page 73

Preview Pages

Have students preview these pages and predict the topics.

Teach Pages

Read the text and captions, or call on students to read them. Help students understand and pronounce any new words. Elicit the key word (festivals), the sentence it's in, and its definition.

Understand Information Have students reread the pages. Ask, *What pictures did you visualize?* Ask, *Which words helped you visualize?*

Language Tip: Pronouns

Read the text in the box on page 72 aloud, or call on a volunteer to read it. Write the word *Pronouns* on the board, and then write the example sentences. Have students copy this into their notebooks. Ask, *How do I know the pronoun for* Greek cities *is* they? (*Greek cities* is plural) Write *Plural* on the board. Ask, *How do I know*

(continued)

the pronoun for <u>laws</u> *is* <u>them</u>? (it's plural and it's the subject) Ask, *How do I know the pronoun for* <u>democracy</u> *is* <u>it</u>? (it's not plural; it's uncountable) Write *Not plural* and *Uncountable* on the board.

Have students look at the second paragraph on page 72. Read the first sentence and ask, *What's a pronoun for* <u>life</u>? Elicit pronouns for *historians, this period, the Greeks, the idea of democracy, Pericles, poor people, the government of Athens, equal justice,* and *all people.* Write these words and their pronouns on the board as you elicit them. Have students copy them into their notebooks.

Ask comprehension, picture, and thinking questions. Help and encourage students to use pronouns in their answers. For example, *What were early Greek cities like?* (<u>They</u> were like small countries.) *Why was a city like a small country?* (<u>It</u> had its own government and made its own laws.) *What's a government?* (<u>It's</u> the people who control what happens in a country.) *Where is the government of the United States?* (<u>It's</u> in Washington, D.C.)

Organize Information Say, *Let's do a Main Idea and Details chart of the first paragraph on page 72.* Ask, *What's the main idea? What are the details?* Write the responses onto a Main Idea and Details chart on the board, and have students copy it into their notebooks. The chart might look like this:

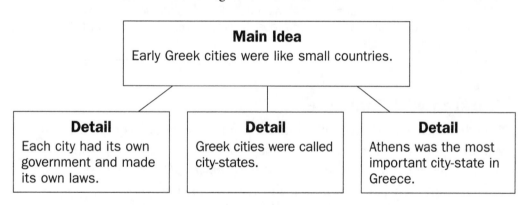

REACHING ALL STUDENTS: Visual Learners

Have students copy the picture of the Greek home on page 72 into their notebooks and label it. Then draw a cutaway view of a modern American house on the board. Have students copy this into their notebooks and, in pairs or small groups, have them label it. Circulate to help with vocabulary. To check, elicit the labels and write them on the board.

CONNECT TO TODAY: The Olympic Games

Have students look at the box on page 73. Practice <u>previewing</u>. Ask, *What's the heading? Have you ever seen the Olympic Games on TV? Can you see the Olympics symbol in the picture? The word on the poster is Greek. It's the name of a Greek city.* Say and write on the board, *The letter* Θ *is pronounced /th/. Can you guess which city this is?* (Athens) Read the text, or call on students to read it.

(continued)

Elicit or explain the meanings of any new words, and help students pronounce them. Have students read the section again silently. Alternatively, assign pairs or small groups and have students take turns reading aloud to each other.

Ask questions such as, *When did the first Olympic Games take place? Where did they take place? What is the earliest recorded date of the games?* Encourage students to use pronouns in their answers.

Bring in photos of different Olympic sports and teach or elicit their English names. Ask students which sports they like to watch, and why.

Before You Go On

Have students read the first two questions. Pair students and have them write the answers in their notebooks. Check the answers. Do the third question together as a class. Write the answers on the board and have students copy them into their notebooks.

Answers

1. Athens was a city-state and a democracy.
2. Pericles was an important leader and warrior in Athens during the Golden Age. He made it possible for poor people to be in the government. He said there should be equal justice for all people.
3. Answers will vary. Possible answers: Women and slaves were not allowed to vote. They probably didn't discuss politics as much. Slaves did much of the work in Athens. The other men and women probably didn't have to work as hard. They had time for many festivals.

Working with Timelines

Read the timeline entries, or call on students to read them. Ask comprehension and review questions such as, *What's important about 776 B.C.E.? How did the Olympic Games begin? When did the Golden Age of Greece begin?* Have students copy the Unit Events timeline onto their Lesson 1 Timelines page.

Choose World Events that your students will find interesting. Bring in pictures and maps to help teach these events.

Greek Life (continued), page 74
Sparta, page 75

Preview Pages

Have students underline preview these pages and predict the topics.

Teach Pages

Read the text and captions, or call on students to read them. Help students understand and pronounce any new words. Elicit the key words (amphitheater, pottery, sculptures), the sentences they're in, and their definitions.

Ask, *What's the reading strategy for this lesson? What do you do when you <u>visualize</u>? Visualize as you read. Stop for a few seconds after each sentence. Visualize a picture in your mind.*

Understand Information Have students reread the pages. Ask, *What pictures did you visualize?* Ask, *Which words helped you visualize?* Ask comprehension, picture, and thinking questions. Help and encourage students in the use of pronouns when answering.

Organize Information Say, *Let's do a word web about the first paragraph on page 74.* Say, *The subject is the ancient Greeks. What can we write on our word web?* Help students abbreviate their sentences. Write these onto a word web on the board, and have students copy it into their notebooks. The word web might look like this:

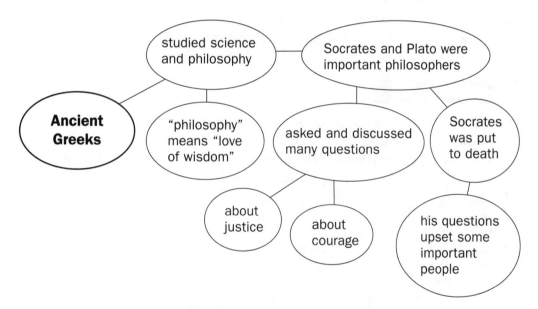

REACHING ALL STUDENTS: Visual Learners

Help students find websites showing Greek art from the Golden Age. Alternatively, bring in pictures to pass around and discuss.

DRAMA CONNECTION: Greek Drama

Have students look at the box on page 74. Practice <u>previewing</u>. Ask, *What's the heading? What do you see in the picture?* Read the text, or call on students to read it. Elicit or explain the meanings of any new words and help students pronounce them.

(continued)

Have students read the section again silently. Alternatively, assign pairs or small groups and have students take turns reading aloud to each other. Ask questions such as, *What was the birthplace of drama? Where does the word* drama *come from?* Encourage students to use pronouns in their answers.

Bring in photos or help students find pictures of ancient Greek drama masks on the Internet. Ask, *Which feeling do you think this mask shows? Why?*

ELSEWHERE IN THE WORLD: The Celts

Have students look at the box on page 75. Practice underlining previewing. Ask, *What's the heading? What do you see in the picture? Do you think the Celts made it?* Read the text, or call on students to read it. Elicit or explain the meanings of any new words and help students pronounce them. Have students read the section again silently. Alternatively, assign pairs or small groups and have students take turns reading aloud to each other.

Ask questions such as, *Who were the Celts? Do we know much about their culture or religion? What's an example of a religion today? What's an example of a culture?* Encourage students to use pronouns in their answers.

Bring in photos or help students find pictures of Celtic artifacts on the Internet.

Before You Go On

Have students read the first two questions. Pair students and have them write the answers in their notebooks. Check the answers. Do the third question together as a class. Help students with the *would like to have* structure. Write the answers on the board, and have students copy them into their notebooks.

Answers
1. Socrates and Plato were two important philosophers in Athens.
2. Spartan boys began to train to be soldiers when they were only seven years old.
3. Answers will vary. Possible answers: Yes, because I would like to have trained to be strong and healthy; *or* No, because I wouldn't like to have had to go to war and gotten killed.

Working with Timelines

Read the timeline entries, or call on students to read them. Ask comprehension and review questions such as, *When was the Parthenon completed?* Say, *Look at the picture of the Parthenon on page 66. What are two other words to describe the Parthenon?* (monument, temple) *Who do you think built the Parthenon?* (probably slaves) *Were arts very important to the Greeks?* Have students copy the Unit Events timeline onto their Lesson 1 Timelines page.

Choose World Events that your students will find interesting. Bring in pictures and maps to help teach these events.

Macedonia, pages 76–77

Preview Pages

Have students <u>preview</u> these pages and <u>predict</u> the topic.

Teach Pages

Read the text and captions, or call on students to read them. Help students understand and pronounce any new words. Show Afghanistan and India on a map or globe. At the end of page 76, ask students to <u>predict</u>. Ask, *What do you think will happen to Alexander's empire after he dies? Do you think it will be one empire for a long time?*

Ask, *What's the reading strategy for this lesson? What do you do when you <u>visualize</u>? Visualize as you read. Stop for a few seconds after each sentence. Visualize a picture in your mind.*

PROFILE: Alexander the Great

This Profile is integral to the text content on these pages. Teach it after the first paragraph on page 76. Read the text, or call on students to read it aloud. Elicit or explain the meanings of any new words and help students pronounce them. Have students read the section again silently. Alternatively, assign pairs or small groups and have students take turns reading aloud to each other.

Ask questions such as (pointing to the picture of Alexander), *Who is this man? Was he well educated? Who was his teacher? What did Alexander learn to be? What did he want to do? What countries did Alexander lead his army through? Did he respect other cultures? What did he encourage his soldiers to do? What did he establish?*

Understand Information Have students reread the pages. Ask, *What pictures did you visualize?* Ask, *Which words helped you visualize?* Ask comprehension, picture, and thinking questions. Help and encourage students in the use of pronouns when answering.

Organize Information Say, *Let's do a flowchart about the most important historical events on these pages. Let's label it "King Philip and Alexander the Great." What important things did they do?* Continue to ask questions to elicit the most important events. Help students condense information into shorter sentences. Write these onto a flowchart on the board, and have students copy it into their notebooks. The flowchart might look like this:

King Philip and Alexander the Great

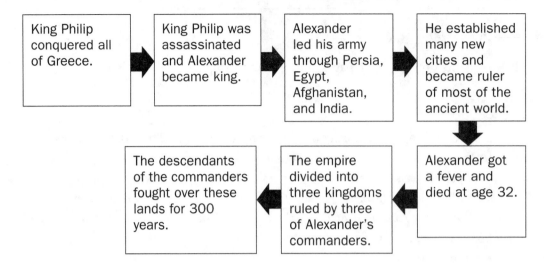

King Philip conquered all of Greece. → King Philip was assassinated and Alexander became king. → Alexander led his army through Persia, Egypt, Afghanistan, and India. → He established many new cities and became ruler of most of the ancient world. ↓ Alexander got a fever and died at age 32. ← The empire divided into three kingdoms ruled by three of Alexander's commanders. ← The descendants of the commanders fought over these lands for 300 years.

Optional Activity

This activity will allow students to see the breadth of Alexander's empire and review locations in the ancient world. Before class, label six Post-It© Notes with these countries: *Macedonia, Greece, Persia, Egypt, Afghanistan,* and *India.* Review locations of Persia (Iran) and Macedonia (northern Greece). In class, give one to each of six students. Have them place these on the appropriate countries on a world map.

Before You Go On

Have students read the first two questions. Pair students and have them write the answers in their notebooks. Check the answers. Do the third question together as a class. Write the answers on the board, and have students copy them into their notebooks.

Answers
1. King Philip was the king of Macedonia. He built a strong army and succeeded in conquering all of Greece.
2. The Chavin culture was located in Peru.
3. Answers will vary. Possible answers: He led his army through Persia, Egypt, Afghanistan, and India. His soldiers admired him because he always fought at the front of the battle. He respected the cultures of his enemies. He established many new cities. He became the ruler of the ancient world.

Working with Timelines

Read the timeline entries, or call on students to read them. Help students understand and pronounce any new words. Ask comprehension and review questions such as, *What happened in 359 B.C.E.? Where was Macedonia? What did King Philip do next? What did Macedonia become?* Have students copy the Unit Events timeline onto their Lesson 1 Timelines page.

   Choose World Events that your students will find interesting. Bring in pictures and maps to help teach these events.

Go to www.longmanusa.com/socialstudies for links to interesting websites about the Golden Age of Greece.

Review and Practice, pages 78–79

Vocabulary

If your students need additional help in reviewing this vocabulary, see the Optional Vocabulary Activities (pages vii–viii) to choose an appropriate activity.

Suggest to students that they copy all the sentences into their notebooks before they begin writing the answers. Have students work individually to complete this exercise. Check by calling on students to read their sentences aloud. Write the correct answers on the board. Have students correct their work, if needed.

> **Answers**
> 1. monuments
> 2. festivals
> 3. amphitheater
> 4. pottery
> 5. drama
> 6. sculptures

Check Your Understanding

Depending upon the language level and abilities of your students, have them work individually, in pairs, or in small groups to answer the questions. Let students look back at the text, as needed. Then have students share their answers with the whole class. Write the answers on the board. Have students correct or add to their answers, if needed.

> **Answers**
> 1. Athens was a city-state and a democracy.
> 2. Arts such as pottery, jewelry, and sculptures were important to the Greeks.
> 3. Spartan boys began to train to be soldiers when they were only seven years old. Girls also had to train to be strong and healthy.
> 4. He led his army through Persia, Egypt, Afghanistan, and India. He encouraged his soldiers to settle and marry local women. He established many new cities.

Apply Social Studies Skills

Content Reading Strategy: Visualize Read the instructions aloud, or call on a student to read them. Ask comprehension questions to make sure students understand the instructions. Say, *There are some new words in this reading. Visualizing will help you understand them. Pause after each sentence and make a picture in your mind. Visualize as you read.* Tell students to read the paragraph, and then close their books and write three things they visualized. You may want to have students draw a picture next to their description.

Elicit a variety of student visualizations and write these on the board. Have students open their books and elicit the meanings of *catapult, fireballs, horsemen,* and *navy* using students' visualizations.

Using Visuals: Use a Map Key Read the heading. Tell students, *You'll learn more about Alexander the Great's empire using this map and key.* Read the instructions and information on the map, or call on students to read it aloud. Help students understand and pronounce any new words.

Elicit the answer for number 1 and write it on the board. Then have students work in pairs or small groups to ask and answer the rest of the questions. Have them write their answers in their notebooks. Check by eliciting the answers and writing them on the board. Have students correct or add to their answers, if needed.

Answers
1. The map key gives us the original area of Macedonia, Alexander's empire at its height, the route of Alexander, and cities.
2. Alexander's journey began in Macedonia.
3. Alexander's journey ended in Babylon.
4. Alexander's empire was at its height in 323 B.C.E.

Discuss

Read the discussion question aloud. Have students discuss the question together as a class. If students have not been to plays, discuss movies they've seen recently.

 Workbook pages 37–38 may now be assigned.

Evaluation

Self-Assessment Questions

Write the following questions on the board and have students respond in their notebooks. Then have them share their responses in small groups.
1. How can I use visualizing to help me in reading?
2. How can map keys help me to understand maps?
3. What was difficult for me in this lesson?
4. What was easy for me in this lesson?
5. What was most enjoyable to learn?

Lesson ❷

Before You Read, pages 80–83

Have students <u>preview</u> these pages individually or in pairs. Then ask, *What are you going to learn about on these pages?*

Vocabulary

Read the captions, or call on students to read them aloud. Help students understand and pronounce any new words. Have students read the captions again silently. Ask picture and comprehension questions for each item to make sure students have understood. For example, ask (pointing to the Colosseum), *What's this? Who built it? How many people did it hold? What did people watch there? What's a gladiator? What's an example of a wild animal? Do we still use this kind of building today? What do we watch?*

Point out the key words in the box on page 81. Read them aloud and have students say them after you. Say, *These words are important in this lesson. Let's learn these words.* Have students close their books. Hold up your book so all students can see. Point to pictures illustrating the key words. Ask questions to elicit each key word. Encourage all students to answer together.

Practice

Read the instructions, or call on a student to read them aloud. Make sure students understand the words *bridges* in question 2 and *entertainment* in question 3. Model by writing sentence 1 on the board, and then elicit the answer. Have students work individually to fill in the blanks. When students have finished, have them compare their answers with a classmate. Check by calling on students to read their sentences aloud. Write the letters of the correct answers on the board.

Answers		
1. b. government	**3.** a. Colosseum	**5.** c. senate
2. b. structures	**4.** c. prison	**6.** a. aqueduct

 Workbook page 39 may now be assigned. This workbook page provides practice in understanding and using the key words.

Social Studies Skills

 Content Reading Strategy: Ask Questions Write *Ask questions* on the board. Tell students, *When you read, it's important to <u>ask questions</u>.* Read the information on the page, or call on students to read it. Have students reread it silently. Ask comprehension questions to make sure students understand. For example, *When do successful readers ask questions? What will asking yourself questions help you do? What questions can you ask before you read?*

Have students copy the three headings and six questions onto a new page in their notebooks labeled *Ask Questions.* Say, *You'll practice asking these questions as you read this lesson.*

 Workbook page 40 may now be assigned.

Using Visuals: Use a Compass Rose Have students read the heading on the top of the page. Ask, *What visuals did you practice using in earlier lessons?* (timelines, map keys) *What visual will you practice using in this lesson?* Point to the compass rose and ask, *What is this?* Read the introduction, or call on a student to read it aloud. Have students reread silently. Ask comprehension questions. Then help students pronounce the place names on the map. Elicit the fact that the bold, capital names are countries, and that Rome is in the country of Italy.

Have students study the map for a moment. Then assign pairs. Say, *Ask and answer the questions, and write the answers in your notebook.* When students have finished, elicit the answers and write them on the board.

Workbook pages 41–42 may now be assigned.

Reading ②

The Beginning of Rome, pages 84–85

Preview Pages

Have students <u>preview</u> these pages and <u>predict</u> the topic.

Teach Pages

Have the key words on the board before the students begin. Read the text and captions, or call on students to read them. Elicit or explain the meanings of any new words, and help students pronounce them. Elicit the key words (government, senators [related to *senate*]), the sentences they're in, and their definitions.

As You Read: Ask Questions

Point to the box on page 84. Read it aloud, or call on a student to read it. Say, *Ask yourself these questions as you read the pages again.*

Understand Information Have students reread the pages. When students have finished, ask the two As You Read questions and elicit different answers. Important ideas might be, *People settled in the area of Rome because of the river and the fertile land. Romans formed a republic so people could choose their leaders. Roman society included rich and poor people.* Then ask, *Are there any words you don't understand? What do you remember about what you read?* Ask comprehension, picture, and thinking questions.

Optional Activity

Point to different sections of the Roman house illustration and elicit the room names. Draw a Venn diagram on the board for comparing and contrasting a Roman house and a house of today. Label one circle *Roman house*, the other circle *Modern house*, and label the overlapping space *Both*. Ask, *How is the Roman house the same as houses now? How is it different from houses now?* Write students' answers into the diagram, and have students copy the diagram into their notebooks.

Organize Information Say, *Let's do a flowchart about Julius Caesar and the Roman Empire. What important things did Caesar do?* Continue to ask questions to elicit the most important events. Help students condense information into shorter sentences. Write these onto a flowchart on the board, and have students copy it into their notebooks. The flowchart might look like this:

Julius Caesar and the Roman Empire

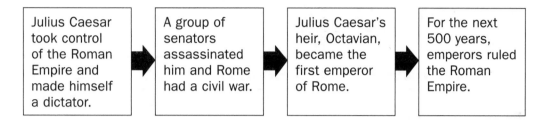

| Julius Caesar took control of the Roman Empire and made himself a dictator. | A group of senators assassinated him and Rome had a civil war. | Julius Caesar's heir, Octavian, became the first emperor of Rome. | For the next 500 years, emperors ruled the Roman Empire. |

CONNECT TO TODAY: The Senate

Have students look at the box on page 85. Practice <u>previewing</u>. Ask, *What's the heading? What do you see in the picture?* Read the text, or call on students to read it. Elicit or explain the meanings of any new words and help students pronounce them. Have students read the section again silently. Alternatively, assign pairs or small groups, and have students take turns reading aloud to each other.

Ask questions such as, *What was an important part of the Roman government? What were the members of the senate called? What did they do? Who were Cato and Cicero?* Explain that the United States has a Congress with two parts: the Senate and the House of Representatives.

Bring in photos or help students navigate the Internet to find pictures of the United States Senate.

Before You Go On

Have students read the first two questions. Pair students and have them write the answers in their notebooks. Check the answers. Do the third question together as a class. Write the answers on the board, and have students copy them into their notebooks.

Answers

1. People probably settled in the area of Rome because of the river and the fertile land.
2. The senators assassinated Caesar because he made himself a dictator (and many senators did not like this idea).
3. Answers will vary. Possible answers: Guatemala had a civil war from 1960 to 1996. Israel and Palestine have a civil war that began in 1967 and continues today. Sudan has a civil war that began in 1983 and continues today.

Life after Caesar, pages 86–87

Preview Pages

Have students <u>preview</u> these pages and <u>predict</u> the topic.

Teach Pages

Read the text and captions, or call on students to read them. Elicit or explain the meanings of any new words, and help students pronounce them. Elicit the key words (government, structures, prisons, Colosseum), the sentences they're in, and their definitions.

Practice the reading strategy, <u>asking questions</u>. On the board, write, *What do I think about this? What are the most important ideas I can learn from these pages?* Say, *Ask yourself these questions as you read the pages again.*

Understand Information Have students reread the pages. When students have finished, ask the two reading questions and elicit different answers. Then ask, *Are there any words you don't understand? What do you remember about what you read?* Ask comprehension, picture, and thinking questions. Be sure to elicit the fact that the dates are now in the Common Era.

Organize Information Say (pointing to the paragraph), *Look at the second paragraph on page 87. Let's do a Main Idea and Details chart about gladiator fights.* Draw a blank Main Idea and Details chart on the board, and have students copy it into their notebooks. Students should be able to complete this by themselves. Depending on student ability, assign pairs or small groups. The chart might look like this:

Main Idea
Gladiator fights were a main form of entertainment for the Roman people.

Detail
Many gladiator fights were held at the Colosseum.

Detail
People from all over Rome came to watch.

Optional Activity

Give students a more in-depth look at the Colosseum. Bring in more pictures, or help students find interesting websites. Point out interesting facts about the structure: there were underground rooms for gladiators and cages for animals below the Colosseum arena; animals often entered the arena through hidden trap doors in the wooden floor; for ship battles, the Colosseum arena was filled with water taken from a lake; etc.

CONNECT TO TODAY: Aqueducts

Have students look at the box on page 86. Practice <u>previewing</u>. Ask, *What's the heading? What do you see in the picture?* Read the text, or call on students to read it. Elicit or explain the meanings of any new words, and help students pronounce them. Have students read the section again silently. Alternatively, assign pairs or small groups and have students take turns reading aloud to each other.

Ask questions such as, *Did people have water in their homes in ancient times? What brought fresh water to the cities? Where did they bring the water from?*

Have students look back at the illustration of the Roman aqueduct on page 80. Have students compare and contrast that with the modern aqueduct on page 86. Ask, *How are these aqueducts the same? How are they different?* You may want to draw a Venn diagram on the board and write the responses into it.

Before You Go On

Have students read the first two questions. Pair students and have them write the answers in their notebooks. Do the third question together as a class. Write the answers on the board, and have students copy them into their notebooks.

Answers
1. Hadrian tried to build a good government. He made laws to protect women, children, and slaves. Many important structures were built while he was emperor.
2. The gladiators were fighters in ancient Rome. They fought each other or wild animals such as tigers. Most gladiators were either criminals from the prisons or slaves.
3. Answers will vary. Possible answers: Except for bullfights, we don't have real fights with dangerous animals or weapons for entertainment. Some people go to boxing and wrestling matches where people fight each other. People play video games and watch movies and TV shows about dangerous fights. Sports teams play in arenas similar to the Colosseum.

Working with Timelines

Read the timeline entries, or call on students to read them. Ask comprehension and review questions such as, *What happened in 14 c.e.? What does c.e. stand for? What year is it now? Who was Augustus?* Have students copy the Unit Events timeline onto their Lesson 2 Timelines page.

Choose World Events that your students will find interesting. Bring in pictures and maps to help teach these events.

Primary Source, page 88

Have students <u>preview</u> this page and <u>predict</u> the topic.

Teach Page

Read the text, or call on students to read it. Elicit or explain the meanings of any new words, and help students pronounce the words.

Understand Information Have students reread the pages. Ask comprehension and picture questions such as, *How many characters did the Roman alphabet have by the end of the first century* B.C.E.*? What did they add later? How many characters were there then? How many characters does the English alphabet have?*

   Have students work in pairs or small groups to write the answers to the questions in their notebooks. When students have finished, elicit the answers and write them on the board.

Answers
1. All of the letters look like the letters we use today.
2. There were twenty-four letters in the Roman alphabet.

Optional Activity

Have students work in pairs to rewrite the second answer in the manner Romans first wrote—writing right to left and left to right. The second answer might look like this:

> letters twenty-four were There
>
> in the Roman alphabet.

The Fall of the Roman Empire, page 89

Preview Page

Have students <u>preview</u> this page and <u>predict</u> the topic.

Teach Page

Read the text and captions, or call on students to read them. Elicit or explain the meanings of any new words, and help students pronounce them. Elicit the key word (government), the sentence it's in, and its definition.

As You Read: Ask Questions

Point to the box on page 89. Read the text aloud, or call on a student to read it. Say, *Ask yourself these questions as you read the pages again.*

Understand Information Have students reread the pages. When students have finished, ask the two As You Read questions and elicit different answers. Then ask, *Are there any words you don't understand? What do you remember about what you read?* Ask comprehension, picture, and thinking questions.

Organize Information Say, *Let's do a flowchart about the fall of the Roman Empire. What important things happened to the empire?* Continue to ask questions to elicit the most important events. Help students condense information into shorter sentences. Write these onto a flowchart on the board, and have students copy it into their notebooks. The flowchart might look like this:

The Fall of the Roman Empire

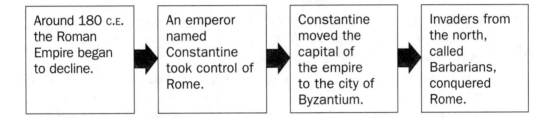

| Around 180 C.E. the Roman Empire began to decline. | → | An emperor named Constantine took control of Rome. | → | Constantine moved the capital of the empire to the city of Byzantium. | → | Invaders from the north, called Barbarians, conquered Rome. |

Before You Go On

Have students read the first two questions. Pair students and have them write the answers in their notebooks. Check the answers. Do the third question together as a class. Write the answers on the board, and have students copy them into their notebooks.

Answers
1. Rome was too large to defend. The government did not have enough money to pay its soldiers. The emperors were corrupt and did not care about the people.
2. The Chinese invented paper in 105 C.E.
3. Answers will vary. Possible answers: The Roman Empire had a government with a senate. People could vote. There were some good emperors, like Hadrian. There were structures like aqueducts, the Colosseum, and many nice houses.

Working with Timelines

Read the timeline entries, or call on students to read them. Ask comprehension and review questions such as, *What happened in 180 C.E.? What are some reasons the empire declined? What did Constantine do? When?* Have students copy the Unit Events timeline onto their Lesson 2 Timelines page.

　　Choose World Events that your students will find interesting. Bring in pictures and maps to help teach these events.

The Byzantine Empire, page 90
The Muslim Empire, page 91

Preview Pages

Have students <u>preview</u> these pages and <u>predict</u> the topics.

Teach Pages

Have students open their notebooks to reread their reading strategy questions. Then ask, *Do you already know something about this?* Call on several students to say what they know about the Byzantine or Muslim empires. Ask, *How can the pictures help you understand?* Read the text and captions, or call on students to read them. Elicit or explain the meanings of any new words, and help students pronounce them. On the board, write, *What do I think about this? What are the most important ideas I can learn from these pages?* Say, *Ask yourself these questions as you read the pages again.*

Understand Information Have students reread the pages. When students have finished, ask the two reading questions and elicit different answers. Then ask, *Are there any words you don't understand? What do you remember about what you read?* Ask comprehension, picture, and thinking questions.

Have students focus on the map and key. Ask, *What information does the map key give us? What color is the Byzantine Empire? What color is the Islamic world? Which was larger, the Byzantine or Muslim Empire? What happened to the Roman Empire? What cities can you see on the map?* (help students with pronunciation) *What were the capitals of the Byzantine and Muslim empires? What seas and oceans can you see?*

Organize Information Say, *Let's do a chart about the Byzantine and Muslim empires.* Draw a chart on the board with the subheadings *Area, Capital, Golden Age,* and *Scholars.* Using the map, help students fill in the area of the Byzantine Empire. Then, depending on student ability, complete the chart in pairs, in small groups, or as a class. The chart might look like this:

The Byzantine Empire		The Muslim Empire	
Area:	Greece, present-day Turkey	**Area:**	Arabian Peninsula, North Africa, Persia, present-day Spain
Capital:	Constantinople	**Capital:**	Baghdad
Golden Age:	from about 900 until 1050 C.E.	**Golden Age:**	from about 900 until 1050 C.E.
Scholars:	copied important writings from the ancient Greeks	**Scholars:**	studied mathematics, science, literature, and history

ELSEWHERE IN THE WORLD: Chichen Itza

Have students look at the box on page 90. Practice previewing. Ask, *What's the heading? What do you see in the picture?* Read the text, or call on students to read it. Elicit or explain the meanings of any new words, and help students pronounce them. Be sure students understand century dates: the tenth century is the 900s, the thirteenth century is the 1200s, and we live in the twenty-first century (2000s). Have students read the section again silently. Alternatively, assign pairs or small groups and have students take turns reading aloud to each other.

Ask questions such as, *Where is Chichen Itza? What developed there? When did it develop? Which years make up the tenth century? What was the culture a mixture of?*

Bring in photos or help students navigate the Internet to find pictures of Chichen Itza and the stone carvings there. Discuss the sacrifices performed at the temple.

MATH CONNECTION: Al-Khawarizmi

Have students preview the box on page 91. *What's this section about?* Read the text, or call on students to read it. Elicit or explain the meanings of any new words, and help students pronounce them. Have students read the section again silently. Alternatively, assign pairs or small groups, and have students take turns reading aloud to each other.

Ask questions such as, *Who was Al-Khawarizmi? Where was he born? What does a mathematician study? What does an astronomer study? What does a geographer study?*

Write a simple algebra problem on the board and elicit or teach math terms. (variable, multiplied by, plus, minus, equals, etc.) Then solve the problem with the class.

Before You Go On

Have students read the first two questions. Pair students and have them write the answers in their notebooks. Check the answers. Do the third question together as a class. Elicit the early civilizations students have studied and write them on the board. Elicit a variety of student responses and reasons, writing the first on the board as a model for structure. (*I would like to have lived in . . . because . . .*) Have students work individually, in pairs, or in small groups to write their own response in their notebooks.

Answers

1. Justinian's Code was a fair system of laws.
2. The Muslim Empire spread to North Africa, Persia, and present-day Spain.
3. Answers will vary. Possible answers: I would like to have lived during the Roman Empire. There were aqueducts for water, nice houses, and great structures, such as the Colosseum. There was also exciting entertainment.

Go to www.longmanusa.com/socialstudies for links to interesting websites about the ancient Roman, Byzantine, and Muslim empires.

Review and Practice, pages 92–93

Vocabulary

If your students need additional help in reviewing this vocabulary, see the Optional Vocabulary Activities (pages vii–viii) to choose an appropriate activity.

Suggest to students that they copy all the sentences into their notebooks before they begin writing the answers. Have students work individually to complete this exercise. Check by calling on students to read their sentences aloud. Write the correct key word on the board. Have students correct their answers, if needed.

Answers

1. senate
2. prison
3. aqueducts
4. Colosseum
5. government
6. structures

Check Your Understanding

Depending upon the language level and abilities of your students, have them work individually, in pairs, or in small groups to answer the questions. Let students look back at the text, as needed. Then have students share their answers with the whole class. Write the answers on the board. Have students correct or add to their answers.

Answers

1. The Romans and the Greeks had a government, laws, and (some) people could vote. Both had different classes, and both had slaves. Both built many new structures, and liked art and entertainment.
2. Julius Caesar was assassinated.
3. The Roman Empire declined because it was too large to defend. The government did not have enough money to pay its soldiers. The emperors were corrupt and did not care about the people.
4. Muslim scholars studied mathematics, science, literature, and history. The Muslims conquered many lands, including North Africa, Persia, and present-day Spain. Baghdad was an important center for trade.

Apply Social Studies Skills

Content Reading Strategy: Ask Questions Review the reading strategy. Ask students, *What questions do we ask before we read? While we read? After we read? How does this help us understand and remember?* Read the instructions and choices, or call on a student to read them aloud. Ask comprehension questions to make sure students understand the task. Have students work individually to reread and write questions and answers. To check, elicit some of these from students.

Using Visuals: Use a Compass Rose Read the heading. Tell students, *This map and its compass rose will show you some new information.* Read the instructions, or call on students to read them aloud. Have students identify the compass rose. Elicit or teach new words, and help students pronounce them. Then have them work in pairs to find the answers to the questions and write them in their notebooks. Tell students, *Look at the questions. Then look at the map and compass rose to find the answers.* Check by eliciting the answers and writing them on the board. Then go through the timeline with the students chronologically.

> **Answers**
> 1. The sea south of Constantinople is the Sea of Marmara.
> 2. The building north of the palace is the Hagia Sophia.
> 3. No, the Bosporus Strait is east of the city.
> 4. There are more forums in the south of the city.

Discuss

Read the discussion question. Ask, *Do you play video games or watch movies about fights or battles? What are some examples? Do you like to go to a sports stadium and watch two teams play against each other? What games do you like to watch? Why?* Then assign small groups to discuss the question. Circulate to help and comment on students' responses. Allow time for students to share their answers with the class.

Workbook pages 43–44 may now be assigned.

Evaluation

Self-Assessment Questions

Write the following questions on the board. Have students respond in their notebooks. Then have them share their responses in small groups.
1. How can asking questions help me in reading?
2. How can a compass rose help me to understand a map?
3. What was difficult for me in this lesson?
4. What was easy for me in this lesson?
5. What was most enjoyable to learn?

Unit Review, pages 94–95

Vocabulary

Read the instructions, or call on a student to read them aloud. Model by eliciting the answer for question 1 and writing it on the board. Have students work individually, in pairs, or in small groups, depending on how much support they need. After they have finished, check answers together as a class, writing the answers on the board.

Answers

1. festivals	**4.** prisons	**7.** amphitheater	**10.** monuments
2. aqueducts	**5.** structures	**8.** sculptures	**11.** drama
3. Colosseum	**6.** government	**9.** senate	**12.** pottery

Timeline Check

Read the instructions, or call on a student to read them aloud. Have students write the sentences (not the answers yet) in their notebooks. Then suggest that they find the dates for all the events before numbering the list. Model by eliciting the date for the top event. Have students work individually, in pairs, or in small groups. After they have finished, check answers together as a class, writing the numbers on the board.

Answers

  _2_   The first Olympic Games were held in Greece.
  _5_   Julius Caesar became the dictator of the Roman Empire.
  _7_   Justinian developed a system of laws in the Byzantine Empire.
  _1_   The New Kingdom of Egypt began.
  _4_   Romans formed a republic.
  _3_   The Greeks created a democracy during their Golden Age.
  _6_   Constantine took control of Rome.

Apply Social Studies Skills

Using Visuals: Use a Map Key Read the instructions aloud, or call on a student to read them. Elicit or teach the pronunciation of new people and place names. Have students work individually or in pairs to write the answers in their notebooks. Then call on students to answer the questions. Write the answers on the board.

Extension Project

Help students find information on the Internet or in the library on Greek and Roman artifacts. Have students work in small groups or as a class to choose items and draw pictures. Help students with the usage of the object and related vocabulary.

Read More About It

Bring at least one of the suggested books to class. Show the cover and some of the inside pages to students as a preview. Ask students to predict what the book is about.

Read an excerpt aloud to the class. Then ask several comprehension questions. Read the excerpt again before calling on students to answer. Encourage students to find this or another suggested book in their school library or local bookstore.

Workbook pages 45–46 may now be assigned.

Writing Skills, pages 96–97

Write a Paragraph

Preview

Have students <u>preview</u> these two pages individually or in pairs. Then ask, *What do you think you will be writing?*

Present the Model

Read the information at the top of page 96 aloud, or call on students to read it. Help students understand and pronounce any new words. (topic sentence, indentation, architecture) Have students reread. Then ask comprehension questions such as, *What do most paragraphs begin with? What does a topic sentence tell the reader? Is this similar to a main idea? What does a new paragraph begin with? What's an indentation?*

Read the paragraph and possible topic sentences, or call on students to read them. Then have students work in pairs or small groups to choose a topic sentence. Elicit the topic sentence. (The Romans were famous for their excellent architecture.) Elicit why this is the best sentence. (it contains the main idea) Have students copy the topic sentence and paragraph into their notebooks as a model.

Practice

Read the instructions and paragraph aloud, or call on students to read them. Say, *Two sentences are out of order. The first sentence should be the topic sentence—but it's not. Find the real topic sentence, and then switch the two sentences.* Have students work in pairs or small groups to find the topic sentence. (The Muslims had a huge empire.) Elicit it and write it on the board. Ask, *Which sentence should we put last?* (The Muslims became rich from trading.) Have students write the corrected paragraph in their notebooks.

Read the instructions, and then give students a few minutes to look at the list of people on page 65. For students who need more support, pair them and have them choose a person, and then write their paragraphs together. You may want to have students do a word web before they begin writing. Model this by choosing a person and eliciting information for a word web you write on the board. Then have students compose their own word webs.

Have students complete their paragraphs, and then exchange it with a classmate for feedback. Ask them to make any corrections before handing the paragraph in to you. Check and correct errors in the paragraphs. If a student's paragraph had errors, have the students rewrite the corrected paragraphs.

Workbook pages 47–48 may now be assigned.

Unit 3 The Middle Ages

Unit Overview

Lesson	Content	Social Studies Skills		Writing Skills
		Reading Strategies	Using Visuals	
1	• The Byzantine and Muslim Empires • Charlemagne • The Manor System • The Crusades • The Growth of Cities	Monitor Comprehension	Read a Map	Make an Outline
2	• China in the Middle Ages • The Mongol Empire • Japan in the Middle Ages • Early Civilizations of the Americas	Predict	Use a Map Scale	

Objectives

Vocabulary
- Develop new vocabulary related to the Middle Ages
- Use newly acquired vocabulary in context

Concepts
- Acquire knowledge of the Middle Ages in Europe and the Middle East
- Acquire knowledge of the Middle Ages in China, Japan, and the Americas

Reading Strategies
- Monitor comprehension to understand and remember what you read
- Use sequence words to help understand chronological order
- Practice previously learned strategies

Using Visuals
- Understand how to read latitude and longitude on a map
- Understand how to use a map scale

Writing Skills
- Practice making an outline

Unit Opener, pages 98–99

Preview Topic

Point to and read the unit title aloud or call on a student to read it. Say, and write on the board, *In this unit, we'll study the Middle Ages. The Middle Ages lasted from about 500 to about 1500 C.E. We'll study the Middle Ages in Europe, the Middle East, China, Japan, and the Americas.* Point out each area on a map or globe. Point to the art (an illuminated manuscript page showing Louis IX of France and his mother, Blanche of Castile). Say, *This is a picture from the Middle Ages.* Ask picture, thinking, and background knowledge questions to get students interested in this period. Help with vocabulary, as needed.

Unit Contents

Point to page 99 and say, *These are the people, places, and events we will learn about in this unit.* Help students pronounce the list of names. Say each name and have students repeat. When students feel comfortable, call on students to read names on the list. Ask if students recognize any names. Ask what they know about them. Write that information on the board. Follow the same procedures with place names. Use a world map or globe to teach or elicit the locations of these places.

For key events, say, *These are the key, or most important, events we will learn about.* Read the list of key events aloud, or call on a student to read them. Give simple definitions of new words. Have students copy the key events into their notebooks.

Get Ready

Say, *Before we start this unit, let's review some dates from Unit 2.* Read the instructions, or call on a student to read them. Ask, *What do you need to do first? What do you write on the timeline?* Draw the timeline on the board as students copy it into their notebooks.

Have students look back at the Unit 2 Unit Events timeline to find the answers. Elicit the caption for the first date (776 B.C.E. on page 72) and write it on the board. Have students work in pairs or small groups to find the information and write it on their timelines. Check by eliciting the captions and writing them on the board. The timeline might look like this:

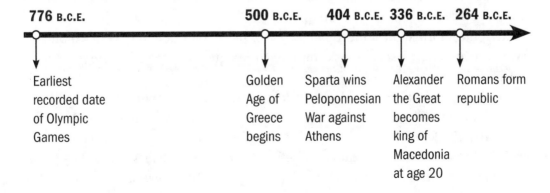

776 B.C.E.	500 B.C.E.	404 B.C.E.	336 B.C.E.	264 B.C.E.
Earliest recorded date of Olympic Games	Golden Age of Greece begins	Sparta wins Peloponnesian War against Athens	Alexander the Great becomes king of Macedonia at age 20	Romans form republic

Lesson ❶

Before You Read, pages 100–103

Have students <u>preview</u> these pages individually or in pairs. Ask, *What will you learn about in this lesson?*

Vocabulary

Read the captions, or call on students to read them aloud. Help students understand and pronounce any new words. Use pictures, props, and mime. Have students reread the captions. Ask picture and comprehension questions for each item to make sure students have understood.

Point out the key words in the box on page 101. Read them aloud and have students say them after you. Say, *Let's learn these words.* Have students close their books. Point to pictures illustrating the key words. Ask questions to elicit each key word. Encourage all students to answer together.

Practice

Make sure students understand the words *estate* in question 2 and *laborers* in question 3. Have students fill in the blanks, and then compare their answers with another student. Check by calling on individual students. Write the letters of the correct answers on the board.

> **Answers**
> **1.** c. knight   **3.** b. peasants   **5.** c. crusade
> **2.** b. manor   **4.** a. cathedral   **6.** b. feudalism

Workbook page 49 may now be assigned for homework or done in class. This workbook page provides practice in understanding and using the key words.

Social Studies Skills

Content Reading Strategy: Monitor Comprehension Write *Monitor Comprehension* on the board. Tell students, *When we <u>monitor comprehension</u>, we make sure we understand.* Say and write on the board, *Ask yourself: Do I understand this? Can I tell about it in my own words?*

Read the information at the top of page 102, or call on students to read it aloud. Have students <u>reread</u> it silently. Ask comprehension questions to make sure students understand.

Read the paragraph aloud. Model by doing a think-aloud: *Pause after each sentence, ask yourself a question, and then answer it. For example: Where were Gothic cathedrals built? What does the word* gothic *mean? Who were the cathedrals built for? What did people do in cathedrals? Where were the biggest and most beautiful cathedrals? What does this picture show?* Depending on student level and ability, you might want to write the questions on the board as you ask them.

Say, *Read the paragraph again silently. Ask yourself questions as you read. Make sure you understand.* When students have finished reading, point to and read the information at the bottom of page 102 aloud. Have students close their books. Say, *Tell me about this paragraph in your own words.* Call on several different students to elicit the main ideas.

 Workbook pages 50–51 may now be assigned.

Using Visuals: Read a Map Ask, *What visuals did you practice using in earlier lessons?* (timelines, map keys, compass roses) *What will you practice using in this lesson?* Read the introduction, or call on an individual student to read it aloud. Help students with any new words. Have students reread silently. Ask comprehension questions using a map or globe. Then help students pronounce new place names on the map.

Have students study the map for a moment. Then assign pairs. Make sure students understand *coasts*. Elicit the answer to question 1 and write it on the board so that the answer format is clear. Say, *Ask and answer the questions, and write the answers in your notebook.* When students have finished, elicit the answers and write them on the board. Have students compare this map of Europe in 1400 with a current map of Europe. Ask, *Which countries are the same? Which are different?*

Answers
1. 10°W longitude is near the coasts of Portugal and Ireland.
2. London is located at 0° longitude, 54° latitude.
3. 40°N latitude goes through the middle of Sardinia.

 Workbook page 52 may now be assigned.

Reading ❶

The Byzantine and Muslim Empires, pages 104–105

Preview Pages

Have students <u>preview</u> these pages and <u>predict</u> the topics.

Teach Pages

Have the key words on the board before the students begin. Read the text and captions, or call on students to read them. Help students with any new words.

As You Read: Monitor Comprehension

Point to the box on page 105. Read the text aloud, or call on a student to read it. Say, *Ask yourself these questions as you read. <u>Monitor your comprehension</u>.*

Understand Information Have students reread the pages. Point to and read the first sentence on page 104 aloud. Ask, *What questions can I ask myself to make sure I understand this sentence?* Elicit one or more questions for the sentence and write them on the board. Point to the picture of Justinian and ask, *What can I ask myself about this picture?* If students need support in forming questions, elicit questions for the sentences on this page and write them on the board. Assign pairs or small groups and have them take turns asking and answering questions about the reading. When students have finished, ask the class comprehension, picture, and thinking questions.

   Say, *Close your books. Can you tell me about the reading in your own words?* Elicit the main ideas from different students until the content has been adequately covered.

Organize Information Say, *Let's do a word web about Muhammad.* As a model, begin a word web on the board. Ask, *What can you tell me about Muhammad?* Elicit a couple of responses, write them into the word web, and have students copy them into their notebooks. Then assign small groups and have them complete their word webs. When students have finished, ask, *What did you write about Muhammad?* Write this into a word web on the board. Say, *If this is not on your word web, add it.* The word web might look like this:

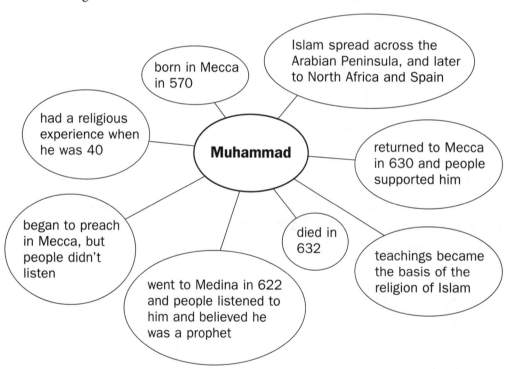

Language Tip: Irregular Verbs

Read the text in the box on page 104 aloud, or call on a volunteer to read it. Write *Regular Past Tense Verbs* on the board. Ask (pointing to the text on page 104), *What are examples of regular past tense verbs on this page?* (created, divided) Write *Irregular Verbs* on the board and ask, *What are examples of irregular past tense verbs on this page?* Elicit these and write them on the board with their present tense forms. (These are in the Language Tips box.) Have students copy this into their notebooks.

(continued)

Say, *Now find the irregular verbs on page 105. Write them in your notebook.* Have students work in pairs or small groups to find these. (bear → born, begin → began, become → became, spread → spread, [possibly do → did, will → would]) Elicit these, teaching any verbs that students missed, and write them on the board.

Before You Go On

Have students do the first two questions in pairs. Do the third critical-thinking question as a class.

Answers

1. The major religion of the Byzantine Empire was Christianity.
2. The major religion of the Arabian Peninsula was Islam.
3. Answers will vary. Possible answers: Yes, because it helps us understand our own religion and the religions of others. It helps us see the similarities in religions and understand people from different cultures.

Working with Timelines

Read the timeline entries, or call on students to read them. Ask comprehension and review questions such as, *What's important about the year 534? Who was Justinian? What is the Justinian Code the basis of?* Have students write the heading *Unit 3, Lesson 1 Timelines* on a new page in their notebooks. Then have them copy the Unit Events timeline.

Choose World Events that your students will find interesting. Bring in pictures and maps to help teach these events.

Primary Source, page 106

Preview Page

Have students preview this page and predict the topic.

Teach Page

Read the text, or call on students to read it. Help students with any new words.

Understand Information Write *Monitor Comprehension* on the board. Ask, *Do I understand this? Can I tell about this in my own words?* Encourage students to monitor their comprehension as they read. Have students reread the page silently.

Ask comprehension, picture, and thinking questions. Then ask students to close their books. Ask, *Can you tell me about the reading in your own words?* Elicit the main ideas.

Have students open their books and work in pairs or small groups to write the answers to the questions in their notebooks. Then elicit the answers and write them on the board.

REACHING ALL STUDENTS: Kinesthetic Learners

Have students act out the excerpt from *The Battle of Maldon*. Write the following script on the board.

VIKING 1: Bold seamen have sent me to you. They have commanded me to say to you that you must quickly send treasure to protect yourself.

VIKING 2: There is no need for us to destroy one another, if you are rich enough to pay.

EARL: Hold the bridge!

WULFSTAN: All right!

Have students copy this into their notebooks. Then assign groups of four, and ask them to stand. Say, *Take turns acting out the parts.* Call on a group to model for the class. To check, call on one or more groups to come to the front and act out their rendition of the script.

Charlemagne, page 107

Preview Page

Have students preview this page and predict the topic.

Teach Page

Read the text and captions, or call on students to read them. Help students with any new words. Ask, *Do I understand this? Can I tell about this in my own words?* Encourage students to monitor their comprehension as they read. Have students reread the page silently.

Understand Information Point to and read the first sentence on page 107 aloud. Ask, *What questions can I ask myself to make sure I understand this sentence?* Elicit one or more questions for the sentence. Point to the picture of Charlemagne and ask, *What can I ask myself about this picture?* If students need support in forming questions, elicit questions for the sentences on this page and write them on the board. Assign students to pairs or small groups and have them take turns asking and answering questions about the reading. When students have finished, ask the class your own comprehension, picture, and thinking questions.

Say, *Close your books. Tell me about the reading in your own words.* Elicit the main ideas from different students until the content has been adequately covered.

Organize Information Say, *Let's do a word web about Charlemagne.* Begin a word web on the board. Elicit a couple of details, write them into the word web, and have students copy them into their notebooks. Then assign small groups and have them complete their word webs. When students have finished, ask, *What did you write about Charlemagne?* Add their answers to the word web on the board. The word web might look like this:

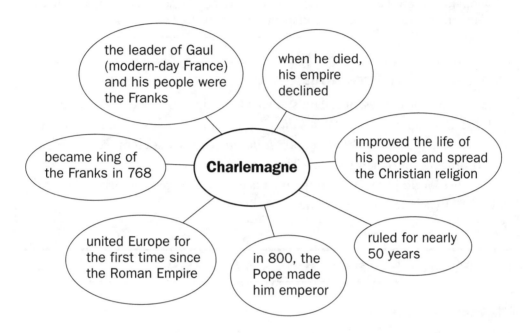

ELSEWHERE IN THE WORLD: Pala Dynasty

Practice <u>previewing</u> the box on page 107 and <u>predicting</u> the topic. Ask, *What's the heading? What do you see in the picture? Where do you think Pala is?* Read the text, or call on students to read it. Help students with any new words. Have students reread the section silently. Then ask comprehension, picture, and thinking questions to help students understand and remember.

Bring in photos or help students find pictures of Pala art on the Internet.

Optional Activity

Bring in recordings or help students find websites featuring audios of 1) a Catholic mass in Latin, and 2) a recitation of the Qu'ran (Koran) in Arabic. Let students listen to a few minutes of each. Then discuss the similarities and differences.

Have students do the first two questions in pairs. Do the third critical-thinking question as a class.

Answers

1. Charlemagne united Europe for the first time since the Roman Empire. He improved the life of his people and spread the Christian religion.
2. (Charlemagne died and) Vikings attacked for the next 300 years.
3. Answers will vary. Possible answers: It is called the Middle Ages because it is between early/ancient history and today/modern history.

Working with Timelines

Read the timeline entries, or call on students to read them. Ask comprehension and review questions such as, *When did Charlemagne become king of the Franks? Where did the Franks live? What country is this today?* Have students copy the Unit Events timeline onto their Lesson 1 Timelines page.

Choose World Events that your students will find interesting. Bring in pictures and maps to help teach these events.

The Manor System, pages 108–109

Preview Pages

Have students preview these pages and predict the topic.

Teach Pages

Read the text and captions, or call on students to read them. Help students with any new words. Elicit the key words (feudalism, knights, peasants, manors), the sentences they're in, and their definitions.

Understand Information Ask, *Do I understand this? Can I tell about this in my own words?* Encourage students to monitor their comprehension as they read. Have students reread the page. Ask, *What questions can I ask about the manor system?* Elicit one or more questions. Assign students to pairs or small groups, and have them take turns asking and answering questions about the reading. When students have finished, ask the class your own comprehension, picture, and thinking questions.

Say, *Close your books. Tell me about the reading in your own words.* Elicit the main ideas from different students until the content has been adequately covered.

Organize Information Say, *Let's draw a pyramid diagram of the feudal system.* Draw a pyramid on the board. Ask, *Who was at the very top of the feudal system? Who was next?* Elicit the different classes in the feudal system and add these to the diagram. Point out that lords were vassals of the king, and knights were vassals of the lords and kings. The diagram might look like this:

Feudalism

king

lords

knights

peasants / serfs

vassals

MORE ABOUT IT: Knights

Practice <u>previewing</u> the box on page 108. Ask, *What's the heading? What do you see in the picture?* Read the text, or call on students to read it. Help students with any new words. Have students reread the section silently. Then ask comprehension, picture, and thinking questions to help students understand and remember.

Have students look back at the shining suit of armor on page 100. Ask, *What are good and bad points about armor? Do soldiers today wear armor in battle?*

Before You Go On

Have students do the first two questions in pairs. Do the third critical-thinking question as a class.

Answers

1. A vassal was a person who held land for their king or lord in exchange for protection. A peasant was the poorest person in the feudal system. A peasant (or serf) lived and worked on the manor.
2. A serf belonged to the vassal, or lord of the manor.
3. Answers will vary. Possible answers: No, because serfs and peasants weren't free. Also, they gave most of the harvest to their vassal.

Working with Timelines

Read the timeline entries, or call on students to read them. Ask comprehension and review questions such as, *When did the Holy Roman Empire divide? How was life different after this? What new system of government developed?* Have students copy the Unit Events timeline onto their Lesson 1 Timelines page.

Choose World Events that your students will find interesting. Bring in pictures and maps to help teach these events.

The Crusades, page 110
The Growth of Cities, page 111

Preview Pages

Have students <u>preview</u> these pages and <u>predict</u> the topics.

Teach Pages

Read the text and captions, or call on students to read them. Help students with any new words. Elicit the key words (crusades, manors), the sentences they're in, and their definitions.

Understand Information Ask, *Do I understand this? Can I tell about this in my own words?* Encourage students to <u>monitor their comprehension</u> as they read. Have students reread the page. Ask, *What questions can I ask about the Crusades and the growth of cities?* Elicit one or more questions. Assign pairs or small groups and have them take turns asking and answering questions about the reading. When students have finished, ask the class your own comprehension, picture, and thinking questions.

Say, *Close your books. Tell me about the reading in your own words.* Elicit the main ideas from different students until the content has been adequately covered.

Organize Information Say, *Let's draw a flowchart of how the Crusades started.* Draw a box on the board. Ask, *What happened first?* Write this response on the board. Ask, *What happened next?* Then assign small groups and have them complete their flowcharts. When students have finished, elicit the rest of the information and add it to the flowchart. The flowchart might look like this:

The Crusades

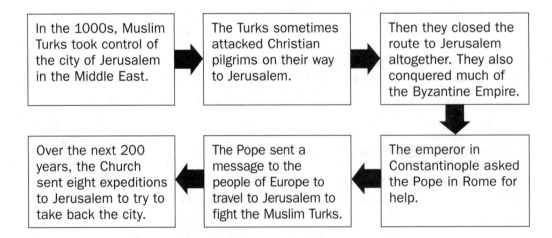

In the 1000s, Muslim Turks took control of the city of Jerusalem in the Middle East. → The Turks sometimes attacked Christian pilgrims on their way to Jerusalem. → Then they closed the route to Jerusalem altogether. They also conquered much of the Byzantine Empire. ↓ The emperor in Constantinople asked the Pope in Rome for help. ← The Pope sent a message to the people of Europe to travel to Jerusalem to fight the Muslim Turks. ← Over the next 200 years, the Church sent eight expeditions to Jerusalem to try to take back the city.

ART CONNECTION: Stained Glass

Practice <u>previewing</u> the box on page 110. Ask, *What's the heading? What do you see in the picture?* Read the text, or call on students to read it. Help students with any new words. Have students reread the section silently. Then ask comprehension, picture, and thinking questions to help students understand and remember.

Bring in pictures or help students navigate the Internet to find pictures of medieval stained glass in cathedrals such as Notre Dame in Paris.

MORE ABOUT IT: The Black Death

Practice <u>previewing</u> on page 111. Ask, *What's the heading? What do you see in the picture? What do you think the Black Death is?* Read the text, or call on students to read it. Help students with any new words. Have students reread the section silently. Then ask comprehension, picture, and thinking questions to help students understand and remember. Be sure to elicit why the Bubonic plague was called the Black Death.

Connect this section back to the main reading by eliciting how population, trade, and the growth of cities helped create and spread the Bubonic plague.

Before You Go On

Have students do the first two questions in pairs. Do the third critical-thinking question as a class.

Answers
1. The Crusaders went to Jerusalem to fight the Muslim Turks and to try to take back the city.
2. People moved to towns because manors could not feed everyone who lived on them.
3. Answers will vary. Possible answer: Yes, there are diseases like the Ebola virus in Africa.

Working with Timelines

Read the timeline entries, or call on students to read them. Ask comprehension and review questions such as, *What happened in 1071? When did the Pope call for a crusade?* Have students copy the Unit Events timeline onto their Lesson 1 Timelines page.

Choose World Events that your students will find interesting. Bring in pictures and maps to help teach these events.

 Go to www.longmanusa.com/socialstudies for links to interesting websites about the Middle Ages in Europe.

Review and Practice, pages 112–113

Vocabulary

If your students need additional help in reviewing this vocabulary, see the Optional Vocabulary Activities (pages vii–viii) to choose an appropriate activity. Have students work individually. Check by calling on students to read their sentences. Write the correct answers on the board.

Answers
1. manor
2. cathedral
3. peasants
4. knight
5. feudalism
6. crusade

Check Your Understanding

Have students work individually, in pairs, or in small groups. Let students look back at the text, as needed. Then have students share their answers with the class. Write the answers on the board. Have students correct or add to their answers.

Answers
1. Charlemagne was an emperor. He united Europe for the first time since the Roman Empire.
2. The Crusaders went to Jerusalem to fight the Muslim Turks and to try to take back the city.
3. Towns grew into cities because the Crusades encouraged trade. Manors could not feed everyone who lived on them, so people moved off the manors and lived in towns along trade routes.
4. Fleas on rats spread the Bubonic plague to humans.

Apply Social Studies Skills

Content Reading Strategy: Monitor Comprehension Read the instructions aloud, or call on a student to read them. Ask, *Do I understand this? Can I tell about this in my own words?* Encourage students to monitor their comprehension as they read. Have students reread the page silently. Ask, *What questions can I ask about chivalry?* Elicit one or more questions. Assign pairs or small groups and have them take turns asking and answering questions about the reading. When students have finished, ask the class your own comprehension and thinking questions.

Say, *Close your books. Write what chivalry means in your own words.* Check by eliciting what chivalry means from different students. Ask if students think chivalry exists today.

Using Visuals: Read a Map Read the heading. Review the meaning of *longitude* and *latitude*. Tell students, *You'll learn more about the Crusades using this map and the lines of longitude and latitude.* Read the instructions and information on the map, or call on students to read them. Help students with any new words and place names.

Have students work in pairs or small groups to ask and answer the questions. Have them write their answers in their notebooks. Check by eliciting the answers and writing them on the board. Have students correct or add to their answers, if needed.

Elicit information about where the four crusade routes shown on the map started and ended. Have students compare the map of 1095 with the map of the crusader states in 1130. Ask, *How have the borders changed?*

Answers
1. Jerusalem is near 30°N latitude.
2. Constantinople is located at about 28° longitude and 41° latitude.
3. Rome is located at about 13° longitude and 43° latitude.

Discuss

Read the discussion question. Then assign small groups to discuss the question. Circulate to help and comment on students' responses. Allow time for students to share their answers with the class.

Workbook pages 53–54 may now be assigned.

Evaluation

Self-Assessment Questions

Write the following questions on the board and have students respond in their notebooks. Then have them share their responses in small groups.
1. How can I use monitoring comprehension to help me in reading?
2. How can longitude and latitude help me to understand maps?
3. What was difficult for me in this lesson?
4. What was easy for me in this lesson?
5. What was most enjoyable to learn?

Lesson ❷

Before You Read, pages 114–117

Have students <u>preview</u> these pages individually or in pairs. Then ask, *What are you going to learn about in this lesson?*

Vocabulary

Read the captions, or call on students to read them aloud. Help students with any new words. Have students reread the captions. Ask picture and comprehension questions for each item to make sure students have understood.

Point out the key words in the box on page 115. Read them aloud and have students say them after you. Say, *Let's learn these words.* Have students close their books.

Point to pictures illustrating the key words. Ask questions to elicit each key word. Encourage all students to answer together.

Practice

Make sure students understand the words *process* in question 2, *in order to* in question 4, and *thread, fabric,* and *secretions* in question 5. Have students fill in the blanks, and then compare their answers with another student. Check by calling on individual students. Write the letters of the correct answers on the board.

Answers		
1. c. samurai	**3.** a. cliff dwellers	**5.** b. silk
2. c. trade	**4.** b. canal	**6.** a. dynasty

 Workbook page 55 may now be assigned. This workbook page provides practice in understanding and using the key words.

Social Studies Skills

 Content Reading Strategy: Understand Chronological Order Write the words *first, began, later, now, then, before, after,* and *finally* on the board. Draw a timeline on the board and label *now*. Ask students to tell you which words might come before and after *now*. The timeline might look like this:

began	before	first	then	**NOW**	later	finally	after

Write *Understand Chronological Order* on the board. Tell students, *Words like this, as well as dates, will help you understand the order of events. They will help you understand chronological order.* Have students copy the timeline into their notebooks.

Read the introduction and paragraph, or call on students to read them. Help students understand and pronounce any new words. Have students reread the paragraph. Ask comprehension questions, focusing on the chronological adverbs. For example, *When people think about exploring or invading, what do they think about first? What do they think about after that?* Say, *Understanding chronological order is very important when you read about social studies.*

 Workbook pages 56–57 may now be assigned.

Using Visuals: Use a Map Scale Ask, *What visuals did you practice using in earlier lessons?* (timelines, map keys, longitude and latitude) *What visual will you practice using in this lesson?* Point out the scale on the map. Read the introduction, or call on an individual student to read it aloud. Have students reread silently. Ask comprehension questions. Then help students pronounce the place names on the map. Show students how to use a ruler, or other straight object, to align with the scale, and then apply to the map. Ask students to estimate the distance in miles from Beijing in China to Tokyo in Japan. (about 1,000 miles)

Assign pairs or small groups and have them take turns asking and answering the questions. Have them write the answers in their notebooks. Tell students to write the answers in <u>miles</u>. When students have finished, elicit the answers and write them on the board. Using the map key, elicit other information about places and empires on the map.

Answers
1. It's about 2,000 miles from Kashi to Xi'an.
2. Japan is about 1,000 miles from north to south.
3. It's about 2,000 miles from Delhi in India to Beijing in China.

 Workbook page 58 may now be assigned.

Reading ❷

China in the Middle Ages, pages 118–119

Preview Pages

Have students <u>preview</u> these pages and <u>predict</u> the topic.

Teach Pages

Have the key words on the board before the students begin. Read the text and captions, or call on students to read them. Help students with any new words. Elicit the key words (dynasty, canal, silk, traded), the sentences they're in, and their definitions.

Understand Information Encourage students to <u>visualize</u>, to <u>monitor their comprehension</u>, and to <u>understand chronological order</u> as they read. Have students reread the page silently. Then have them take turns asking and answering questions about the reading in pairs or small groups. When students have finished, ask the class your own comprehension, picture, and thinking questions. Begin your questions by saying, *Let's be sure we understand chronological order. When was the Tang dynasty? When did the Song dynasty begin?* Use the map on page 118 to elicit where the Huang and Chiang rivers are, where the Grand Canal is, what the names of the capitals of the Tang and Song dynasties were, and what the length of the Great Wall of China is. Be sure to elicit why the trading route is called the Silk Road. Say, *Close your books. Tell me about the reading in your own words.* Elicit the main ideas from different students until the content has been adequately covered.

Bring in photos of Song porcelain and art, or help students find websites featuring these. Ask students which pieces they like best and why.

Organize Information Say, *Let's make a chart about the Tang and Song dynasties.* Draw a chart on the board with the bold headings and subheadings shown below. Model by eliciting the sentence for one subheading and writing it on the board. Then assign pairs and have them complete their charts. When students have finished, elicit the rest of the information verbally. The chart might look like this:

The Tang Dynasty	The Song Dynasty
When: The Tang dynasty ruled China from 618 to 907. **Built:** China built a 1,000-mile-long canal that connected the Huang and Chiang rivers. The Grand Canal connected northern and southern China. **Great Ruler:** A man named Tang Taizong was a great ruler during the Tang dynasty. He followed the wise and peaceful teachings of Confucius and helped reform China's government.	**When:** By 960 the Song dynasty ruled China. **Valued:** They valued art, books, and beautiful objects. **Made:** For a long time, only the Chinese knew how to make silk. For hundreds of years, Chinese artists made the finest kinds of clay dishes and figures. **Traded:** Porcelain and silk were traded.

CONNECT TO TODAY: The Panama Canal

Practice previewing the box on page 118. Ask, *What's the heading? What do you see in the picture?* Read the text, or call on students to read it. Help students with any new words. Have students reread the section silently. Then ask comprehension, picture, and thinking questions to help students understand and remember. Begin by saying, *Let's understand chronological order. When did the French begin the canal? Who finally finished it? When was it finished? How many years did it take?*

Have students locate the Panama Canal on a world map. Help students navigate the Internet to find animations of how the locks in the Panama Canal work.

SCIENCE CONNECTION: Silkworms

Practice previewing the box on page 119 and predicting the topic. Ask, *What's the heading? What do you think the picture shows?* Read the text, or call on students to read it. Help students with any new words. Have students reread the section silently. Then ask comprehension, picture, and thinking questions to help students understand and remember. Emphasize chronological order in the silk-making process.

Bring in pictures of silkworms and silk-making, or help students navigate the Internet to find them. Pass around a piece of silk for students to look at and touch. Ask, *Why do you think people like silk?*

Have students do the first two questions in pairs. Do the third critical-thinking question as a class.

Answers

1. A canal is used for irrigation and for boats and ships to pass through.
2. Silk, porcelain, gunpowder, the compass, and the printing press were Chinese inventions.
3. Answers will vary. Possible answers: Silk was so expensive because it took a long time and a lot of work to make it. Also, only the Chinese could make silk.

Working with Timelines

Read the timeline entries, or call on students to read them. Ask comprehension and review questions such as, *When did the Tang dynasty begin? What did China build during the Tang dynasty? What did the Grand Canal connect?* Have students write the heading *Unit 3, Lesson 2 Timelines* on a new page in their notebooks. Then have them copy the Unit Events timeline.

Choose World Events that your students will find interesting. Bring in pictures and maps to help teach these events.

The Mongol Empire, pages 120–121

Preview Pages

Have students <u>preview</u> these pages and <u>predict</u> the topic.

Teach Pages

Read the text, or call on students to read it. Help students with any new words. Elicit the key words (dynasty, trade/trader), the sentences they're in, and their definitions. Teach the Profile box after students have read page 121.

Language Tip: Northern, Southern, Eastern, Western

Read the words on the compass in the box on page 120 aloud, or call on a student to read them. Write on the board, *The Grand Canal connected <u>northern</u> and <u>southern</u> China.* Say, *The words* northern *and* southern *are adjectives. They come before, and modify, the noun* China. *When we want to talk about the north part of a country, we use the adjective* northern *before the country name.* Ask, *What part of the United States do we live in?* Write the words *Noun* and *Adjective* on the board. Under *Noun*, write *west.* Ask, *What's the adjective for the noun* west? (western) Write this on the board, along with the other noun forms: *west, east, south.* Say, *Write the noun and adjective forms in your notebook.* When students have finished, elicit several examples of usage by asking questions such as, *Is Los Angeles in the eastern or western United States? Is Miami in the northern or southern United States?*

Understand Information Encourage students to <u>visualize</u>, to <u>monitor their comprehension</u>, and to <u>understand chronological order</u> as they read. Have students reread the page. Then have them take turns asking and answering questions about the reading in pairs or small groups. When students have finished, ask the class your own comprehension, picture, and thinking questions. Begin your questions by saying, *Let's be sure we understand chronological order. When did the Mongols have a large army? Who was their leader? Who was the next leader of the Mongols? When did he become ruler? What did he overthrow? When did China decline? What happened in 1368?* Then ask more detailed questions.

Say, *Close your books. Tell me about the reading in your own words.* Elicit the main ideas from different students until the content has been adequately covered.

Organize Information Say, *Let's make a word web about Genghis Khan and Kublai Khan.* Draw a circle on the board for each leader. Model by eliciting the sentence for one or two pieces of information and writing it on the board. Then assign pairs and have them complete their charts. When students have finished, elicit the rest of the information verbally. The word web might look like this:

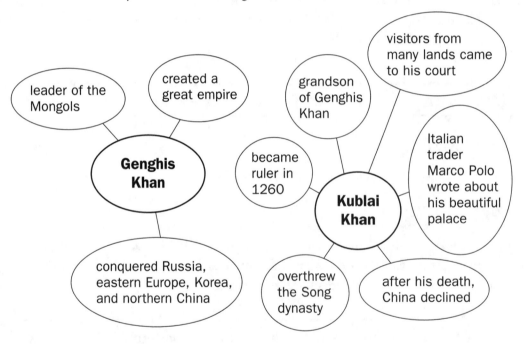

PROFILE: Marco Polo

Practice <u>previewing</u> the box on page 120 and <u>predicting</u> the topic. Ask, *Who do you think the man in the picture is?* Read the text, or call on students to read it. Help students with any new words. Have students reread the section silently. Then ask comprehension, picture, and thinking questions to help students understand and remember. Begin by saying, *Let's <u>understand chronological order</u>. When was Marco Polo born? When did he first go to China? How old was he? When did he sail home? How many years did he work for Kublai Khan? What did he write later? When do you think Marco Polo probably died?* Then ask more detailed questions.

Ask students if they <u>visualized</u> as they read. Ask, *What images do you remember?*

REACHING ALL STUDENTS: Visual and Kinesthetic Learners

This exercise will further familiarize students with the legendary fierceness of the Mongols. Before class, make copies of the following information (one copy per group of 3–4 students):

The Mongols

A historian once wrote: "The Mongols made the fullest use of the terror inspired by their physique [bodies], their ugliness, and their stench [smell]."

- The Mongols had small feet and big heads. They never washed their clothes.
- The Mongols shaved their hair short on the backs and tops of their heads, and left it long at the sides.
- The Mongols drank horses' milk, and would sometimes open a vein in their horses' necks and drink the blood. They ate rats and dogs.
- The Mongols made meat soft by putting it under their saddles and sitting on it during long trips. Then they would eat it.

Tell the groups they will make a presentation on the Mongols. Say, *Draw pictures or act out the information to present it to the class.* Model by eliciting how students could draw or act out one piece of information. Have each group choose a leader to give the presentation. Then circulate to help groups with words and concepts. When students are ready, call on each group to make their presentation to the class. Have the class vote on the best presentation.

Before You Go On

Have students do the first two questions in pairs. Do the third critical-thinking question as a class.

Answers
1. The Mongols were nomads. They were also great horsemen and fierce warriors.
2. Kublai Khan, the grandson of Genghis Khan, became the ruler of the Mongol Empire in 1260.
3. Answers will vary. Possible answers: Kublai Khan was probably interested in visitors from other lands because he could learn about their countries, goods, and inventions, and China could trade more with those countries.

Working with Timelines

Read the timeline entries, or call on students to read them. Ask comprehension and review questions such as, *What happened in 1218? Who were the Mongols? Who was their leader? Who did the Mongols conquer?* Have students copy the Unit Events timeline onto their Lesson 2 Timelines page.

Choose World Events that your students will find interesting. Bring in pictures and maps to help teach these events.

Japan in the Middle Ages, pages 122–123

Preview Pages

Have students <u>preview</u> these pages and <u>predict</u> the topic.

Teach Pages

Read the text, or call on students to read it. Help students with any new words. Elicit the key word (samurai), the sentences it's in, and its definition.

Understand Information Encourage students to <u>visualize</u>, to <u>monitor their comprehension</u>, and to <u>understand chronological order</u> as they read. Have students reread the pages. Then have them take turns asking and answering questions about the reading in pairs or small groups. When students have finished, ask the class your own comprehension, picture, and thinking questions. Begin your questions by saying, *Let's be sure we understand chronological order. What dates do you see on these pages? What happened on those dates?* Then ask more detailed questions. Use the map on page 122 to elicit the modern and ancient capitals of Japan, as well as the names of the northern and southern islands. Have students use the scale to figure out the distance from Japan to Korea, and Japan to southern China.

Say, *Close your books. Tell me about the reading in your own words.* Elicit the main ideas from different students until the content has been adequately covered.

Organize Information Say, *Let's make a diagram about Japanese feudalism.* Draw a pyramid with four sections on the board and the title *Japanese Feudalism.* Ask, *What two people were at the very top of this pyramid?* Write this into the chart, and then have students complete their pyramids in pairs or small groups. When students have finished, elicit the rest of the information, and write it on the board. Have students compare this pyramid with the one they did for European feudalism. The pyramid might look like this:

Japanese Feudalism

emperor/
shogun

daimyo

samurai

peasants

CONNECT TO TODAY: Martial Arts

Practice <u>previewing</u> the box on page 122 and <u>predicting</u> the topic. Ask, *What's the heading? What do you see in the picture? What do you think martial arts are?* Read the text, or call on students to read it. Help students with any new words. Have students reread the section silently. Then ask comprehension, picture, and thinking questions to help students understand and remember.

Ask a local jujitsu, kendo, or karate school to give a demonstration of the art for the class. Alternatively, help students find streaming video of one of these martial arts on the Internet.

MORE ABOUT IT: The Shogun

Practice <u>previewing</u> the box on page 123 and <u>predicting</u> the topic. Ask, *What's the heading? Who do you think this man in the picture is?* Read the text, or call on students to read it. Help students with any new words. Have students reread the section silently. Then ask comprehension, picture, and thinking questions to help students understand and remember. Emphasize <u>chronological order</u> in the silk-making process.

Ask if students have seen any samurai movies. Discuss these. Show an excerpt from a samurai battle from a film.

Before You Go On

Have students do the first two questions in pairs. Do the third critical-thinking question as a class.

Answers
1. Korea and China are close to Japan.
2. A samurai is a warrior. The samurai were very skilled fighters, and they were members of clans.
3. Answers will vary. Possible answers: A knight was supposed to be brave in battle, loyal, kind, and humble. Like knights, samurai warriors had a strict code of honor. They could not surrender to an enemy. They promised to die for the daimyo.

Working with Timelines

Read the timeline entries, or call on students to read them. Ask comprehension and review questions such as, *When was Kyoto declared the capital of Japan? Who was Japan ruled by then? When did feudalism become the way of life in Japan? What was Japanese feudalism like?* Have students copy the Unit Events timeline onto their Lesson 2 Timelines page.

Choose World Events that your students will find interesting. Bring in pictures and maps to help teach these events.

Early Civilizations of the Americas, pages 124–125

Preview Pages

Have students <u>preview</u> these pages and <u>predict</u> the topic.

Teach Pages

Read the text and captions, or call on students to read them. Help students with any new words. Elicit the key words (cliff dwellers, canals), the sentences they're in, and their definitions.

Understand Information Encourage students to <u>visualize</u>, to <u>monitor their comprehension</u>, and to <u>understand chronological order</u> as they read. Have students reread the pages silently. Then have them take turns asking and answering questions about the reading in pairs or small groups. When students have finished, ask the class your own comprehension, picture, and thinking questions.

Organize Information Say, *Let's make a chart about the early civilizations of the Americas.* Draw a chart on the board with the heading and subheadings shown below. Model by eliciting the sentence for one subheading and writing it on the board. Then assign pairs and have students complete their charts. When students have finished, elicit the rest of the information verbally. The chart might look like this:

Early Civilizations of the Americas			
Mayas	**Aztecs**	**Mound Builders**	**Anasazi**
• lived in Mesoamerica • built great cities such as Tikal in modern-day Guatemala • developed a calendar and invented a written language • were very successful farmers • they abandoned their cities, but no one knows why	• lived in the area where Mexico City is today • their capital was Tenochtitlán • built a large empire • by the 1470s, they had conquered the lands around them • ruled until the Spanish invaded	• lived in the eastern half of the United States • built large and small mounds made of piles of dirt • some mounds have nothing in them • other mounds have human bones, weapons, tools, and art objects	• lived in the southwest United States • they were cliff dwellers • they also built canals and grew cotton • when droughts hit the area, they abandoned their buildings

MORE ABOUT IT: Mayan Calendars

Practice <u>previewing</u> the box on page 124. Ask, *What's the heading? What do you think the picture shows?* (The photo shows an Aztec stone calendar. This one is in the National Museum in Mexico City and was made in about 1500. It's 12 feet high.) Then read the text, or call on students to read it. Help students with any new words. Have students reread the section silently. Then ask comprehension, picture, and thinking questions to help students understand and remember.

Bring in photographs of other Mayan and Aztec art and artifacts or help students find websites featuring these.

As You Read: Understand Chronological Order

Read the information in the box on page 125, or call on a student to read it. Model by drawing a timeline on the board. Ask (pointing to the text), *What's the earliest date in our reading? What's the latest date in our reading?* Write these at the beginning and end of the timeline on the board. Ask, *How long did the Mayas live in Mesoamerica?* Write *the Mayas* in a box spanning the two dates (250 and 900). Have students complete their timelines in pairs or small groups. Check by eliciting the other dates and labels and writing them on the timeline on the board. The timeline might look like this:

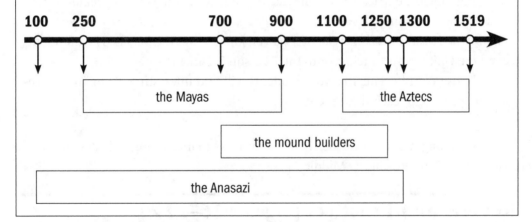

Optional Activity

This activity will further familiarize students with the important dates in this lesson. Tell students, *We will play a game using the dates and events on the Unit Events Timeline for Lesson 2. Study these dates and try to remember them.* As students study, write the main unit headings on the board: *China in the Middle Ages, The Mongol Empire, Japan in the Middle Ages,* and *Early Civilizations of the Americas.* When you think students are ready, have them close their books. Organize them into 3–4 mixed-ability teams. Write the team names on the board. (Team 1, Team 2, etc.) Tell the first team (pointing at the categories on the board), *Choose a category and I'll ask you a question.* When the team has chosen a category, say, *You have 10 seconds to answer the question. If you can't answer, I'll*

(continued)

*ask the same question to Team 2. If Team 2 can't answer, I'll ask the same question
to Team 3.* Using one of the dates on the timeline that the team has chosen,
ask, *What happened in ~ ?* If the team can answer successfully, give them one
point (write this next to the team name on the board), and ask the next team to
choose a category. If the team can't answer successfully, ask the question to the
following teams until it is answered correctly. Continue playing until all dates
have been covered.

Before You Go On

Have students do the first two questions in pairs. Do the third critical-thinking
question as a class.

Answers
1. The Mayas invented a written language (and a calendar).
2. Some mounds have nothing inside. Other mounds have human bones, weapons,
   tools, and art objects.
3. Answers will vary. Possible answers: The Anasazi probably built their homes under
   cliffs to protect them from the sun and rain. The cliffs also may have protected
   them from enemies and wild animals.

Working with Timelines

Read the timeline entries, or call on students to read them. Ask comprehension
and review questions such as, *When did the Mayan city of Tikal have nearly 50,000
inhabitants? Where is Tikal? What else do you know about the Mayas?* Have students
copy the Unit Events timeline onto their Lesson 2 Timelines page.

Choose World Events that your students will find interesting. Bring in pictures
and maps to help teach these events.

 Go to www.longmanusa.com/socialstudies for links to interesting websites about
Asia and the Americas in the Middle Ages.

Review and Practice, pages 126–127

Vocabulary

If your students need additional help in reviewing this vocabulary, see the Optional
Vocabulary Activities (pages vii–viii) to choose an appropriate activity.

Have students work individually. Check by calling on students to read their
sentences aloud. Write the correct answers on the board.

Answers
1. cliff dwellers	3. samurai	5. trade
2. canal	4. silk	6. dynasty

Check Your Understanding

Have students work individually, in pairs, or in small groups. Let students look back at the text, as needed. Then have students share their answers with the class. Write the answers on the board. Have students correct or add to their answers, if needed.

> **Answers**
> 1. The Huang and Chiang rivers were connected by the Grand Canal in China.
> 2. Europeans read about China in Marco Polo's book (*The Book of Travels*).
> 3. A samurai warrior had a strict code of honor. He could not surrender to an enemy. He was a member of a clan. He promised to die for the daimyo.
> 4. Some of the early civilizations of the Americas were in Mesoamerica, the eastern half of the United States, and the southwest United States.

Apply Social Studies Skills

Content Reading Strategy: Understand Chronological Order Review the reading strategy. Ask students, *What are some words that can help you understand chronological order? What else helps you understand?* Read the instructions and paragraph, or call on a student to read them aloud. Ask comprehension questions to make sure students understand the task. Have students work individually or in pairs to underline words and dates. To check, elicit these from students. (began, 794, before this time, 800s, began, after 894, before, lasted, 500 years)

Using Visuals: Use a Map Scale Read the heading. Tell students, *This map and scale will show you some new information.* Read the instructions, or call on students to read them aloud. Have students identify the scale. Go over the map key and map, eliciting or teaching new words and helping students pronounce them. Be sure to elicit that Chaco Canyon is where the Anasazi lived in cliffs, and Cuzco is where the Incas lived.

Have students work in pairs to find the answers to the questions and write them in their notebooks. Tell students, *Look at the questions. Then look at the map and scale to find the answers.* Check by eliciting the answers and writing them on the board.

> **Answers**
> 1. Tenochtitlán is about 1,500 miles from Chaco Canyon.
> 2. Cuzco is about 200 miles from the most southern part of South America.
> 3. The Amazon River is longer than the Mississippi River.

Discuss

Read the discussion question. Then assign small groups to discuss the question. Circulate to help and comment on students' responses. Allow time for students to share their answers with the class.

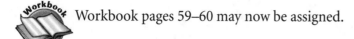

Evaluation

Self-Assessment Questions

Write the following questions on the board. Have students respond in their notebooks. Then have them share their responses in small groups.

1. How can understanding chronological order help me in reading?
2. How can a scale help me to understand a map?
3. What was difficult for me in this lesson?
4. What was easy for me in this lesson?
5. What was most enjoyable to learn?

Unit Review, pages 128–129

Vocabulary

Have students work individually, in pairs, or in small groups, depending on how much support they need. After they have finished, check answers as a class, writing the answers on the board.

Answers

1. crusade
2. trade
3. knight
4. silk
5. peasant
6. canal
7. cathedral
8. cliff dwellers
9. feudalism
10. dynasty
11. samurai
12. manor

Timeline Check

Draw the timeline on the board as students copy it into their notebooks. Elicit the first event and write it on the timeline on the board. Then have students work individually, in pairs, or in small groups to complete the timeline. Check by eliciting the events and writing them on the board.

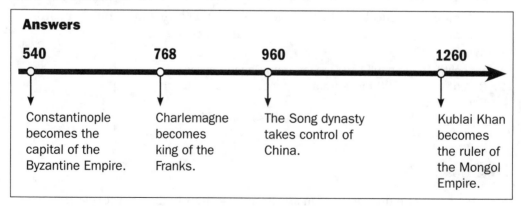

Answers

540	768	960	1260
Constantinople becomes the capital of the Byzantine Empire.	Charlemagne becomes king of the Franks.	The Song dynasty takes control of China.	Kublai Khan becomes the ruler of the Mongol Empire.

Apply Social Studies Skills

Using Visuals: Read a Map Read the instructions aloud, or call on a student to read them. Review the importance of the place names on the map. (the mound builders lived in Cahokia, the Anasazi lived in Chaco Canyon, the Aztecs lived in Tenochtitlán, and the Incas lived in Cuzco) Have students work individually or in pairs to write the answers in their notebooks. Then call on students to read their answers aloud. Write the answers on the board.

> **Answers**
> 1. Tenochtitlán is nearest 20°N.
> 2. Tenochtitlán, Chaco Canyon, and Cahokia are north of the equator.
> 3. Cuzco is south of the equator.

Extension Project

Help students find information on the Internet or in the library, or bring in materials on the Incas. Depending on your resources and student ability, have students work in pairs, in small groups, or as a class. Collect the paragraphs, correct them, and have students write a new version, as needed. Call on several students to share their paragraphs with the class.

Read More About It

Bring at least one of the suggested books to class. Show the cover and some of the inside pages to students as a <u>preview</u>. Ask students to <u>predict</u> what the book is about. Read an excerpt aloud to the class. Then ask several comprehension questions. Read the excerpt again before calling on students to answer. Encourage students to find this or another suggested book in their school library or local bookstore.

 Workbook pages 61–62 may now be assigned.

Writing Skills, pages 130–131

Make an Outline

Preview

Have students <u>preview</u> these two pages individually or in pairs. Then ask, *What do you think you will be writing about?*

Present the Model

Read the information at the top of page 130 aloud, or call on students to read it. Help students with any new words. Have students reread the introduction and study the model outline. Then ask comprehension questions such as (pointing to outline), *What is this? What does the outline help organize? What goes next to the Roman numeral? What goes next to the capital letters? What goes next to the numbers?*

Where does the letter A go on the page? Where does the number 1 go on the page? Have students copy the model outline into their notebooks.

Read the paragraph and outline, or call on students to read them. Help students with any new words. Have students reread the paragraph and study the outline. Then ask comprehension questions such as (pointing to outline), *What is this? What's the main idea? What's a detail to support the main idea? What's the supporting information for that detail? What's another detail to support the main idea? What's the supporting information for that detail?*

Practice

Read the instructions and paragraph aloud, or call on students to read them. Have students reread the paragraph. Ask comprehension, picture, and thinking questions about the paragraph content. Then say, *Let's make an outline.* Begin an outline on the board. Elicit the main idea (I) and the detail to support the main idea (A). Help students join the first two sentences together to make the detail supporting the main idea. Ask, *What is the first sentence about?* (trade) *Does it support the main idea, the Swahili language?* (not really) *Does the second sentence support the main idea?* (yes) *What does "it" refer to in the second sentence?* (trade between East Africans and Arabs) Say, *Let's put these two sentences together to make A, the detail supporting the main idea.* Then, depending on student level and ability, have students work individually, in pairs, or in small groups to complete the outline in their notebooks. Check by eliciting the rest of the outline and writing it on the board. The outline might look like this:

> I. The Swahili Language
>   A. During the Middle Ages, trade between East Africans and Arabs led to the development of a new language called Swahili.
>   1. Swahili was a Bantu (African) language that used some words from the Arabic language.
>   2. Most people on the trade coast spoke Swahili.
>   3. Today Swahili is still spoken in Kenya and Tanzania.
>   4. Most East Africans use Swahili for business.

Workbook pages 63–64 may now be assigned. Make sure that students understand the writing assignment.

Unit 4 The Renaissance

Unit Overview

Lesson	Content	Social Studies Skills		Writing Skills
		Reading Strategies	Using Visuals	
1	• East Meets West • Italian Renaissance • The Printing Press • The Reformation	Reread	Use Physical Maps	Write a First Draft
2	• Portuguese Exploration • Spanish Exploration • Spanish Conquests • The Enlightenment	Use Selective Attention	Use Different Types of Maps	

Objectives

Vocabulary
• Develop new vocabulary related to the Renaissance and major voyages of exploration
• Use newly acquired vocabulary in context

Concepts
• Acquire knowledge of the Renaissance in Europe
• Acquire knowledge of the major voyages of exploration and conquest

Reading Strategies
• Reread to understand and remember what you read
• Use selective attention to find key words and ideas
• Practice previously learned strategies

Using Visuals
• Understand how to read a physical map
• Understand how to differentiate and compare physical and political maps

Writing Skills
• Practice writing a first draft

Unit Opener, pages 132–133

Preview Topic

Point to and read the unit title or call on a student to read it. Say, and write on the board, *In this unit we'll study Europe from the 1300s to the 1600s. This period is called the Renaissance.* Renaissance *is a French word meaning "rebirth," or being born again.* Point to the photograph of the Cathedral (or Duomo) of Florence. Say, *This cathedral was built during the Renaissance in Italy.* Ask picture, thinking, and background knowledge questions to get students interested in this period.

Unit Contents

Point to page 133 and say, *These are the people, places, and events we will learn about in this unit.* Help students pronounce the list of names. Say each name and have students repeat. Ask if students recognize any names. Ask what they know about them. Write that information on the board. Follow the same procedures with place names. Use a world map or globe to teach or elicit the locations of these places. For key events, say, *These are the key events we will learn about.* Read the list of key events, or call on a student to read them. Give simple definitions of any new words. Have students copy the key events into their notebooks.

Get Ready

Say, *Before we start this unit, let's review some events from Unit 3.* Draw the timeline on the board as students copy it into their notebooks. Elicit the caption for the first date (540 on page 104) and write it on the board. Have students work in pairs or small groups to find the information and write it on their timelines. The completed timeline might look like this:

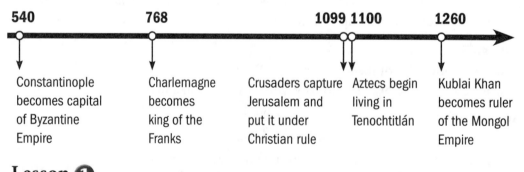

540	768	1099 1100	1260
Constantinople becomes capital of Byzantine Empire	Charlemagne becomes king of the Franks	Crusaders capture Jerusalem and put it under Christian rule / Aztecs begin living in Tenochtitlán	Kublai Khan becomes ruler of the Mongol Empire

Lesson ❶

Before You Read, pages 134–137

Have students <u>preview</u> these pages individually or in pairs. Ask, *What will you learn about in this lesson?*

Vocabulary

Read the captions, or call on students to read them. Help students understand and pronounce any new words. Use pictures, props, maps, and mime. Have students read the captions again silently. Ask picture and comprehension questions for each item to make sure students have understood. Read the key words again and have students say them after you. Then have students close their books. Point to the pictures and ask questions to elicit the key words.

Practice

Make sure students understand the words *public* in question 1 and *machine* in question 4. Have students fill in the blanks, and then compare their answers with another student. Check by calling on individual students. Write the letters of the correct answers on the board.

Answers
1. c. protests 3. a. clergy 5. a. manuscript
2. b. explorer 4. b. printing press 6. c. Movable type

 Workbook page 65 may now be assigned.

Social Studies Skills

 Content Reading Strategy: Reread Write *Reread* on the board. Tell students, *When we <u>reread</u>, we read again to make sure we understand the details.* Write on the board and ask, *Do you understand and remember the main idea and some details when you reread?* Read the information at the top of page 136, or call on students to read it. Have students reread it silently. Ask comprehension questions to make sure students understand. Read the paragraph about Lorenzo de Medici, or call on a student to read it. Help students understand and pronounce any new words.

Have students close their books. Ask detail questions such as, *Where was Lorenzo de Medici from? What was his family like? What did his family own?* Say, *Read the paragraph again silently. Make sure you understand.* When students have finished reading, have them close their books again. Ask the same questions you asked earlier. Point to the question on the board and ask, *Do you understand and remember the main idea and some details when you reread?*

 Workbook pages 66–67 may now be assigned.

Using Visuals: Use Physical Maps Ask, *What visuals did you practice using in earlier lessons?* (timelines, map keys, compass roses, longitude and latitude, map scales) *What will you practice doing in this lesson?* Read the introduction, or call on a student to read it. Help students with any new words. Then help students pronounce new place names on the map and understand the key. Elicit or explain the meaning of *R.* (river), *Alps, Channel, Peninsula, Mont* (French for mount/mountain), *elevation, sea level,* and *national border.*

Have students work in pairs to find the answers to the questions, and write them in their notebooks. Make sure students understand the word *range* in question 1. Check by eliciting the answers and writing them on the board.

Ask questions to bring out more map details and review use of the compass rose and the map scale. For example, *What three peninsulas can you see on the map? What mountain ranges can you see? What islands are east of the Iberian Peninsula? How far is Great Britain from the northern border of the Iberian Peninsula?*

 Workbook page 68 may now be assigned.

Reading ❶

East Meets West, pages 138–139

Preview Pages

Have students underline preview these pages and predict the topic.

Teach Pages

Read the text and captions, or call on students to read them. Help students with any new words. Elicit the key word (explorer), the sentence it's in, and its definition.

Understand Information Encourage students to visualize, to monitor their comprehension, and to understand chronological order as they reread the pages. Write on the board and ask, *Do you understand and remember the main idea and some details when you reread?* Have students take turns asking and answering questions about the reading in pairs or small groups. When students have finished, ask comprehension, picture, and thinking questions.

Say, *Close your books. Tell me about the reading in your own words.* Elicit the main ideas and details from different students until the content has been adequately covered.

Organize Information Say, *Let's do a Main Idea and Details chart about the text on page 139.* As a model, draw a blank Main Idea and Details chart on the board. Depending on student level and ability, you may want to elicit the main idea, or let students find it by themselves. The chart might look like this:

Main Idea

During the Middle Ages, trade grew between Africa, Europe, and Asia.

Detail	Detail	Detail	Detail	Detail
The Italian explorer Marco Polo traveled to Asia.	When he returned to Europe, he told people stories about the spices, silk, and other goods that he saw in China.	European people wanted these goods.	Traders traveled along trade routes called the Silk Road to trade for spices, silk, and rugs from Asia.	Trading between different countries brought different cultures and languages together.

Language Tip: Phrasal Verbs

Read the text in the box on page 138, or call on a student to read it. Write *Phrasal Verbs* on the board, and have students copy this into their notebooks. Ask, pointing to the text on page 138, *Can you find a sentence with a phrasal verb on this page?* (Crusaders traveled to the Middle East to <u>take back</u> the city of Jerusalem from the Muslims.) Write this sentence on the board, underlining the phrasal verb. Ask, *What does* take back *mean here?* (control again, conquer again) Write the definition on the board. Ask, pointing at the box, *Which phrasal verbs do you know? Can you give me an example sentence? What does the phrase mean?* Elicit these and write them on the board. Have students copy the example sentences and definitions into their notebooks.

MORE ABOUT IT: The Silk Road

After the reading and comprehension check, draw a long line on the board to represent the Silk Road. Label the ends *Asia* and *Europe*. Elicit or explain how a piece of silk could travel from Asia to Europe by traders trading with people along the way.

Asia ←→ ←→ ←→ ←→ ←→ ←→ ←→ **Europe**

traders

Have students do the first two questions in pairs. Do the third critical-thinking question as a class.

Answers

1. The Crusades were a series of wars during the Middle Ages. Crusaders traveled to the Middle East to take back Jerusalem from the Muslims.
2. European traders wanted spices, silk, and rugs from Asia.
3. Answers will vary. Possible answers: Marco Polo was an important person in history because he told people about China. This helped trade grow between Europe and Asia. Trade brought different cultures together.

Working with Timelines

Read the timeline entries, or call on students to read them. Ask comprehension and review questions. Have students write the heading *Unit 4, Lesson 1 Timelines* on a new page in their notebooks. Then have students copy the Unit Events timeline.

Choose World Events that your students will find interesting. Bring in pictures and maps to help teach these events.

Italian Renaissance, pages 140–141

Preview Pages

Have students underline preview these pages and underline predict the topic.

Teach Pages

Read the text and captions, or call on students to read them. Help students with any new words. Elicit the key word (explorer), the sentence it's in, and its definition.

Understand Information Encourage students to visualize, to monitor their comprehension, and to understand chronological order as they reread the pages. Ask, *Do you understand and remember the main idea and some details when you reread?*

Have students take turns asking and answering questions about the reading in pairs or small groups. When students have finished, ask comprehension, picture, and thinking questions. Say, *Close your books. Tell me about the reading in your own words.* Elicit the main ideas and details.

> ### REACHING ALL STUDENTS: Visual and Auditory Learners
>
> Bring in pictures of Renaissance art and recordings of Renaissance music, or help students locate Internet sites featuring these. Elicit what students think of the art and music, and which pieces they like best. Elicit how art and music are important in students' lives.

Organize Information Say, *Let's make a word web about the Renaissance.* Model by beginning the word web on the board, and then have students copy and complete it. The completed word web might look like this:

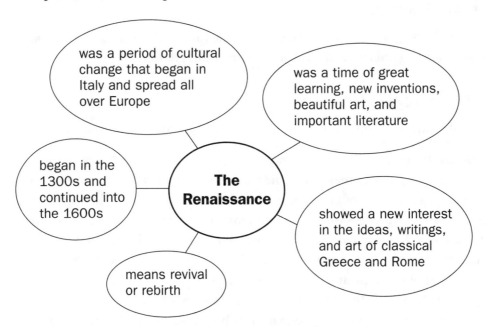

- was a period of cultural change that began in Italy and spread all over Europe
- was a time of great learning, new inventions, beautiful art, and important literature
- began in the 1300s and continued into the 1600s
- **The Renaissance**
- showed a new interest in the ideas, writings, and art of classical Greece and Rome
- means revival or rebirth

MATH AND ART CONNECTION: Perspective and Proportion

After the reading and comprehension check, have students compare the line drawing of *The Last Supper* with the final painting on page 165. Have students draw a simple picture of a room using perspective lines and considering proportion. Draw perspective lines on the board as a model for the walls and ceiling, desk, bookshelf, and other objects.

Before You Go On

Have students do the first two questions in pairs. Do the third critical-thinking question as a class.

Answers
1. The humanists studied the classics (the ideas, writings, and art of classical Greece and Rome).
2. Lorenzo de Medici was a ruler and patron of the arts in Florence, Italy.
3. Answers will vary. Possible answers: Yes, because the arts help us enjoy life. We can learn many things about the world and other cultures through art.

Working with Timelines

Read the timeline entries, or call on students to read them. Help students understand any new words. Ask comprehension and review questions. Have students copy the Unit Events timeline onto their Lesson 1 Timelines page.

Choose World Events that your students will find interesting. Bring in pictures and maps to help teach these events.

Primary Source, page 142

Preview Page

Have students <u>preview</u> this page and <u>predict</u> the topic. Ask, *What do you already know about Leonardo da Vinci? Do you recognize this painting?*

Teach Page

Read the text, or call on students to read it. Help students with any new words.

Understand Information Encourage students to <u>visualize</u> and to <u>monitor their comprehension</u> as they <u>reread</u> the page. Have students take turns asking and answering questions about the reading in pairs or small groups. When students have finished, ask comprehension, picture, and thinking questions. Say, *Close your books. Tell me about the reading in your own words.* Elicit the main ideas and details. Have students open their books and work in pairs or small groups to write the answers to the questions in their notebooks. Then elicit the answers and write them on the board. Elicit several different responses for the second question.

Bring in other paintings by Leonardo, or help students find websites showing these. Discuss Leonardo's use of shadow and light in each painting.

> **Answers**
> 1. Leonardo studied plants (and sunlight) so he could paint flowers better.
> 2. Answers will vary. Possible answer: Yes, the shadows in the painting make *Mona Lisa* more realistic and mysterious.

The Printing Press, page 143

Preview Page

Have students <u>preview</u> this page and <u>predict</u> the topic.

Teach Page

Read the text and captions, or call on students to read them. Help students with any new words. Elicit the key words (printing press, manuscript, movable type), the sentences they're in, and their definitions.

Understand Information Encourage students to <u>visualize</u> and to <u>monitor their comprehension</u> as they <u>reread</u> the page. Have students take turns asking and answering questions about the reading in pairs or small groups. When students have finished, ask comprehension, picture, and thinking questions. Say, *Close your books. Tell me about the reading in your own words.* Elicit the main ideas and details.

Organize Information Say, *Let's do a word web about the printing press.* Model by beginning the word web on the board, and then have students copy and complete it. The completed word web might look like this:

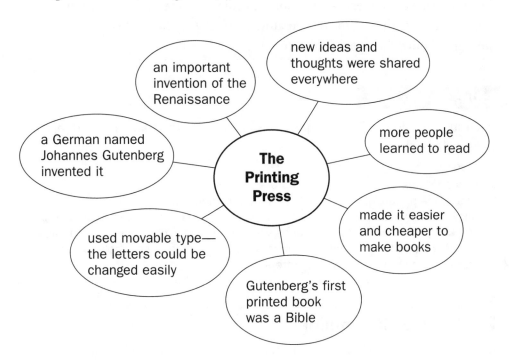

Optional Activity

Write on the board and ask, *How did an early printing press work? What did a printer do with the moveable type?* Have students look closely at the picture of the printing press on page 143, and the related illustrations on page 135. Teach or elicit any helpful vocabulary and write it on the board. (box, ink, handle) Then have students get into small groups and discuss how a printing press worked. To check, elicit student ideas and write them into a flowchart on the board. Have students copy the flowchart into their notebooks. The flowchart might look like this:

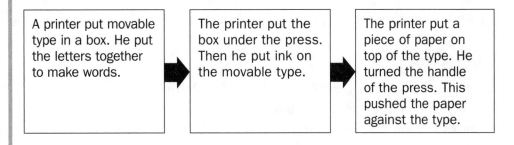

You might like to explain that a more modern form of moveable type was still used by publishers to print books and magazines until the 1980s, when computers revolutionized the printing industry.

After the reading and comprehension check, ask, *What other inventions make life easier?* (the computer, the telephone, the digital camera, the television, the microwave oven, the car, the refrigerator, the electric light, etc.) For each, elicit thoughts about what people did before the item was invented.

Before You Go On

Have students do the first two questions in pairs. Do the third critical-thinking question as a class.

Answers
1. Leonardo was also interested in botany and sunlight.
2. Before the printing press, early books (manuscripts) were written by hand.
3. Answers will vary. Possible answers: The computer compares to the printing press. You can print documents in seconds without having to move type. You can find information on the Internet without having to go to a library or bookstore. E-mail is faster and cheaper than writing letters.

Working with Timelines

Read the timeline entries, or call on students to read them. Ask comprehension and review questions. Have students copy the Unit Events timeline onto their Lesson 1 Timelines page.

Choose World Events that your students will find interesting. Bring in pictures and maps to help teach these events.

The Reformation, pages 144–145

Preview Pages

Have students preview these pages and predict the topic.

Teach Pages

Read the text and captions, or call on students to read them. Help students with any new words. Elicit the key words (protests, clergy), the sentences they're in, and their definitions. Go over the map of the major religions in Europe during the 1500s. Help students pronounce the names of the religions. Ask, *Which areas have only one religion? Which have more than one?*

Understand Information Have students reread page 145. Then have them take turns asking and answering questions about the reading in pairs or small groups. When students have finished, ask comprehension, picture, and thinking questions. Say, *Close your books. Tell me about the reading in your own words.* Elicit the main ideas and details.

As You Read: Reread

Point out the box on page 144. Read the information, or call on a student to read it. Say, *Reread page 144 to find the details and answer the question.* After students have reread the page, have them close their books. Elicit answers to the question. (Martin Luther nailed a list of protests to a church door because he believed the Roman Catholic Church needed to reform its ways.)

Organize Information Say, *Let's draw a flowchart about Martin Luther and the first Protestant church.* Model by beginning the flowchart on the board, and then have students copy and complete it. The completed flowchart might look like this:

Martin Luther and the First Protestant Church

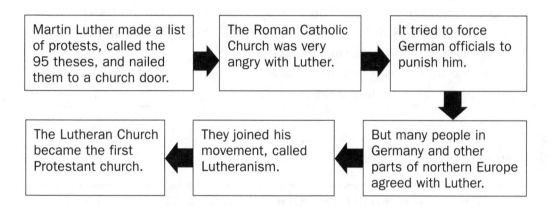

Martin Luther made a list of protests, called the 95 theses, and nailed them to a church door. → The Roman Catholic Church was very angry with Luther. → It tried to force German officials to punish him. ↓ But many people in Germany and other parts of northern Europe agreed with Luther. → They joined his movement, called Lutheranism. → The Lutheran Church became the first Protestant church.

ELSEWHERE IN THE WORLD: William Shakespeare

After the reading and comprehension check, introduce a short, easy dialogue from a famous Shakespearean play, *Romeo and Juliet*. Hand out copies or write the dialogue on the board. Read it aloud. Ask questions to elicit the meanings of the lines. Then have students practice the dialogue in pairs. Call on a few students to perform the dialogue.

From *Romeo and Juliet*, Act 1, Scene 1

BENVOLIO: Good-morrow, cousin.

ROMEO: Is the day so young?

BENVOLIO: But new struck nine.

ROMEO: Ay me! sad hours seem long. Was that my father that went hence so fast?

BENVOLIO: It was. What sadness lengthens Romeo's hours?

ROMEO: Not having that, which, having, makes them short.

BENVOLIO: In love?

ROMEO: Out—

BENVOLIO: Of love?

ROMEO: Out of her favour, where I am in love.

Have students do the first two questions in pairs. Do the third critical-thinking question as a class.

Answers

1. Martin Luther was a Roman Catholic monk in Germany. In the early 1500s, he began the Reformation and a new movement called Lutheranism.
2. In Europe during the 1500s, there were the Roman Catholic, Anglican, Lutheran, Calvinist, Eastern Orthodox, and Muslim religions.
3. Answers will vary. Possible answers: This period is called the Reformation because the Roman Catholic Church made some reforms, and Luther created the first Protestant church.

Working with Timelines

Read the timeline entries, or call on students to read them. Help students understand any new words and concepts. Have students copy the Unit Events timeline onto their Lesson 1 Timelines page.

Choose World Events that your students will find interesting. Bring in pictures and maps to help teach these events.

For more information, go to www.longmanusa.com/socialstudies for links to interesting websites about the Renaissance in Europe.

Review and Practice, pages 146–147

Vocabulary

If your students need additional help in reviewing this vocabulary, see the Optional Vocabulary Activities (pages vii–viii). Have students work individually. Check by calling on students to read their sentences. Write the correct answers on the board.

Answers

1. printing press	3. explorer	5. manuscript
2. clergy	4. protests	6. movable type

Check Your Understanding

Have students work individually, in pairs, or in small groups. Let students look back at the text, as needed. Then have students share their answers with the class. Write the answers on the board. Have students correct or add to their answers, if needed.

> **Answers**
> 1. Francesco Petrarch was a poet and one of the first humanists of the Renaissance.
> 2. Martin Luther began the Reformation and a new movement called Lutheranism.
> 3. The printing press that used moveable type was an important invention created during the Renaissance.
> 4. The Jesuits were a group of clergy. The group was formed to strengthen the Catholic faith in Europe.

Apply Social Studies Skills

Content Reading Strategy: Reread Read the instructions, or call on a student to read them. Ask students to close their books and write in their notebooks what they remember about the printing press. Then have them open their books and read the paragraph again silently. Then have them close their books again and write down any additional details. Ask, *What details did you remember before you reread? What details did you remember after you reread?*

Using Visuals: Use Physical Maps Read the heading. Review the features on a physical map by asking, *What kind of things does a physical map show?* Tell students, *You'll learn more about Italy using this map.* Read the instructions and information on the map, or call on students to read them. Help students with any new words and place names. Have students work in pairs or small groups to ask and answer the questions, and then write their answers in their notebooks. Check by eliciting the answers and writing them on the board.

As a review, elicit other information about the map using the compass rose, lines of latitude and longitude, scale, and key.

> **Answers**
> 1. Two seas surround Italy. They are the Adriatic Sea and the Mediterranean Sea.
> 2. The Alps are north of Italy.
> 3. Answers will vary. Possible answer: Italy is long and narrow. Two seas surround Italy. Italy can trade by sea with the countries to the east and west. It is close to northern European countries and to Africa.

Discuss

Read the discussion question. Then assign small groups to discuss the question. Circulate to help and comment on students' responses. Allow time for students to share their answers with the class.

Workbook pages 69–70 may now be assigned.

Self-Assessment Questions

Write the following questions on the board and have students respond in their notebooks. Then they can share their responses in small groups.

1. How can I use rereading to help me understand and remember details?
2. How can using a physical map help me to understand maps?
3. What was difficult for me in this lesson?
4. What was easy for me in this lesson?
5. What was most enjoyable to learn?

Lesson ❷

Before You Read, pages 148–151

Have students <u>preview</u> these pages individually or in pairs. Then ask, *What are you going to learn about in this lesson?*

Vocabulary

Read the captions, or call on students to read them. Help students with any new words. On the map showing Columbus's route, you may want to point out that the straight line shows Columbus's first voyage, while the dotted line shows a later voyage. Have students read the captions again silently. Ask picture and comprehension questions for each item to make sure students have understood. Read the key words again and have students say them after you. Then have students close their books. Point to the pictures and ask questions to elicit the key words.

Practice

Make sure students understand *original* and *native* in question 2. Have students fill in the blanks, and then compare their answers in pairs. Check by calling on individual students. Write the letters of the correct answers on the board.

Answers		
1. b. Voyages	**3.** b. diseases	**5.** c. route
2. a. indigenous	**4.** c. conquered	**6.** a. Navigation

 Workbook page 71 may now be assigned.

Social Studies Skills

 Content Reading Strategy: Use Selective Attention Write *Selective Attention* on the board. Ask, *What's green in this room?* Elicit several responses. Ask, *Did you look at each object and think, "What color is that?" No, you thought of green and looked for green. This is called* selective attention. *Green was the key word. We can use this strategy in reading, too.*

Have students preview the page. To teach *helicopter*, ask, *What does the picture show?* Read the introduction, or call on students to read it. Help students understand and pronounce any new words. Write the reading question on the board. Say, *Look for the answer as you read. Look for key words.* Have students read the paragraph silently. Then elicit the answer to the question. (flying machines) Elicit, *What key words in the question helped you find the key words for the answer?* (design, machines) Say, *We'll practice using selective attention as we read this lesson.*

Workbook pages 72–73 may now be assigned.

Using Visuals: Use Different Types of Maps Ask, *What visuals did you practice using in earlier lessons?* (timelines, map keys, compass roses, longitude and latitude, map scales, physical maps) *What visual will you practice using in this lesson?* Read the introduction, or call on a student to read it. Then help students pronounce the place names and physical features on the maps. Assign pairs and have students take turns asking and answering the questions, and then have them write the answers in their notebooks. When students have finished, elicit the answers and write them on the board.

Using the maps, elicit other information about places and physical features. For example, *What two countries are on the Iberian Peninsula? What Spanish city is by the Guadalquivir River? What elevation is most of the Iberian Peninsula? What mountains are on Spain's border?*

Answers
1. A physical map names the rivers and mountain ranges.
2. A political map names the countries and cities.
3. The capital of Portugal is Lisbon, and the capital of Spain is Madrid.

Workbook page 74 may now be assigned.

Reading ❷

Portuguese Exploration, pages 152–153

Preview Pages

Have students <u>preview</u> these pages and <u>predict</u> the topic.

Teach Pages

Ask, *What is the reading strategy in this lesson?* Write *Selective Attention* on the board. Say, *Let's practice using selective attention.* (pointing to the Before You Go On box on page 153) *What's the second question? What are the key words in this question?* (Vasco da Gama, sail) Say, *Find the answer on page 152. Use selective attention. Look for the key words. You don't have to understand everything on the page. Just look for the key words to answer the question. Raise your hand when you've found the answer.*

When most students have raised their hands, elicit the answer. (Vasco da Gama sailed around the Cape of Good Hope to India.)

Read the text and captions, or call on students to read them. Help students with any new words. Be sure to show or elicit routes on a globe or world map. Elicit the key word (navigation), the sentence it's in, and its definition.

Understand Information Encourage students to <u>visualize</u>, to <u>monitor their comprehension</u>, and to <u>understand chronological order</u> as they <u>reread</u> the pages. Have students take turns asking and answering questions about the reading in pairs or small groups. When students have finished, ask comprehension, picture, and thinking questions. Say, *Close your books. Tell me about the reading in your own words.* Elicit the main ideas and details.

Organize Information Say, *Let's make an outline about Portuguese exploration.* Have students look at the model outline on page 130. Ask questions to review the format. Model by beginning the outline on the board, and then have students copy and complete it. Have them list one or two pieces of supporting information per paragraph. The completed outline might look like this:

> I. Spanish Exploration
>   A. Portugal was the first European country to sail far south on the Atlantic Ocean.
>   1. Prince Henry was the Portuguese leader.
>   2. He became an expert on navigation.
>   B. In 1497 a Portuguese explorer named Vasco da Gama sailed around the Cape of Good Hope to India.
>   1. Before that, people thought it was impossible to sail around Africa.
>   C. Unfortunately, the Portuguese were the first Europeans to bring people from Africa to be sold as slaves.
>   1. In the 1400s slave traders captured or bought African people and transported them to Europe.
>   2. The buying and selling of people from Africa spread to countries on both sides of the Atlantic Ocean.

CONNECT TO TODAY: Maps

After the reading and comprehension check, have students work in pairs or small groups to find websites featuring interactive and 3-D maps. Encourage students to explore and talk about what they see on the maps.

ELSEWHERE IN THE WORLD: The Kingdom of Mali

After the reading and comprehension check, have students locate the modern-day country of Mali on a map. Bring in or help students find photos of current-day Mali on the Internet.

Before You Go On

Have students do the first two questions in pairs. Do the third critical-thinking question as a class.

Answers

1. Prince Henry was the Portuguese leader. He sailed to parts of Africa that Europeans had never been to.
2. Vasco da Gama sailed around the Cape of Good Hope to India.
3. Answers will vary. Possible answers: The slave trade was a sad thing. African men, women, and children were captured or bought, and sent on long, dangerous trips. They were owned by others and forced to work for no money.

Working with Timelines

Read the timeline entries, or call on students to read them. Help students with any new words. Have students write the heading *Unit 4, Lesson 2 Timelines* on a new page in their notebooks. Then have them copy the Unit Events timeline.

Choose World Events that your students will find interesting. Bring in pictures and maps to help teach these events.

REACHING ALL STUDENTS: Visual Learners

This exercise will further emphasize the importance of Vasco da Gama's voyage to Calcutta. Create handouts of a current political map showing Portugal, Africa, and India. Pass these out to students. Then have students, in pairs or small groups, draw lines to show Portuguese voyages on the map.

Spanish Exploration, pages 154–155

Preview Pages

Have students <u>preview</u> these pages and <u>predict</u> the topic.

Teach Pages

Read the text and captions, or call on students to read them. Help students with any new words. Elicit the key words (voyage, route, diseases, indigenous [in caption]), the sentences they're in, and their definitions. After teaching page 154, do the As You Read activity.

As You Read: Use Selective Attention

Ask, *What is the reading strategy in this lesson?* Read the information in the box on page 155, or call on a student to read it. Say (pointing to the Before You Go On box), *What's the second question? What is the key word in this question?* (Taino) Say, *Now read the two paragraphs on page 155 and find the answers. Use selective attention. Remember, you don't have to understand everything on the page. Just look for the key word to answer the question. Raise your hand when you've found the answers.* When most students have raised their hands, elicit the answers.

Understand Information Encourage students to visualize, to monitor their comprehension, and to understand chronological order as they reread the pages. Have students take turns asking and answering questions about the reading in pairs or small groups. When students have finished, ask comprehension, picture, and thinking questions. Say, *Close your books. Tell me about the reading in your own words.* Elicit the main ideas and details.

Organize Information Say, *Let's make an outline about Spanish Exploration.* Model by beginning the outline on the board, and then have students copy and complete it. Have students list one or two pieces of supporting information per paragraph. The completed outline might look like this:

I. Spanish Exploration
  A. An Italian sailor named Christopher Columbus tried to get money from Italy to plan a voyage to India.
    1. When Italy refused to give him money, Columbus decided to ask Spain for help.
    2. The rulers of Spain wanted to sail to India as the Portuguese had done.
  B. People called the Tainos were living on the islands where Columbus landed, in present-day Bahamas. Columbus thought he had landed in India, so he called the Tainos Indians. When Columbus returned to Spain, he brought gold, pearls, parrots, and some Taino people to show to Queen Isabella and King Ferdinand.
  C. The Spanish made the islands a colony and the Tainos became slaves.
    1. The Spanish brought diseases to the islands.
    2. Many Tainos died from these diseases.

SCIENCE CONNECTION: Smallpox

After the reading and comprehension check, discuss with students why the Europeans were not as affected by smallpox as the indigenous population. Discuss how current diseases (Asian flu, Ebola, AIDS, etc.) can be spread very rapidly with modern transportation and lack of effective vaccinations or cures.

Before You Go On

Have students do the first two questions in pairs. Do the third critical-thinking question as a class. Make sure students understand the words *positive* and *negative* in the third question.

Answers
1. Columbus wanted to go to India.
2. The Taino people were living on the islands where Columbus landed, in present-day Bahamas. The Tainos became slaves. The Spanish brought diseases, and many Taino people died. After 100 years, the Taino people and their culture almost disappeared.
3. Answers will vary. Possible answers: Positives: Columbus found a route to the Americas. He brought Spanish culture to the Americas. Negatives: The Tainos became slaves and many died of diseases. The Taino culture almost disappeared.

Working with Timelines

Read the timeline entries, or call on students to read them. Ask comprehension and review questions. Have students copy the Unit Events timeline onto their Lesson 2 Timelines page.

Choose World Events that your students will find interesting. Bring in pictures and maps to help teach these events.

Spanish Conquests, pages 156–157

Preview Pages

Have students <u>preview</u> these pages and <u>predict</u> the topic. Ask, *What do you already know about this topic?*

Teach Pages

Read the text and captions, or call on students to read them. Elicit the key words (conquered, diseases), the sentences they're in, and their definitions. After teaching page 156, ask, *What is the reading strategy in this lesson?* Say (pointing to the Before You Go On box on page 157), *What's the second question? What are some key words in this question?* (Incas, build) Say, *Now read the paragraph on page 157 and find the answer. Use selective attention. Raise your hand when you've found the answer.* When most students have raised their hands, elicit the answer.

Understand Information Encourage students to visualize, to monitor their comprehension, and to understand chronological order as they reread the pages. Have students take turns asking and answering questions about the reading in pairs or small groups. When students have finished, ask comprehension, picture, and thinking questions. Begin your questions by saying, *Let's be sure we understand chronological order. What dates do you see on these pages? What happened on those dates?* Then ask more detailed comprehension, picture, and thinking questions. Say, *Close your books. Tell me about the reading in your own words.* Elicit the main ideas and details.

Organize Information Say, *Let's make a T-chart about the Aztec and Inca empires.* Draw a T-chart on the board. Elicit information about the Aztec Empire, write it into the chart, and have students copy it as a model. The completed chart might look like this:

The Aztec Empire	The Inca Empire
Tenochtitlán in Mexico was the center of the Aztec Empire.	Cuzco in Peru was the center of the Inca Empire.
It was ruled by an emperor called Moctezuma.	In the 1400s the Incan population was 10 million.
The Aztecs were powerful warriors.	The Incas built great temples and cities in the mountains.
They studied the stars and planets, and their ancestors had invented an accurate calendar.	The Incas built the city of Machu Picchu in about 1470.
	They built roads that were hundreds of miles long.
	The Incas grew maize, cocoa, and tobacco on large farms.

MORE ABOUT IT: Tenochtitlán

After the reading and comprehension check, have students look at the illustration of Tenochtitlán on page 156. Explain that this is an artist's idea of the city. It doesn't exist today. Say, *Study the picture a moment, and then close your eyes and imagine living in Tenochtitlán.* Elicit what students imagined. Bring in pictures of Aztec art, or help students navigate the Internet to find examples.

Optional Activity

This exercise will further emphasize the importance of the Spanish conquests in the history of the Americas. Create handouts of a current political map showing Central and South America. Pass these out to students. Have students mark an X on Spanish-

(continued)

speaking countries. If a large number of your students are from Latin America, first have students work in pairs or small groups to complete this exercise, and then elicit the country names and write them on the board. If Latin American students are in the minority, you may want to do this exercise as a class, eliciting the country names, writing them on the board, and then having students mark their maps.

Before You Go On

Have students do the first two questions in pairs. Do the third critical-thinking question as a class.

Answers

1. The Spanish conquered Tenochtitlán and Cuzco.
2. The Incas built great temples and cities in the mountains, such as Machu Picchu. They built roads that were hundreds of miles long.
3. Answers will vary. Possible answers: The Aztecs thought Cortés was a god because they had never seen white men before. Cortés and his army wore strange clothes and came in strange ships. They probably had strange tools and weapons.

Working with Timelines

Read the timeline entries, or call on students to read them. Ask comprehension and review questions. Have students copy the Unit Events timeline onto their Lesson 2 Timelines page.

Choose World Events that your students will find interesting. Bring in pictures and maps to help teach these events.

The Enlightenment, pages 158–159

Preview Pages

Have students preview these pages and predict the topic.

Teach Pages

Ask, *What is the reading strategy in this lesson?* Say (pointing to the Before You Go On box on page 159), *What's the second question? What are some key words in this question?* (discovered, basics, modern chemistry) Say, *Find the answer on page 158. Use selective attention. Raise your hand when you've found the answer.* When most students have raised their hands, elicit the answer.

Teach the Profile box either before moving on to page 159, or as a separate reading. Read the text, or call on students to read it. Help students with any new words.

Understand Information Encourage students to visualize, to monitor their comprehension, and to understand chronological order as they reread the pages. Have students take turns asking and answering questions about the reading in pairs or small groups. When students have finished, ask comprehension, picture, and thinking questions. Say, *Close your books. Tell me about the reading in your own words.* Elicit the main ideas and details.

Organize Information Say, *Let's make a word web about the discoveries of the Enlightenment.* Model by beginning the word web on the board, and then have students copy and complete it. The completed word web might look like this:

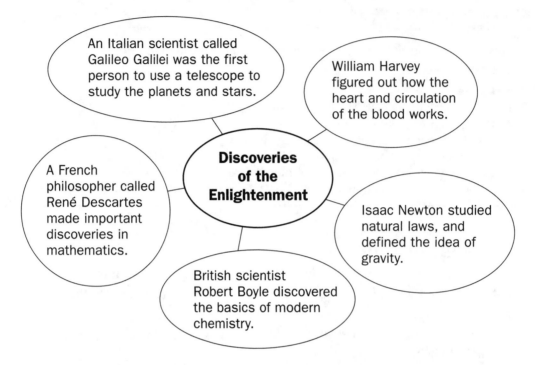

An Italian scientist called Galileo Galilei was the first person to use a telescope to study the planets and stars.

William Harvey figured out how the heart and circulation of the blood works.

Discoveries of the Enlightenment

A French philosopher called René Descartes made important discoveries in mathematics.

Isaac Newton studied natural laws, and defined the idea of gravity.

British scientist Robert Boyle discovered the basics of modern chemistry.

PROFILE: Galileo Galilei

Before the reading and comprehension check, practice <u>asking the question</u>, *Do I know something about this already?* Ask, *What do you already know about Galileo?*

MORE ABOUT IT: The Inquisition

After the reading and comprehension check, discuss with students what they think about the Inquisition. Ask, *Should people ever be punished for their beliefs? Why or why not?*

Before You Go On

Have students do the first two questions in pairs. Do the third critical-thinking question as a class.

Answers
1. Italian scientist Galileo Galilei observed that the earth revolves around the sun.
2. British scientist Robert Boyle discovered the basics of modern chemistry.
3. Answers will vary. Possible answers: It was probably used for torturing people. It probably was put around a person's neck. Then someone pulled the two sides closer together and the spikes went into the person's neck.

Working with Timelines

Read the timeline entries, or call on students to read them. Help students with any new words. Ask comprehension and review questions. Have students copy the Unit Events timeline onto their Lesson 2 Timelines page.

Choose World Events that your students will find interesting. Bring in pictures and maps to help teach these events.

For more information, go to www.longmanusa.com/socialstudies for links to interesting websites about the Renaissance, exploration, and the Enlightenment.

Review and Practice, pages 160–161

Vocabulary

If your students need additional help in reviewing this vocabulary, see the Optional Vocabulary Activities (pages vii–viii). Have students work individually. Check by calling on students to read their sentences. Write the correct answers on the board.

Answers
1. conquered
2. route
3. voyages
4. diseases
5. navigation
6. indigenous

Check Your Understanding

Have students work individually, in pairs, or in small groups. Let students look back at the text, as needed. Then have students share their answers with the class. Write the answers on the board. Have students correct or add to their answers, if needed.

Answers
1. Students may write about any three of the following scientists:
   - Galileo Galilei discovered that the earth revolved around the sun. He made a telescope that magnified objects to thirty times their real size. He found many new stars and changed people's ideas about the universe.
   - René Descartes made important discoveries in mathematics.
   - Robert Boyle discovered the basics of modern chemistry.
   - Isaac Newton studied natural laws and defined the idea of gravity.
   - William Harvey figured out how the heart and circulation of blood works.
2. Spanish explorer Hernán Cortés and his small army conquered the Aztecs.
3. Columbus found people called the Tainos on the islands where he landed.
4. Galileo was brought before the Inquisition because he observed that the earth revolved around the sun. At that time, the Church believed that the earth was the center of the universe, and that the planets and stars revolved around the earth. For many years, Galileo's views annoyed the Church.

Apply Social Studies Skills

Content Reading Strategy: Use Selective Attention Review the reading strategy. Ask students, *How do you use selective attention to help find answers?* (look for key words) Read the instructions, or call on a student to read them. Remind students that they don't have to understand every word in the paragraph—they just have to find the answer. Have students work individually to read the paragraph, and find the answer to the question. Have students raise their hands when they've found the answer. When most students have raised their hands, elicit the answer. (Spanish viceroys ruled Spanish land in the Americas. The Roman Catholic Church and its missionaries helped.)

Direct students' attention to the questions below the paragraph. Have students individually write the answers in their notebooks. To check, elicit one or more responses.

Using Visuals: Use Different Types of Maps Read the heading. Tell students, *These two maps will show you some new information.* Read the instructions, or call on students to read them. Help students learn and pronounce any new words after they've answered the questions. For question 3, tell students to write the features (mountains, lakes, etc.), but not the names of the features. Have students work in pairs to find the answers to the questions and write them in their notebooks. Check by eliciting the answers and writing them on the board.

Answers

1. The map on the left is a political map. The map on the right is a physical map.
2. Canada, the United States, Mexico, Guatemala, Honduras, Belize, Jamaica, Haiti, Cuba, the Bahamas, the Dominican Republic, and Puerto Rico are shown on the political map.
3. Plains, mountains, rivers, lakes, gulfs, bays, seas, straits, peninsulas, and elevations are shown on the physical map.
4. The physical map tells you the elevation of Mt. McKinley.

Discuss

Read the discussion question. Then assign small groups to discuss the question. Circulate to help and comment on students' responses. Allow time for students to share their answers with the class.

 Workbook pages 75–76 may now be assigned.

Evaluation

Self-Assessment Questions

Write the following questions on the board. Have students respond in their notebooks. Then they can share their responses in small groups.

1. How can using selective attention help me in reading?
2. How can using different types of maps help me to learn about countries?
3. What was difficult for me in this lesson?
4. What was easy for me in this lesson?
5. What was most enjoyable to learn?

Unit Review, pages 162–163

Vocabulary

Have students work individually, in pairs, or in small groups, depending on how much support they need. Check answers as a class, writing the answers on the board.

Answers

1. printing press	5. indigenous	9. protests
2. conquered	6. manuscript	10. diseases
3. route	7. clergy	11. voyages
4. movable type	8. explorer	12. navigation

Timeline Check

Draw the timeline on the board as students copy it into their notebooks. Elicit the first event and write it on the timeline on the board. Then have students work individually, in pairs, or in small groups to complete the timeline. Check by eliciting the events and writing them on the board.

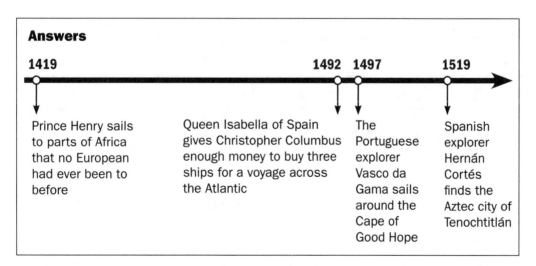

Answers

1419	1492	1497	1519
Prince Henry sails to parts of Africa that no European had ever been to before	Queen Isabella of Spain gives Christopher Columbus enough money to buy three ships for a voyage across the Atlantic	The Portuguese explorer Vasco da Gama sails around the Cape of Good Hope	Spanish explorer Hernán Cortés finds the Aztec city of Tenochtitlán

Apply Social Studies Skills

Using Visuals: Read a Map Read the instructions, or call on a student to read them. Have students work individually or in pairs to write the answers in their notebooks. Then call on students to answer the questions. Write the answers on the board.

After checking the last question, draw a compass rose on the board and elicit or teach *northwest, northeast, southwest, southeast*. Explain that these points are halfway between the main four points on the compass rose. Have students copy this into their notebooks.

Extension Project

Help students find information about ships on the Internet or in the library. Depending on your resources and student ability, have students work in pairs, in small groups, or as a class. Have them write the answers to the questions as a paragraph. Collect the paragraphs, correct them, and have students write a new version, as needed. Then call on several students to share their paragraphs with the class.

Read More About It

Bring at least one of the suggested books to class. Show the cover and some of the inside pages to students as a preview. Ask students to predict what the book is about. Read an excerpt to the class. Then ask several comprehension questions. Read the excerpt again before calling on students to answer. Encourage students to find this or another suggested book in their school library or local bookstore.

Workbook pages 77–78 may now be assigned.

Writing Skills, pages 164–165

Write a First Draft

Preview

Have students preview these two pages. Then ask, *What will you practice writing?*

Present the Model

Read the information on page 164, or call on students to read it. Have students reread the introduction and study the model outline and first draft. Then ask comprehension questions such as (pointing to the outline), *What should your outline show? What's the topic of the example outline? What symbol shows it's the most important idea? What is the main idea of the first paragraph? What letter is written next to it in the outline? What are some supporting ideas? What's the main idea of the second paragraph?* (pointing to the first draft) *Did the student change some sentences from the outline? What are some mistakes in spelling or punctuation in the first draft?*

Practice

Read the instructions, or call on students to read them. Have students reread the instructions, and then ask comprehension questions to make sure students understand. Say, *First I'll choose the topic.* Do a think-aloud as a model. As you look through the unit pages, say, *What's a topic I find very interesting? I know, I think I'll write about the printing press on page 143.* Have students choose a topic and write it in their notebooks. If students need extra support for this writing assignment, have them choose the topic and complete the practice in pairs.

Elicit the format of an outline and write it on the board. (I. A. 1. 2. 3.) Say, *Now I'm going to reread the information about the printing press on page 143.* Have students reread this page also. Then say, *Now I'm going to close my book and write my outline. I'm going to close my book because I need to write this in my own words. First, I need to write the main idea. My main idea is that the printing press made it easier for people to have books.* Write this into the outline. Say, *Now I need some details to support this idea.* Say, and write on the board, *Only rich people had books before the printing press.*

Tell students to close their books as they write their outline. Tell them they can open their books if they've forgotten a detail, but then they should close them again. Circulate to monitor and help students with their outlines. When students have completed their outlines, model the writing part of a first draft of the outline on the board. Remind students that they don't need to worry about spelling or punctuation now—they just have to get their ideas written down. As students complete their drafts, circulate to help.

 Workbook pages 79–80 may now be assigned.

Unit 5 Early United States

Unit Overview

Lesson	Content	Social Studies Skills		Writing Skills
		Reading Strategies	Using Visuals	
1	• The New World • The English Colonists • Pilgrims and Puritans • The French and Indian War • Southern Plantations	Use What You Know	Read a Chart (Part 1)	Write a Three-Paragraph Essay
2	• American Independence • The Boston Tea Party • The War for Independence • The Declaration of Independence • The United States Constitution	Look for Cause and Effect	Read a Chart (Part 2)	

Objectives

Vocabulary
- Develop new vocabulary related to early United States history
- Use newly acquired vocabulary in context

Concepts
- Acquire knowledge of early colonization in North America
- Acquire knowledge of the founding of the United States government

Reading Strategies
- Use what you know to understand what you read
- Understand cause-and-effect relationships
- Practice previously learned strategies

Using Visuals
- Understand how to read charts for information

Writing Skills
- Practice writing a three-paragraph essay

Unit Opener, pages 166–167

Preview Topic

Point out the unit title and the pictures on the page. Ask students, *What do you think the word* early *means in the title?* Elicit that the unit is about the beginning years of the United States.

Have students describe the pictures. Ask, *Who are all these people? Are they getting on a ship or off? Where do you think they are? What are they building? What else can you see in the picture?* Ask picture, thinking, and background knowledge questions to get students interested in this period. Help with vocabulary, as needed.

Unit Contents

Help students pronounce the list of names. Say each name and have students repeat. Ask if students recognize any names. Ask what they know about them. Write that information on the board. Follow the same procedures with place names. Use a U.S. map to teach or elicit the locations of these places. For key events, say, *These are the key events we will learn about.* Read the list of key events, or call on a student to read them. Give simple definitions of any new words. Have students copy the key events into their notebooks.

Get Ready

Say, *Before we start this unit, let's review some events from Unit 4.* Draw the timeline on the board as students copy it into their notebooks. Elicit the caption for the first date (on page 152) and write it on the board. Have students work in pairs or small groups to find the information and write it on their timelines. The completed timeline might look like this:

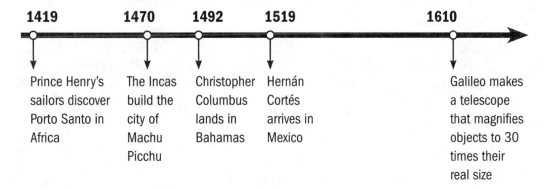

1419	1470	1492	1519	1610
Prince Henry's sailors discover Porto Santo in Africa	The Incas build the city of Machu Picchu	Christopher Columbus lands in Bahamas	Hernán Cortés arrives in Mexico	Galileo makes a telescope that magnifies objects to 30 times their real size

Lesson ❶

Before You Read, pages 168–171

Have students <u>preview</u> these pages individually or in pairs. Ask, *What will you learn about in this lesson?*

Vocabulary

Read the captions, or call on students to read them. Help students understand and pronounce any new words. Use pictures, props, maps, and mime. Have students read the captions again silently. Ask picture and comprehension questions for each item to make sure students have understood. Read the key words and have students say them after you. Then have students close their books. Point to the pictures and ask questions to elicit the key words.

Practice

Have students fill in the blanks, and then compare their answers in pairs. Check by calling on individual students. Write the letters of the correct answers on the board.

> **Answers**
> **1.** b. settlers   **3.** b. slaves   **5.** c. colony
> **2.** c. plantation   **4.** a. territory   **6.** a. indentured servant

Workbook page 81 may now be assigned.

Social Studies Skills

Content Reading Strategy: Use What You Know To prepare students for this reading strategy, ask, *What do you know about this school?* Write responses on the board. Elicit information such as grade levels, subject classes, rules, class schedules, students with different backgrounds, after-school activities, and so on. Then ask, *If you move to another school tomorrow, what do you know that will help you in your next school?* Point out that we automatically use what we already know to help us understand new situations and new information.

Read the information on page 170, or call on a student to read it. Make a T-chart on the board with these headings:

What I Learned About Indigenous People in Unit 4	What I Think Happened to Indigenous People in North America

Elicit what students learned about indigenous people in the Americas to fill in the left side of the T-chart. Also, encourage students to express what they have learned from other sources. Then ask students, *What do you think happened to indigenous people in North America when the English came?* List that information on the right side of the T-chart. Accept all plausible guesses without comment or confirmation. Have students copy this information into their notebooks to confirm or correct their guesses later when they read the section about Native Americans and the English settlers. Remind students to use the <u>use what you know</u> strategy as they read the lesson.

Workbook page 82 may now be assigned.

Using Visuals: Read a Chart Ask, *What visuals did you learn about and use in earlier units?* (timelines, map keys, compass roses, longitude and latitude, map scales, physical maps, political maps) Read the introduction, or call on a student to read it. Help students with any new words in the chart. Have students work in pairs to find the answers to the questions and write them in their notebooks. Check by eliciting the answers and writing them on the board.

REACHING ALL STUDENTS: Visual and Kinesthetic Learners

Bring in real-life examples of food: a potato, an ear of corn, a tomato, and beans for students to look at and hold. Tell students, *These foods were new to Europeans. Columbus brought them from the New World to Europe.* Show pictures of cocoa pods growing on trees and sugarcane growing in fields.

Workbook pages 83–84 may now be assigned.

Reading ❶

The New World, pages 172–173

Preview Pages

Have students <u>preview</u> these pages and <u>predict</u> the topic.

Teach Pages

Read the text and captions, or call on students to read them. Help students with any new words. Elicit the key word (territory), the sentence it's in, and its definition.

Understand Information Ask, *What's the reading strategy in this lesson? What do we already know about explorers from the previous unit?* Encourage students to <u>use what they know</u> as they <u>reread</u> the pages. Have students take turns asking and answering questions about the reading in pairs or small groups. When students have finished, ask comprehension, picture, and thinking questions. Say, *Close your books. Tell me about the reading in your own words.* Elicit the main ideas and details from students until the content has been adequately covered.

Organize Information Say, *Let's make a word web about Christopher Columbus using the paragraph on page 173.* Model by beginning the word web on the board, and then have students copy and complete it. The completed word web might look like this:

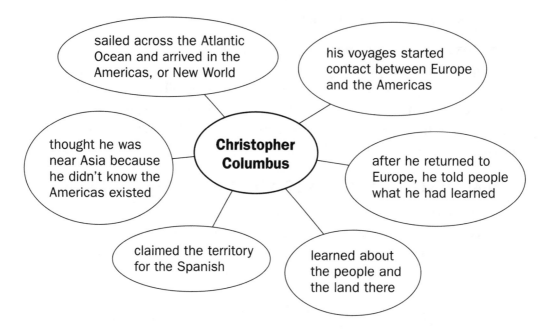

Language Tip: Conjunctions

Read the text in the box on page 173, or call on a student to read it. Write *Conjunctions* on the board and have students copy it into their notebooks. On the board, write, *Columbus sailed across the Atlantic Ocean. Columbus arrived in the Americas, or the New World.* Have students find an example of these two sentences joined with a conjunction in the reading. Write this on the board, have students copy it in their notebooks, and then find and write down other sentences with conjunctions. To check, elicit the sentences and have students tell you what words or sentences are joined with conjunctions.

Have students write two compound sentences about themselves in their notebooks—one with *and* and one with *because*. Model by writing a sentence about yourself. When students have finished, call on several students to share their sentences with the class.

Before You Go On

Have students do the first two questions in pairs. Do the third critical-thinking question as a class.

Answers
1. Columbus was looking for a faster trade route to Asia.
2. Columbus found the Americas, or New World (at San Salvador in the modern-day Bahamas).
3. Answers will vary. Possible answers: Columbus didn't know there were other lands between Europe and Asia. He didn't know the world was so large.

Working with Timelines

Read the timeline entries, or call on students to read them. Help students understand any new words. Ask comprehension and review questions. Have students write the heading *Unit 5, Lesson 1 Timelines* on a new page in their notebooks. Then have them copy the Unit Events timeline.

Choose World Events that students will find interesting. Bring in pictures and maps to help teach these events.

The English Colonists, pages 174–175

Preview Pages

Have students preview these pages and predict the topic.

Teach Pages

Read the text and captions, or call on students to read them. Help students with any new words. Elicit the key words (colonies, settlers, indentured servants, slaves), the sentences they're in, and their definitions.

Understand Information Ask, *What's the reading strategy in this lesson? The settlers were newcomers, people who just arrived in a new place. What do you know about being a newcomer? What do you know about religious freedom from earlier units?* Encourage students to use what they know as they reread the pages.

Have students take turns asking and answering questions about the reading in pairs or small groups. When students have finished, ask comprehension, picture, and thinking questions. Say, *Close your books. Tell me about the reading in your own words.* Elicit the main ideas and details.

Organize Information Say, *Let's make a chart about the Jamestown colony.* Model by writing the chart and headings on the board, and then have students copy and complete it. The completed chart might look like this:

The Jamestown Colony	
When and where:	The settlers formed the Jamestown colony in Virginia in 1607.
First winter:	Many of the colonists got sick and died during the first winter.
Land and labor:	The colonists used the Native Americans' land and labor.
Government and laws:	Jamestown started its own government in 1619. The government made laws. The colonists had to follow the laws.
Slaves:	In 1619 a ship arrived in Jamestown. The ship carried the first slaves from Africa to the colonies.

Before You Go On

Have students do the first two questions in pairs. Do the third critical-thinking question as a class.

Answers
1. Some people wanted to own land. Other people came for religious freedom. (Alternates: Some people came to America as indentured servants. Some people came to North America as slaves.)
2. They had many problems. Many of the colonists got sick and died during the winter.
3. Answers will vary. Possible answers: The new settlers didn't know how to grow food. They didn't know the area. They had to make everything they needed. The Native Americans found new and different people living near them. The colonists used the Native Americans' land and labor. The new settlers thought they "owned" the land.

Working with Timelines

Read the timeline entries, or call on students to read them. Help students understand any new words. Ask comprehension and review questions. Have students copy the Unit Events timeline onto their Lesson 1 Timelines page.

Choose World Events that students will find interesting. Bring in pictures and maps to help teach these events.

Pilgrims and Puritans, page 176
The French and Indian War, page 177

Preview Pages

Have students preview these pages and predict the topics. Point to the picture of the *Mayflower* and tell them that this ship had 102 passengers and took two months to sail from Plymouth, England, to Cape Cod, Massachusetts. Then have students close their eyes and visualize being on a small ship with 101 other passengers. *Where would you sleep? What would you eat? What would you do all day?*

Teach Pages

Read the text and captions, or call on students to read them. Help students with any new words. Elicit the key words (colony, territory), the sentences they're in, and their definitions.

Understand Information Have students reread the pages. Then have them take turns asking and answering questions about the reading in pairs or small groups. When students have finished, ask comprehension, picture, and thinking questions. Say, *Close your books. Tell me about the reading in your own words.* Elicit the main ideas and details.

Organize Information Say, *Let's make a Venn diagram to compare and contrast the Pilgrims and the Puritans.* Model by beginning the diagram on the board, and then have students copy and complete it. The completed diagram might look like this:

Pilgrims
- in 1620 sailed to the Americas
- their ship was the *Mayflower*
- they called their colony Plymouth

Both
- English settled in Massachusetts
- wanted religious freedom

Puritans
- in 1630 settled in the Americas
- Puritan leaders made strict laws
- they did not allow people to practice other religions

CONNECT TO TODAY: Blue Laws

After the reading and comprehension check, ask students if they have any kind of "blue laws" in their home countries. Discuss with students what they think of blue laws.

Language Tip: British, French, American

Read the text in the box on page 177 and have students repeat. Ask students which words are names of countries and which are the names of the people who live there. Write the headings *Country* and *Nationality* on the board. Then write *He is from France. He is French* underneath the headings. Have students copy this into their notebooks. Elicit other countries and nationalities and write them on the board. Have students write pairs of sentences in their notebooks using a country and a nationality.

As You Read: Use What You Know

Read the text in the box on page 177. Brainstorm a list on the board by asking, *What do you already know about moving to a new place?* Then ask, *What things on this list might be true for the Pilgrims and Puritans?* Place a check next to those items. Say, *As you reread the pages, think about how your experience helps you understand the lives of the Pilgrims and Puritans.*

Have students do the first two questions in pairs. Do the third critical-thinking question as a class.

Answers

1. The Pilgrims and Puritans left England because they wanted religious freedom.
2. The French and British fought a war because both wanted the territory west of the Appalachian Mountains.
3. Answers will vary. Possible answers: Yes, because religion is important in my life. *or* No, because religion is not so important to me.

Working with Timelines

Read the timeline entries, or call on students to read them. Help students understand any new words. Ask comprehension and review questions. Have students copy the Unit Events timeline onto their Lesson 1 Timelines page.

Choose World Events that students will find interesting. Bring in pictures and maps to help teach these events.

Primary Source, page 178

Preview Page

Have students preview this page and predict the topic.

Teach Page

Read the text, or call on students to read it. Help students with any new words.

Understand Information Encourage students to visualize and to monitor their comprehension as they reread the page. Have students take turns asking and answering questions about the reading in pairs or small groups. When students have finished, ask comprehension, picture, and thinking questions. Say, *Close your books. Tell me about the reading in your own words.* Elicit the main ideas and details. Then have students open their books and work in pairs or small groups to write the answers to the questions in their notebooks. Then elicit the answers and write them on the board.

Bring in pictures of life on a slave ship or help students find websites showing this. Discuss the conditions on the ship, and how many slaves died on the journey.

Answers

1. The "poor chained men" are the other African men on the slave ship.
2. Some men tell Equiano that they were to be carried to these white people's country to work for them.

Southern Plantations, page 179

Southern Plantations, page 179

Preview Page

Have students <u>preview</u> this page and <u>predict</u> the topic. Ask students, *What's the reading strategy in this lesson? What do you already know about farming? What do you know about slaves?*

Teach Page

Read the text and captions, or call on students to read them. Help students with any new words. Elicit the key words (plantation, slaves), the sentences they're in, and their definitions.

Understand Information Encourage students to <u>use what they know</u> as they <u>reread</u> the page. Have students take turns asking and answering questions about the reading in pairs or small groups. When students have finished, ask comprehension, picture, and thinking questions. Say, *Close your books. Tell me about the reading in your own words.* Elicit the main ideas and details.

Organize Information Say, *Let's do a word web about slave plantations.* Model by beginning the word web on the board, and then have students copy and complete it. The completed word web might look like this:

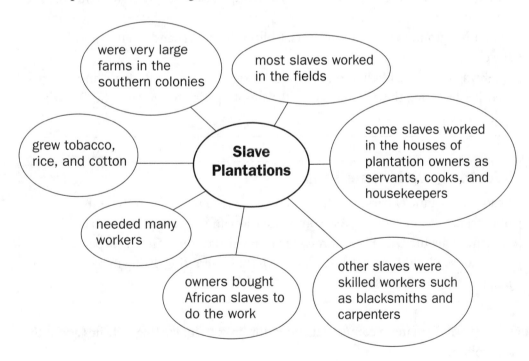

Have students do the first two questions in pairs. Do the third critical-thinking question as a class. Use a Venn diagram for question 3.

Answers

1. People grew tobacco, rice, and cotton on the plantations.
2. The plantation owners bought so many slaves because the plantations needed many workers.
3.

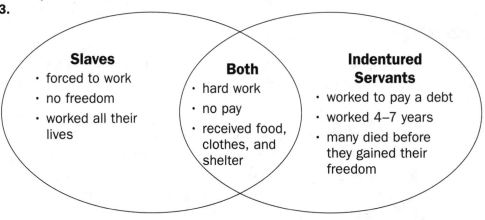

Slaves
- forced to work
- no freedom
- worked all their lives

Both
- hard work
- no pay
- received food, clothes, and shelter

Indentured Servants
- worked to pay a debt
- worked 4–7 years
- many died before they gained their freedom

MORE ABOUT IT: The Quakers

After the reading, assign students to small groups. Ask each group to write three questions about the Quakers on a piece of paper. Have them pass their questions to another group to write the answers. Collect the papers and ask the questions to the class.

Bring in photos of Quaker houses and furniture, or help students find websites featuring these. Discuss how the simple, plain style reflects the Quakers' beliefs in equality.

Working with Timelines

Read the timeline entries, or call on students to read them. Help students understand any new words. Ask comprehension and review questions. Have students copy the Unit Events timeline onto their Lesson 1 Timelines page.

Choose World Events that students will find interesting. Bring in pictures and maps to help teach these events.

Go to www.longmanusa.com/socialstudies for links to interesting websites about the early colonies.

Review and Practice, pages 180–181

Vocabulary

Help students review the key vocabulary in Lesson 1 before they complete this exercise. For additional practice, see Optional Vocabulary Activities (pages vii–viii) to choose an appropriate activity. Have students work individually. Check by calling on students to read their sentences. Write the correct answers on the board.

Answers
1. settlers
2. Plantation
3. territory
4. colony
5. Indentured servants
6. Slaves

Check Your Understanding

Depending on the language level and abilities of your students, have them work individually, in pairs, or in small groups to answer the questions. Let students look back at the text, as needed. Then have students share their answers with the whole class. Write the answers on the board. Have students correct or add to their answers, if needed.

Answers
1. English settlers came to North America for different reasons. Some people wanted to own land, and others came for religious freedom. Some were indentured servants.
2. The first lasting English settlement was Jamestown in Virginia.
3. African slaves were brought to the southern colonies to work on the plantations.
4. After 1763 life in North America changed for the French because they lost almost all their land.

Apply Social Studies Skills

Content Reading Strategy: Use What You Know Review the reading strategy <u>use what you know</u>. Ask students, *What does it mean to use what you know? How does using what you know help you?* Have students reread page 177, which tells about the French and Indian War. Then have them copy the two boxes into their notebooks and work individually to write their predictions. Then assign small groups so that students can share their ideas. Elicit the ideas from different groups and write them on the board.

Using Visuals: Read a Chart Point to the title of the chart and ask, *What do you think colonial jobs were?* Elicit that they are jobs people did in the colonies. Have students look at the small pictures in the chart as you read the chart from left to right. Ask students to repeat. Then have them work in pairs or small groups to ask and answer the questions, and then write their answers in their notebooks. Check by eliciting the answers and writing them on the board.

Discuss

Read the discussion question. Check for comprehension. Have students discuss the question in groups or as a class. Make sure they offer reasons for their opinions.

Optional Activity

Show an example of *unfair*. Choose two student volunteers. Give a smaller number of something (e.g., cookies, pencils, coins, etc.) to one student than to the other. Then say to the class, *That's not fair. I gave five cookies to [Tomás] and only three cookies to [Maria]. That's not equal.* Fair *means equal.* Unfair *means not equal.*

 Workbook pages 85–86 may now be assigned.

Evaluation

Self-Assessment Questions

Write the following questions on the board and have students respond in their notebooks. Then have them share their responses in small groups.

1. How can I use what I know to help me in reading?
2. How can charts help me to understand new ideas?
3. What was difficult for me in this lesson?
4. What was easy for me in this lesson?
5. What was most enjoyable to learn?

Lesson ②

Before You Read, pages 182–185

Have students <u>preview</u> these pages individually or in pairs. Ask, *What will you learn about in this lesson?*

Vocabulary

Read the captions, or call on students to read them. Help students with any new words. Have students read the captions again silently. Ask picture and comprehension questions for each item to make sure students have understood. Read the key words and have students say them after you. Then have students close their books. Point to the pictures and ask questions to elicit the key words.

Practice

Make sure students understand the word *formally* in question 1. Have students fill in the blanks, and then compare their answers in pairs. Check by calling on individual students. Write the letters of the correct answers on the board.

Workbook page 87 may now be assigned.

Social Studies Skills

 Content Reading Strategy: Look for Cause and Effect To prepare students for this reading strategy, write the words *Cause* and *Effect* on the board. Under *Effect*, write *late to school.* Under *Cause,* write a question mark. Ask students, *What are some reasons for being late to school?* Accept reasonable responses and write them on the board under the question mark. Now write, *Didn't study for a test* under *Cause* and a question mark under *Effect.* Ask students, *What happens if you don't study for a test?* Write their responses under the *Effect* heading. Tell students that there is a relationship between cause and effect. The cause is why something happens, and the effect is what happens.

Read the introduction and examples, or call on students to read them. Ask, *What's the cause? What's the effect? Why did the colonists bring people from Africa? Why did colonists throw boxes of tea into Boston Harbor?*

Tell students that when they read they should look for cause-and-effect relationships. These relationships help them understand what happened and why.

 Workbook pages 88–89 may now be assigned.

Using Visuals: Read a Chart Ask, *What visuals did you practice using in earlier lessons?* (timelines, map keys, compass roses, longitude and latitude, map scales, physical maps, political maps) *What visual will you practice using in this lesson?* Read the introduction, or call on a student to read it. Have students reread, and then ask comprehension questions to make sure students understand. Ask a student to count the colonies in the left-hand column to make sure there are thirteen. Then help students pronounce the place names on the chart. Before students answer the questions below the chart, provide further practice reading the chart. Call out a colony randomly and ask, *What year was it founded? What year did it become a royal colony? What colonies were privately owned?* Assign pairs and have students take turns asking and answering the questions. Then have students write the answers in their notebooks. When students have finished, elicit the answers and write them on the board.

 Workbook page 90 may now be assigned.

Reading ❷

American Independence, page 186
The Boston Tea Party, page 187

Preview Pages

Have students <u>preview</u> these pages and <u>predict</u> the topics.

Teach Pages

Read the text and captions, or call on students to read them. Help students with any new words. Elicit the key words (independence, tax, representatives), the sentences they're in, and their definitions.

Understand Information Have students <u>reread</u> the pages. Then have them take turns asking and answering questions about the reading in pairs or small groups. When students have finished, ask comprehension, picture, and thinking questions. Say, *Close your books. Tell me about the reading in your own words.* Elicit the main ideas and details.

Organize Information Say, *Let's draw a Cause-and-Effect diagram about the effects of the British tax.* Model by beginning the diagram on the board, and then have students copy and complete it. The diagram might look like this:

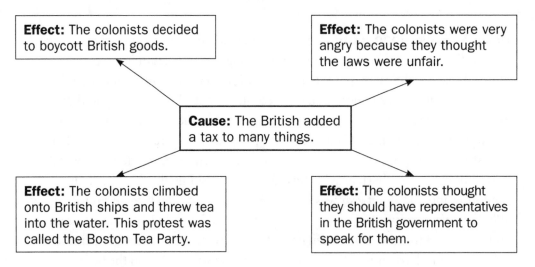

Effect: The colonists decided to boycott British goods.

Effect: The colonists were very angry because they thought the laws were unfair.

Cause: The British added a tax to many things.

Effect: The colonists climbed onto British ships and threw tea into the water. This protest was called the Boston Tea Party.

Effect: The colonists thought they should have representatives in the British government to speak for them.

As You Read: Look for Cause and Effect

Read the information in the box on page 186, or call on a student to read it. Write *Cause* and *Effect* on the board. Under *Cause* write, *The British wanted the colonists to pay for the war with France.* Ask, *What did this cause the British to do?* Elicit the answer and write it under *Effect*.

REACHING ALL STUDENTS: Visual Learners

To make the concept of taxes more concrete, and to help students use what they know, bring in some sales receipts for clothes, food, and other items that are taxed. Show students the line on the receipt where taxes are added to the subtotal. Ask, *What items are taxed? What percent is the tax? Are taxes taken out of your parents' paychecks? What happens to that money? Do you think having to pay tax is fair?*

MORE ABOUT IT: Tea

Before reading the text in the box on page 187, ask students, *Do you or your parents drink tea? What kind of tea? Where does it come from?* After the reading and comprehension check, ask students to close their books and write down three facts they learned. Have students share their facts with a classmate. Then call on different students to tell the class a fact they learned.

Before You Go On

Have students do the first two questions in pairs. Do the third critical-thinking question as a class.

Answers
1. The British taxed molasses, newspapers, and tea.
2. The colonists boycotted British goods because they thought the tax laws were unfair.
3. Answers will vary. Possible answers: People protest about war, about the government, about religion, about things they think are unfair.

Working with Timelines

Read the timeline entries, or call on students to read them. Help students understand any new words. Ask comprehension and review questions. Have students write the heading *Unit 5, Lesson 2 Timelines* on a new page in their notebooks. Then have them copy the Unit Events timeline.

Choose World Events that students will find interesting. Bring in pictures and maps to help teach these events.

The Boston Tea Party (continued), page 188
The War for Independence, page 189

Preview Pages

Have students preview these pages and predict the topics.

Read the text and captions, or call on students to read them. Help students with any new words. Elicit the key words (representatives, revolt, independence), the sentences they're in, and their definitions.

Understand Information Encourage students to look for cause and effect as they reread the pages. Write on the board: *Effect: The colonists begin to think that Britain would never give them freedom. Effect: The colonies sent representatives to Philadelphia.* Say, *Look for the causes.* Elicit the causes when students have finished reading. Have students take turns asking and answering questions about the reading in pairs or small groups. When students have finished, ask comprehension, picture, and thinking questions. Say, *Close your books. Tell me about the reading in your own words.* Elicit the main ideas and details.

Organize Information Say, *Let's do a Cause-and-Effect diagram about the War for Independence.* Draw a box on the board, label it *Cause*, and fill it in. Draw an arrow and a blank box labeled *Effect*. Then have students copy and complete it. The completed diagram might look like this:

The War for Independence

Cause		**Effect**
On April 19, 1775, British troops marched from Boston to Lexington and Concord to take the colonists' weapons.		The colonists fought back. Nearly 100 colonists were killed or wounded. About 250 British soldiers were killed or wounded. This was the beginning of the War for Independence.

Language Tip: Past Progressive

Read the text in the box on page 188, or call on a student to read it. Write *Past Progressive* on the board. Elicit the example in the text, add this on the board, and have students copy it into their notebooks. Review the past progressive tense by talking about the form (*was/were* + verb + *-ing*), the meaning (a continuous action in the past), and the function (describing an action in the past). Elicit examples from students by asking, *What were you doing last night around 9:00 P.M.?* Write their responses on the board, underlining the past progressive forms, and have students copy them into their notebooks.

MORE ABOUT IT: The Musket

After the reading and comprehension check, ask students to close their books and write down three facts they learned. Have students share their facts with a classmate. Then call on different students to tell the class a fact they learned.

Have students do the first two questions in pairs. Do the third critical-thinking question as a class.

Answers

1. The British punished the colonists because the colonists decided to boycott British goods and threw tea into Boston Harbor.
2. The colonists wanted to become an independent country because they began to think that Britain would never give them freedom.
3. Answers will vary. Possible answers: Yes, because freedom is a good reason to have a war. *or* No, because many people are killed or wounded in a war.

Working with Timelines

Read the timeline entries, or call on students to read them. Help students understand any new words. Ask comprehension and review questions. Have students copy the Unit Events timeline onto their Lesson 2 Timelines page.

Choose World Events that students will find interesting. Bring in pictures and maps to help teach these events.

The Declaration of Independence, pages 190–191

Preview Pages

Have students preview these pages and predict the topic.

Teach Pages

Read the text and captions, or call on students to read them. Help students with any new words. Elicit the key words (representatives, document, independence, treaty), the sentences they're in, and their definitions.

Teach the Profile box either before moving on to page 191, or as a separate reading.

Understand Information Encourage students to look for cause and effect as they reread the pages. Write on the board, *Effect: The British signed the Treaty of Paris in 1783.* Ask, *What's the cause?* Elicit the cause when students have finished reading. Have students take turns asking and answering questions about the reading in pairs or small groups. When students have finished, ask comprehension, picture, and thinking questions. Say, *Close your books. Tell me about the reading in your own words.* Elicit the main ideas and details.

PROFILE: Thomas Jefferson

Before the reading and comprehension check, ask, *What do you remember about Thomas Jefferson?* Bring in photos of the Jefferson Memorial in Washington, D.C., or help students find websites showing pictures of it.

Organize Information Say, *Let's do a word web about Thomas Jefferson.* Model by beginning the word web on the board, and then have students copy and complete it. The completed word web might look like this:

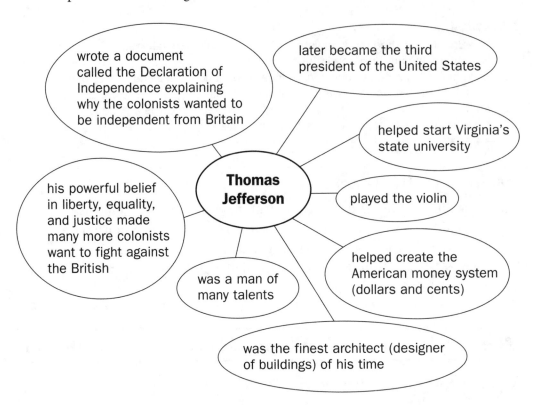

Optional Activity

Bring in a copy of the Declaration of Independence. Read and write on the board some of the key sentences. Help students understand the meaning. Discuss with students why these key ideas are good. Have students copy this in their notebooks.

ELSEWHERE IN THE WORLD: First School for the Blind

Before the reading and comprehension check, encourage students to <u>use what they know</u> to talk about people who are blind. Ask, *How do blind people walk around? How do they do daily chores? How do they read?* If possible, bring in a book written in Braille for students to see and touch.

Before You Go On

Have students do the first two questions in pairs. Do the third critical-thinking question as a class.

Answers
1. Thomas Jefferson and George Washington were two important people in the fight for independence.
2. U.S. citizens celebrate Independence Day on the Fourth of July.
3. Answers will vary. Possible answers: The British ran out of money. There were not enough British soldiers. The colonists were better fighters and knew the land.

The United States Constitution, pages 192–193

Preview Pages

Have students <u>preview</u> these pages and <u>predict</u> the topic. Encourage students to <u>use what they know</u>. Ask, *What do you remember about George Washington?*

Teach Pages

Read the text and captions, or call on students to read them. Help students with any new words. Elicit the key words (independence, representatives, document), the sentences they're in, and their definitions.

Understand Information Encourage students to <u>look for cause and effect</u> as they <u>reread</u> the pages. Ask, *What does* cause *mean?* (why something happened) *What does* effect *mean?* (what happened) Write on the board, *Effect: George Washington was much loved by the people of the United States.* Ask, *Why? (What's the cause?)* Elicit the answer when students have finished reading. Have students take turns asking and answering questions about the reading in pairs or small groups. When students have finished, ask comprehension, picture, and thinking questions. Say, *Close your books. Tell me about the reading in your own words.* Elicit the main ideas and details.

Organize Information Say, *Let's draw a flowchart about what happened after independence.* Model by beginning the flowchart on the board, and then have students copy and complete it. The completed flowchart might look like this:

After Independence

Each colony became a state with its own government.	→	In 1787 the states sent representatives to a meeting in Philadelphia.	→	They wrote a new plan of government. It united the states under one government.

| After the states approved the Constitution, they chose George Washington as the first president of the United States. | ← | They called this plan the United States Constitution. |

HEALTH CONNECTION: Malaria

Before the reading and comprehension check, invite students to say all they know about mosquitoes and/or malaria. Write the information on the board. As an extra challenge, have students find cause-and-effect relationships in the text.

Cause		Effect
A mosquito bit George Washington.	→	Washington got malaria.
Washington did not get treated.	→	Washington was often ill.

Before You Go On

Have students do the first two questions in pairs. Do the third critical-thinking question as a class. For question 3, make two columns with the headings *Yes* and *No*. Ask students to give reasons for either side. Encourage students to express their opinions.

Answers
1. The new plan was called the United States Constitution.
2. The main goal of the Constitution was to unite the states under one government.
3. Answers will vary. Possible answers: Yes, because they fight hard for their country and are ready to die for it. No, because an army leader can sometimes have too much control over the government and the army.

Working with Timelines

Read the timeline entries, or call on students to read them. Help students understand any new words. Ask comprehension and review questions. Have students copy the Unit Events timeline onto their Lesson 2 Timelines page.

Choose World Events that students will find interesting. Bring in pictures and maps to help teach these events.

Go to www.longmanusa.com/socialstudies for links to interesting websites about the U.S. War for Independence.

Review and Practice, pages 194–195

Vocabulary

Help students review the vocabulary in Lesson 2 before they complete this exercise. See Optional Vocabulary Activities (pages vii–viii) to choose an appropriate activity. Suggest to students that they copy all the sentences into their notebooks before they begin writing the answers. Then have students work individually and share their answers together as a class later.

Check Your Understanding

Depending on the language level and abilities of your students, have them work individually, in pairs, or in small groups to answer the questions. Let students look back at the text, as needed. Then have students share their answers with the whole class. Write the answers on the board.

Answers
1. The British taxed the colonists to help pay for the French and Indian War.
2. First, the representatives decided to revolt against Britain. Later, they voted for their independence. After independence, they wrote the Constitution.
3. The Declaration of Independence is a document explaining why the colonists wanted to be independent from Britain.
4. The Constitution was important because it united the states under one government.

Apply Social Studies Skills

Content Reading Strategy: Look for Cause and Effect Review the content reading strategy. Ask students what *cause* and *effect* mean. Ask, *How can this help you understand what you read?* Have students review the Cause-and-Effect charts they made previously in their notebooks. Ask students to copy the chart on this page and to complete the missing items. Allow students to reread sections of their text, if necessary, to find the answers.

Using Visuals: Read a Chart Ask students to find the previous charts in this unit. Say, *There are many different kinds of charts. The chart on this page is called a flowchart. A flowchart is another way to show cause and effect. Sometimes an effect can also be the cause of something new that happens.* Read or have students read the introduction and flowchart. Help students with any new words. Have students follow the arrows with their fingers to help them see the causes and their effects. Have students work individually or in pairs to write the answers in their notebooks. Then call on students to answer the questions. Write the answers on the board.

Discuss

Read the discussion question. Then assign small groups to discuss the question. Circulate to help and comment on students' responses. Allow time for students to share their answers with the class.

Workbook pages 91–92 may now be assigned.

Self-Assessment Questions

Write the following questions on the board and have students respond in their notebooks. Then have them share their responses in small groups.

1. How can understanding cause and effect help me in reading?
2. How are charts helping me to learn?
3. What was difficult for me in this lesson?
4. What was easy for me in this lesson?
5. What was most enjoyable to learn?

Unit Review, pages 196–197

Vocabulary

Have students work individually, in pairs, or in small groups, depending on how much support they need. Check answers as a class, writing the answers on the board.

Answers			
1. territory	**4.** colony	**7.** representatives	**10.** Independence
2. revolt	**5.** plantation	**8.** tax	**11.** document
3. settlers	**6.** slaves	**9.** indentured servant	**12.** Treaty

Timeline Check

Read the instructions, or call on a student to read them. Have students write the sentences (not the answers yet) in their notebooks. Then suggest they find the dates for all the events before numbering the list. After they have finished, check answers as a whole class, writing the numbers on the board.

Answers

_4_	France fought with England in the French and Indian War.
_6_	Thomas Jefferson wrote the Declaration of Independence.
_2_	English settlers formed Jamestown.
_7_	The colonists and the British signed the Treaty of Paris.
_1_	Christopher Columbus sailed to the Americas.
_3_	The Pilgrims sailed from England to Massachusetts.
_5_	The colonists threw British tea into the water.

Apply Social Studies Skills

Using Visuals: Read a Chart Read the instructions, or call on a student to read them. Have students work individually or in pairs to write the answers in their notebooks. Then call on students to answer the question. Write the answer on the board.

Answers
France didn't like Britain because of the French and Indian War. France thought that the American colonists would win the War for Independence.

Extension Project

Ask students to name some of the events they remember from this unit. Have them choose one event and draw a picture of it. They should label their pictures with as much vocabulary as possible from this unit. Assign small groups and invite students to tell about their pictures.

Read More About It

Bring at least one of the suggested books to class. Choose an excerpt that the students will be able to visualize. Have them draw a picture of what you read. Invite students to share their pictures with the class and talk about them. (Note: You may want to point out that *Plimoth* was the original spelling for the place we now spell as *Plymouth*. Plimoth Plantation has kept this original spelling.)

 Workbook pages 93–94 may now be assigned.

Writing Skills, pages 198–199

Write a Three-Paragraph Essay

Preview

Have students <u>preview</u> these two pages. Then ask, *What will you practice writing?*

Present the Model

Ask students, *What's a paragraph?* Have them point to a paragraph on these pages. Explain that an essay consists of several paragraphs about the same topic. Point to the outline. Ask students, *What is this called? What is an outline for?* Elicit from students that an outline organizes their ideas. From an outline, they can write their essay. Review the format of the outline. Elicit that the Roman numerals list the main idea for each paragraph and the letters list the supporting information. Go over the model paragraph and have students point out the details that correspond to the outline.

Practice

Allow time for students to copy the model paragraph and write two more paragraphs using the outline. Have students refer to the bulleted list of questions to make sure they have followed the procedure for writing an essay.

Have students work in pairs to read their essays and receive feedback on whether they included all the details from the outline. Allow time for students to add details before submitting their drafts to you.

 Workbook pages 95–96 may now be assigned.

Unit 6 A New Nation

Unit Overview

Lesson	Content	Social Studies Skills		Writing Skills
		Reading Strategies	Using Visuals	
1	• The First Presidency • Settlers and Explorers • Westward Movement • The Abolitionists	Compare and Contrast	Read a Graph (Circle Graphs)	Revise a Three-Paragraph Essay
2	• The Civil War • Reconstruction • The Reservation System • The Industrial Age	Draw Conclusions	Read a Graph (Bar Graphs)	

Objectives

Vocabulary
- Develop new vocabulary related to the first American presidency through the Industrial Revolution
- Use newly acquired vocabulary in context

Concepts
- Acquire knowledge of America from the first presidency to the 1860s
- Acquire knowledge of America from the Civil War to the Industrial Revolution

Reading Strategies
- Compare and contrast to understand and remember what you read
- Draw conclusions to synthesize and summarize information
- Practice previously learned strategies

Using Visuals
- Understand how to read a circle graph
- Understand how to read a bar graph

Writing Skills
- Practice revising a three-paragraph essay

Unit Opener, pages 200–201

Preview Topic

Point to and read the unit title, or call on a student to read it. Say, and write on the board, *In this unit we'll study America from our first president in 1789 to the start of the modern age in the late 1890s.* Point to the illustration of the wagon train. Say, *These are pioneers. What do you think they're doing?* Ask picture, thinking, and background knowledge questions to get students interested in this period. Help with vocabulary, as needed.

Unit Contents

Point to page 201 and say, *These are the people, places, and events we will learn about in this unit.* Help students pronounce the list of names. Ask if students recognize any names. Ask what they know about them. Write that information on the board. Follow the same procedures with place names. Use a world map or globe to teach or elicit the locations of these places. For key events, say, *These are the key events we will learn about.* Read the list of key events, or call on a student to read it. Give simple definitions of any new words and concepts. Have students copy the key events into their notebooks.

Get Ready

Say, *Before we start this unit, let's review some events from Unit 5.* Draw the timeline on the board as students copy it into their notebooks. Elicit the caption for the first date (on page 174) and write it on the board. Have students work in pairs or small groups to find the information and write it on their timelines. The completed timeline might look like this:

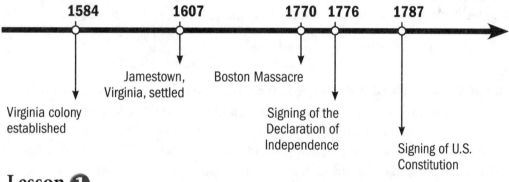

| 1584 | 1607 | 1770 1776 | 1787 |

Virginia colony established

Jamestown, Virginia, settled

Boston Massacre

Signing of the Declaration of Independence

Signing of U.S. Constitution

Lesson ❶

Before You Read, pages 202–205

Have students <u>preview</u> these pages individually or in pairs. Ask, *What will you learn about in this lesson?*

Vocabulary

Read the captions, or call on students to read them. Help students understand and pronounce any new words. Use pictures, props, maps, and mime. Have students read the captions again silently. Ask picture and comprehension questions for each item to make sure students have understood. Read the key words again and have students say them after you. Then have students close their books. Point to the pictures and ask questions to elicit the key words.

Practice

Have students fill in the blanks, and then compare their answers with another student. Check by calling on students. Write the letters of the correct answers on the board.

> **Answers**
> **1.** a. gold rush   **3.** b. Immigrants   **5.** b. wagon train
> **2.** c. tribes   **4.** a. Pioneers   **6.** c. industry

 Workbook page 97 may now be assigned.

Social Studies Skills

 Content Reading Strategy: Compare and Contrast On the board, write, *Compare and Contrast* and *How are things the same? How are things different?* Say, *When we compare and contrast, we ask these two questions. A Venn diagram is helpful when we compare and contrast.* Draw a Venn diagram on the board. Write one male and one female student's name on the outer parts of the ovals, and *Both* on the overlap. Say, *Let's compare and contrast [Student A] and [Student B]. How are they the same? How are they different?* Write student responses onto the diagram.

Read the information on page 204, or call on students to read it. Have students <u>reread</u> it silently. Ask comprehension questions to make sure students understand. Say, *We'll compare and contrast, and use Venn diagrams, as we read this lesson.*

 Workbook pages 98–99 may now be assigned.

Using Visuals: Read a Graph Ask, *What visuals did you practice using in earlier lessons?* (timelines, map keys, compass roses, longitude and latitude, map scales, physical maps, political maps, charts) *What will you practice doing in this lesson?* Read the introduction, or call on a student to read it. Help students with any new words. Ask comprehension questions such as, *Why is this called a circle graph? Why is it sometimes called a pie chart? What does the graph equal?* Write a percent symbol (%) on the board and ask, *What does this symbol mean? What percent of people of English origin are there on the chart? What country are the English from?*

To help students learn nationality and country names, as well as to get a better understanding of the population of early America, you may want to elicit the country name for each nationality on the board. Refer to a map, as needed, and have students write the nationalities and country names into their notebooks.

Have students work in pairs to find the answers to the first two questions and write them in their notebooks. Do the last question as a class. Use a Venn diagram to record student answers.

Answers

1. England had the most colonists in 1775.
2. Africa had the second most colonists in 1775.
3. The diagram might look like this:

English
- some wanted to own land
- some came for religious freedom
- some came as indentured servants

Both
- came by ship
- were immigrants
- had to work hard

Africans
- captured or bought
- taken to America
- forced to work on plantations as slaves

 Workbook page 100 may now be assigned.

Reading ❶

The First Presidency, pages 206–207

Preview Pages

Have students <u>preview</u> these pages and <u>predict</u> the topic.

Teach Pages

Read the text and captions, or call on students to read them. Help students with any new words.

Understand Information Encourage students to <u>use what they know</u>, and to <u>compare and contrast</u> as they <u>reread</u> the pages. Write on the board and ask, *How were the colonists' lives different before and after independence? Compare and contrast as you read.* Have students take turns asking and answering questions about the reading in pairs or small groups. When students have finished, ask the class your own comprehension, picture, and thinking questions. Say, *Close your books. Tell me about the reading in your own words.* Elicit the main ideas and details from different students until the content has been adequately covered.

Organize Information Refer students back to the <u>compare and contrast</u> question on the board. Say, *Let's use a Venn diagram to compare and contrast colonists' lives* *before and after independence.* Since this exercise reviews and compares information from Units 5 and 6, do this diagram as a class. The diagram might look like this:

Before Independence
- had unfair taxes
- didn't have a representative to speak for them
- the British could punish them
- had to feed and house British soldiers
- not enough freedom

Both
- life was hard
- had slaves

After Independence
- had a Constitution and a Bill of Rights
- had certain rights that no one could take away
- had freedom of religion, speech, and assembly
- had a president, vice-president, and a cabinet

ELSEWHERE IN THE WORLD: The Haitian Revolution

Before the reading and comprehension check, point out that there were African slaves and plantations in the Caribbean and South America. Ask if students know of any of these countries. (Jamaica, Dominican Republic, Puerto Rico, Brazil, etc.) Ask, *What do you already know about Haiti?* Have students locate Haiti on a map.

MORE ABOUT IT: First U.S. Coin

After the reading and comprehension check, show photos or have students find websites featuring photos or restrikes of the 1787 Fugio cent. Point out or elicit that these coins were 100% copper, a little over 1 inch in diameter, and had the words *United States* and the mottos *We Are One, Fugio* (Latin for *I fly* or *I escape*), and *Mind Your Business* on them. Pass out modern pennies and have students compare and contrast the coins.

Before You Go On

Have students do the first two questions in pairs. Do the third critical-thinking question as a class.

Answers
1. George Washington served as president for eight years.
2. The first ten amendments are called the Bill of Rights.
3. Answers will vary. Possible answers: Chains reminded people of prisoners and slavery. Americans were free from England, and the chains didn't symbolize this.

Working with Timelines

Read the timeline, helping with any new words. Ask comprehension and review questions, and then have students copy the timeline into their notebooks.

Choose World Events that students will find interesting. Bring in pictures and maps to help teach these events.

Settlers and Explorers, pages 208–209

Preview Pages

Have students <u>preview</u> these pages and <u>predict</u> the topic.

Teach Pages

Read the text and captions, or call on students to read them. Help students with any new words. Help students connect information in the text with the visuals on the map. Point out that America bought the land called the Louisiana Territory from France in 1803. Elicit the key words (pioneers, tribes), the sentences they're in, and their definitions.

Understand Information Encourage students to <u>visualize</u> and to <u>compare and contrast</u> as they <u>reread</u> the pages. Have students take turns asking and answering questions about the reading in pairs or small groups. When students have finished, ask the class your own comprehension, picture, and thinking questions. Say, *Close your books. Tell me about the reading in your own words.* Elicit the main ideas and details.

As You Read: Compare and Contrast

Read the information, or call on a student to read it. Say, *Close your eyes a minute. Imagine how Lewis and Clark lived in their town or city in 1804.* Give students a moment to <u>visualize</u> this, and then say, *Now imagine how Lewis and Clark lived as they explored the new territories.* Then say, *As you reread these pages, think about how different life was for them in the new territories.* See the following page for the Venn diagram.

Organize Information Note: You may want to teach the More About It box on page 209 before organizing information. Say, *Let's make a Venn diagram about what Lewis and Clark were used to, and what they found in the new territories. Use what you know.*

What were they used to? Model by eliciting what they were used to and writing it on the board. Then have students copy and complete the diagram. The completed diagram might look like this:

Lewis and Clark

What They Were Used To
- towns and cities
- nature in the eastern U.S.
- British, European, and Africans who spoke English
- riding horses on roads
- knew or had maps of the land
- homes with beds
- shopping for food or eating out

Both
- had to work hard
- had to work all day
- needed food and clothing

What They Found in the New Territories
- rivers, forests, mountains
- nature in the western U.S.
- Native American tribes who didn't speak English
- no roads, had to walk a lot, and often traveled by boat
- didn't know or have maps of the land
- had to live and sleep outside
- had to hunt or pick fruits and vegetables

MORE ABOUT IT: The Shoshone People

After the reading and comprehension check, have students <u>contrast</u> the life of the Shoshone before and after getting horses, and then how it was different after the settlers moved into the western United States. Ask, *Would you like to live a nomadic life like the Shoshone did? Why or why not?*

REACHING ALL STUDENTS: Visual and Kinesthetic Learners

This exercise will help familiarize students with the Lewis and Clark expedition, maps, and the western United States. Create handouts of a current U.S. map. Have students use the illustration on page 208 to help them draw lines on the map showing the route of Lewis and Clark's expedition. Check by having a student trace the route with a finger on a large U.S. map. If the map has a scale, have students estimate the distance (3,700 miles). Then help students find websites about the Lewis and Clark expedition. Finally, have students close their eyes and <u>visualize</u> what a journey this was.

Have students do the first two questions in pairs. Do the third critical-thinking question as a class. After checking question 3, you may wish to teach students about some of the foods Lewis and Clark ate, which included dogs (this can be easily found on the Internet).

Answers

1. President Jefferson wanted Lewis and Clark to find a water route across the continent to the Pacific Ocean.
2. A Shoshone woman, Sacagawea, and her baby, Jean Baptiste, traveled with them as their guide and translator.
3. Answers will vary. Possible answers: They probably hunted animals, fished, and picked fruit and vegetables. The Native Americans probably gave or sold them some food, too.

Working with Timelines

Read the timeline, helping with any new words. Ask comprehension and review questions, and then have students copy the timeline into their notebooks.

Choose World Events that students will find interesting. Bring in pictures and maps to help teach these events.

Westward Movement, pages 210–211

Preview Pages

Have students preview these pages and predict the topic.

Teach Pages

Read the text and captions, or call on students to read them. Have students look at the illustration of the buffalo on page 233. Elicit the key words (pioneers, wagon trains, gold rush, immigrants), the sentences they're in, and their definitions.

Understand Information Ask, *What's the reading strategy in this lesson?* Encourage students to compare and contrast as they reread the pages. Say, *As you reread, think about how buffalo and cattle were the same and how they were different.* Have students take turns asking and answering questions about the reading in pairs or small groups. When students have finished, begin your questions by saying, *Let's be sure we understand chronological order. What dates do you see on these pages? What happened on those dates?* Then ask more detailed comprehension, picture, and thinking questions. Say, *Close your books. Tell me about the reading in your own words.* Elicit the main ideas and details.

Organize Information Ask, *Did you compare and contrast buffalo and cattle while you were reading? Let's make a Venn diagram about how buffalo and cattle are the same and how they're different.* Model by eliciting what they were used to and writing it on the board, and then have students copy and complete the diagram. The completed diagram might look like this:

Buffalo
- had lived in North America for thousands of years
- Native Americans hunted them for food and to make clothes from their skins
- many buffalo died

Both
- eat grass
- were used for food and clothing
- needed a lot of land

Cattle
- Europeans brought them to North America
- the cattle in the West took over land that was used by the buffalo
- settlers raised them for food and made shoes and clothes from their skins

You may want to bring in photos of American buffalo. Tell students that before Columbus, there were millions of buffalo in North America, but by the 1890s there were under a thousand. There are now several hundred thousand buffalo in the United States, many of them raised for their meat.

MORE ABOUT IT: The Pony Express

Encourage students to <u>visualize</u> as they read. After the reading and comprehension check, you may want to let students listen to Morse code on the Internet. Make handouts of early telegraphic Morse code, or have students find a website showing the code. Give students one or more words to decipher, such as:

$$\bullet \bullet \bullet \bullet / \bullet \bullet / \bullet \bullet \bullet / - / \bullet \bullet / \bullet \bullet \bullet / \bullet \bullet \bullet \bullet$$

which means *history*. Have students compare and contrast the Pony Express with e-mail as a means of communication.

Read the information in the poster. Ask, *Why do you think being a rider on the Pony Express was dangerous?* Explain the word *orphans*. Ask, *Why do you think the poster says "Orphans preferred"?*

CONNECT TO TODAY: Railroad Travel

After reading the text, assign students to pairs and have one student close his or her book. The other student, book open, asks questions about the reading. Then have students change roles. Finally, have all students close their books as you ask questions.

Have students do the first two questions in pairs. Do the third critical-thinking question as a class.

Answers

1. The pioneers were going west because some wanted land and some hoped to find gold and get rich.
2. The buffalo died because cattle in the West took over land that was used by the buffalo for food. (Both cattle and buffalo eat grass.)
3. Answers will vary. Possible answers: The government wanted to build a railroad so that they could help settle and trade with the western part of the United States. The railroad was also faster and safer than wagon trains.

Working with Timelines

Read the timeline, helping with any new words. Ask comprehension and review questions, and then have students copy the timeline into their notebooks.

Choose World Events that students will find interesting. Bring in pictures and maps to help teach these events.

The Abolitionists, pages 212–213

Preview Pages

Have students preview these pages and predict the topic.

Teach Pages

Read the text and captions, or call on students to read them. Help students with any new words. Elicit the key word (industry), the sentence it's in, and its definition. Ask students whether the map on page 213 is a physical map or a political map. (political) Ask, *Was our state a free state, slave state, or territory? Were there more slave states or free states?*

Understand Information Ask, *What's the reading strategy in this lesson?* Encourage students to compare and contrast as they reread the pages. Say, *As you reread, think about how the North and the South were the same and how they were different. Use what you know about the North and the South.* Have students take turns asking and answering questions about the reading in pairs or small groups. When students have finished, ask the class your own comprehension, picture, and thinking questions. Say, *Close your books. Tell me about the reading in your own words.* Elicit the main ideas and details.

Organize Information Ask, *Did you compare and contrast the North and the South while you were reading? Let's make a Venn diagram about the North and the South.* Model by eliciting information about the South and writing it on the board, and then have students copy and complete the diagram. The completed diagram might look like this:

North
- many people worked in industry and were paid for their work
- many northerners wanted to abolish slavery because it was cruel and because the Constitution said people had a right to be free
- most northern states were free states

Both
- were part of America
- didn't agree with each other
- needed to have work

South
- there were many plantations in the South
- most southern states were slave states
- people in the South did not want to stop slavery because they used the slaves to pick cotton and work in the fields
- southerners did not want to change their way of life

PROFILE: Harriet Tubman

Teach the Profile either before going on to page 213, or as a separate reading. After the reading and comprehension check, discuss with students the whippings that a runaway slave could expect if caught. Point out that anyone caught helping a slave escape would be jailed for six months and fined $1,000. Ask about what they think of Tubman's bravery and whether they would do what she did.

Optional Activity

Bring in material or help students find websites about slavery. Let them see the photographs and drawings of slaves and the lives they led. Show students bills of sale, or let them read excerpts of testimony from former slaves taken by the WPA. Explain that these are primary sources. Elicit what students think of slavery.

Language Tip: Suffixes

Read the text in the box on page 212, or call on a student to read it. Point out that -ist and -er at the end of a word can mean "someone who does something or believes in something." Ask comprehension questions to elicit the spelling rules, noting that these rules work for most words. Elicit other examples of each of these suffixes. Have students copy the information in the box into their notebooks. Write the following exercise on the board and have students write any new words in their notebooks:

1. guitar + ist = _____
2. invade + ing = _____
3. help + full = _____
4. explore + er = _____
5. carry + er = _____
6. awe + full = _____
7. environmental + ist = _____
8. copy + er = _____

162 Unit 6

SCIENCE CONNECTION: Environmental Science

After the reading and comprehension check, have students search the Internet for an EPA map of current ozone/smog conditions in the United States. If your students are in an area that experiences high levels of smog, discuss safety precautions and ways of preventing pollution.

Before You Go On

Have students do the first two questions in pairs. Do the third critical-thinking question as a class.

Answers
1. Frederick Douglass was an African-American abolitionist. (He spoke at antislavery meetings across the United States. He published an antislavery newspaper.)
2. A free state was a state without slaves. African Americans could be free there. A slave state was a state with slaves. African Americans couldn't be free there.
3. Answers will vary. Possible answers: I don't agree with [a rule, a law, an issue] because I don't think it's fair. I think . . .

Working with Timelines

Read the timeline, helping with any new words. Ask comprehension and review questions, and then have students copy the timeline into their notebooks.

Choose World Events that students will find interesting. Bring in pictures and maps to help teach these events.

Go to www.longmanusa.com/socialstudies for links to interesting websites about America from the first presidency to the 1860s.

Review and Practice, pages 214–215

Vocabulary

If your students need additional help in reviewing this vocabulary, see the Optional Vocabulary Activities (pages vii–viii). Have students work individually. Check by calling on students to read their sentences. Write the correct answers on the board.

Answers
1. pioneers
2. tribe
3. gold rush
4. industry
5. immigrant
6. wagon train

Check Your Understanding

Have students work individually, in pairs, or in small groups. Let students look back at the text, as needed. Then have them share their answers with the class. Write the answers on the board. Have students correct or add to their answers, if needed.

Apply Social Studies Skills

Content Reading Strategy: Compare and Contrast Read the instructions, or call on a student to read them. Have students look at pages 212–213. Model by eliciting information about the *Both* category and writing it on the board. Then have students copy and complete the Venn diagram. The completed diagram might look like this:

Harriet Tubman
- escaped to the North in 1849
- went back to the South 19 times to help 300 other slaves escape
- from 1862 to 1864 was a spy for the Union army
- she later worked for the poor

Both
- born into slavery in Maryland
- escaped to the North
- against slavery

Frederick Douglass
- was an African-American abolitionist
- defied the rules by learning to read
- escaped to the North in 1838
- spoke at antislavery meetings across the U.S.
- published an antislavery newspaper

Using Visuals: Read a Graph Read the heading. Review circle graphs by asking, *What kind of graph is this? What percent does a circle graph show? What's the title of this circle graph?* Tell students, *You'll learn more about slavery using this graph.* Read the instructions and the graph key, or call on students to read them. Call on students to identify the places on a large map. Have students work in pairs or small groups. Check by eliciting the answers and writing them on the board.

Discuss

Read the discussion question. Have students discuss the question as a class.

 Workbook pages 101–102 may now be assigned.

Evaluation

Self-Assessment Questions

Write the following questions on the board and have students respond in their notebooks. Then they can share their responses in small groups.

1. How can I use comparing and contrasting to help me understand and remember details?
2. How can reading a circle graph help me to understand information?
3. What was difficult for me in this lesson?
4. What was easy for me in this lesson?
5. What was most enjoyable to learn?

Lesson ❷

Before You Read, pages 216–219

Have students <u>preview</u> these pages individually or in pairs. Then ask, *What are you going to learn about in this lesson?*

Vocabulary

Read the captions, or call on students to read them. Help students with any new words. Have students read the captions again silently. Ask picture and comprehension questions for each item to make sure students have understood. Read the key words again and have students say them after you. Then have students close their books. Point to the pictures and ask questions to elicit the key words.

Practice

Make sure students understand the word *imaginary* in question 3. Have students fill in the blanks, and then compare their answers with a classmate. Check by calling on individual students. Write the letters of the correct answers on the board.

Answers

1. b. Union	**3.** b. Mason-Dixon Line	**5.** c. fort
2. a. Confederacy	**4.** c. battle	**6.** a. railroads

Workbook page 103 may now be assigned.

Content Reading Strategy: Draw Conclusions Write *Draw a Conclusion* on the board, and then draw this diagram:

Draw a Conclusion

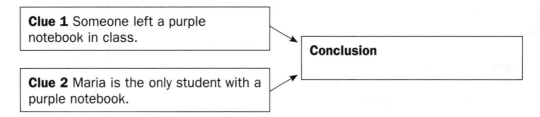

Clue 1 Someone left a purple notebook in class.

Clue 2 Maria is the only student with a purple notebook.

Conclusion

Say, *Clues are pieces of information. We can put these pieces of information together. Then we can make, or draw, a conclusion. What is our conclusion here? Who left a notebook in class?* Write the conclusion on the board. (Maria left her notebook in class.) Say, *Looking for clues and drawing conclusions can help us understand social studies readings, too.*

Read the information on the page, or call on students to read it. Help students understand and pronounce any new words. Stop after each section to ask comprehension questions. Then have students reread the page. Ask, *Can we draw another conclusion? What two groups of people began to dislike each other?* (northerners and southerners) Say, *We'll practice <u>drawing conclusions</u> as we read this lesson.*

Workbook pages 104–105 may now be assigned.

Using Visuals: Read a Graph Ask, *What visuals did you practice using in earlier lessons?* (timelines, map keys, compass roses, longitude and latitude, map scales, physical maps, political maps, charts, circle graphs) *What visual will you practice using in this lesson?*

Read the introduction, or call on a student to read it. Then ask questions to make sure students know what to look at on a graph. Have them look at the graphs. Elicit what each part of the graphs shows, making sure they understand that the numbers shown are in thousands. Have students work in pairs. When students have finished, elicit the answers and write them on the board.

Answers
1. There were about 500,000 slaves in 1800. By 1860 there were about 2,250,000 slaves.
2. The number of bales of cotton grown depended on how many slaves there were. Slavery grew and cotton production grew at the same time.

Workbook page 106 may now be assigned.

Reading ❷

The Civil War, pages 220–221

Preview Pages

Have students <u>preview</u> these pages and <u>predict</u> the topic.

Teach Pages

Read the text and captions, or call on students to read them. Help students with any new words. Elicit the key words (Mason-Dixon Line, Confederacy, Union, battle, fort), the sentences they're in, and their definitions.

> **As You Read:** Draw Conclusions
>
> Read the information in the box on page 220, or call on a student to read it. Ask, *What main groups of people were in the U.S. in the 1800s?* (northerners, southerners, slaves, pioneers, Native Americans, immigrants) Write these groups on the board and have students copy them into their notebooks. For each, ask, *How did this group feel? Draw a conclusion.* Write responses on the board and have students copy them into their notebooks. Say, *Think about the feelings of these groups as you read these pages.* After the reading, students can draw conclusions about each group at the end of the war.

Understand Information Encourage students to <u>visualize</u>, to <u>understand chronological order</u>, and to <u>draw conclusions</u> as they <u>reread</u> the pages. Have students take turns asking and answering questions about the reading in pairs or small groups. When students have finished, ask the class your own comprehension, picture, and thinking questions. Then ask drawing conclusions questions such as, *Why didn't the South like Lincoln's views? Why did General Lee surrender? Why did Lincoln want to help the South rejoin the Union?* Refer back to the As You Read list of groups on the board and ask, *How did each group feel at the end of the war?* Say, *Close your books. Tell me about the reading in your own words.* Elicit the main ideas and details.

Organize Information Say, *Let's make a timeline about the Civil War.* Model by beginning the timeline on the board, eliciting and writing the years from the text on it, and then eliciting information about the first two dates. Show students how to combine information for 1861. Then have students copy and complete the timeline. The completed timeline might look like this:

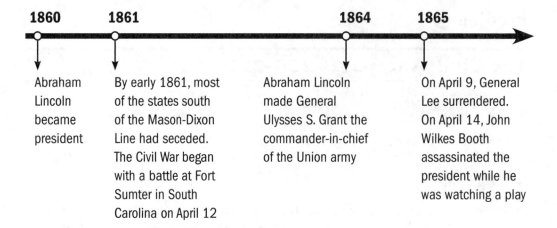

1860	1861	1864	1865

Abraham Lincoln became president

By early 1861, most of the states south of the Mason-Dixon Line had seceded. The Civil War began with a battle at Fort Sumter in South Carolina on April 12

Abraham Lincoln made General Ulysses S. Grant the commander-in-chief of the Union army

On April 9, General Lee surrendered. On April 14, John Wilkes Booth assassinated the president while he was watching a play

---

MUSIC CONNECTION: Songs of the Civil War

After the reading and comprehension check, help students find a website featuring audio and lyrics for "When Johnny Comes Marching Home." Alternatively, hand out lyrics and play a recording of the song. Ask questions to elicit what the lyrics mean, and how students feel listening to the song.

MORE ABOUT IT: Women in the Civil War

After the reading and comprehension check, ask *Do you think there were women soldiers in the Civil War?* Point out that it was against the law for women to serve as soldiers, but some did serve. The women had to take men's names and disguise themselves as men. On the Confederate side, there were probably about 250 women soldiers. Photos of some of these women soldiers can be found on the Internet.

Before You Go On

Have students do the first two questions in pairs. Do the third critical-thinking question as a class.

Answers
1. The southern states called themselves the Confederate States of America, or the Confederacy.
2. President Lincoln gave the Gettysburg Address to honor the men who died (in the battle) there.
3. Answers will vary. Possible answers: Korea had a civil war from 1950 to 1953, and North and South Korea are still separate countries. El Salvador had a civil war from 1980 to 1992. Rwanda had a civil war in 1994, and there are civil wars in many African countries today.

Reconstruction, page 222
The Reservation System, page 223

Preview Pages

Have students <u>preview</u> these pages and <u>predict</u> the topics.

Teach Pages

Read the text and captions, or call on students to read them. Help students with any new words. Teach the Connect to Today box after page 222, and the More About It box after page 223. Elicit the key words (Union, battle), the sentences they're in, and their definitions.

Understand Information Encourage students to <u>visualize</u>, to <u>understand chronological order</u>, and to <u>draw conclusions</u> as they <u>reread</u> the pages. Have students take turns asking and answering questions about the reading in pairs or small groups. When students have finished, ask the class your own comprehension, picture, and thinking questions. Ask drawing conclusions questions such as, *Why did the government want to reconstruct the United States? Why did southern leaders want to stop African Americans from voting? From working? Why didn't the Sioux and Cheyenne want to move to a reservation?* Say, *Close your books. Tell me about the reading in your own words.* Elicit the main ideas and details.

Optional Activity

This exercise will further emphasize the experience of segregation. Cut up two different colored pieces of construction paper, such as red and green, into squares. The total number of squares should equal or exceed the number of students in the class. Put these into an opaque bag or other container. Have each student draw a square. Then say, *The students with the red squares are segregated. You go to the back of the class. The students with the green squares can sit at the front of the class.* After students have rearranged themselves, say, *The green students get to ask questions first, answer first, and get to have most of my attention. Red students need to wait until the green students are finished before I will get to you.* Conduct the rest of the class in this manner. At the end of this activity, ask the different groups how they felt about segregation.

After the reading and comprehension check, ask, *How long after the Civil War did African Americans get true voting rights?*

After the reading and comprehension check, tell students that there were similar schools for the indigenous Aboriginal people of Australia. Show students the short segment from the beginning of the film *Rabbit-Proof Fence,* where Molly and her sisters are captured and brought to school. Discuss how it would feel to be the girls. Encourage students to rent the DVD and see the rest of the film.

Organize Information Say, *Let's make a T-chart about African and Native Americans in the 1860s and 1870s.* Model by beginning the chart on the board, and then have students copy and complete it. The completed chart might look like this:

African Americans in the 1860s and 1870s	Native Americans in the 1860s and 1870s
Southern leaders passed laws to stop them from voting and working.	The United States government decided that they had to live on reservations.
They wanted to keep them segregated.	Farmers and ranchers fenced in the cattle and shot the buffalo.
Congress passed amendments to the Constitution to help them.	In 1876 leaders from the Sioux and Cheyenne tribes refused to move to a reservation.
The Fourteenth Amendment said that states could not deny rights to United States citizens.	The United States government sent General George A. Custer to fight them.
The Fifteenth Amendment said that all men had the right to vote.	The battle took place at Little Big Horn in Montana.
	General Custer and all of his men were killed.
	The Native Americans won this battle, but not the larger fight to keep their lands.

Have students do the first two questions in pairs. Do the third critical-thinking question as a class.

Answers

1. During the Reconstruction period, the government's plan was to reconstruct, or rebuild, the United States. The eleven southern states had to be brought back into the Union.
2. A reservation is an area of land specifically for Native Americans.
3. Answers will vary. Possible answers: People protest about war, human rights, and the environment.

Working with Timelines

Read the timeline, helping with any new words. Ask comprehension and review questions, and then have students copy the timeline into their notebooks.

Choose World Events that students will find interesting. Bring in pictures and maps to help teach these events.

Primary Source, page 224

Preview Page

Have students <u>preview</u> this page and <u>predict</u> the topic.

Teach Page

Read the text, or call on students to read it. Help students with any new words.

Understand Information Encourage students to <u>compare and contrast</u> and <u>draw conclusions</u> as they <u>reread</u> the page. Have students take turns asking and answering questions about the reading in pairs or small groups. When students have finished, ask the class your own comprehension, picture, and thinking questions.

Ask drawing conclusions questions such as, *Why did the government want to reduce the Nez Percé's land? Why were there not many tribe members remaining? What promise did Chief Joseph think the white men broke?* Say, *Close your books. Tell me about the reading in your own words.* Elicit the main ideas and details. Have students open their books and work in pairs or small groups to write the answers to the questions in their notebooks. Then elicit the answers and write them on the board.

Answers

1. Lewis and Clark exchanged presents with the Nez Percé.
2. The Nez Percé promised to let Lewis and Clark pass through their country and never to make war on the white men.

The Reservation System (continued), page 225

The Reservation System (continued), page 225

Preview Page

Have students <u>preview</u> this page and <u>predict</u> the topic.

Teach Page

Read the text and captions, or call on students to read them. Help students with any new words.

Understand Information Encourage students to <u>visualize</u> and to <u>draw conclusions</u> as they <u>reread</u> the page. Have students take turns asking and answering questions about the reading in pairs or small groups. When students have finished, ask the class your own comprehension, picture, and thinking questions. Then ask <u>use what you know</u> and <u>drawing conclusions</u> questions such as, *Why did the U.S. soldiers attack the Nez Percé tribe? Why did Chief Joseph fight back?* Say, *Close your books. Tell me about the reading in your own words.* Elicit the main ideas and details.

Organize Information Say, *Let's do a T-chart about what happened to the Nez Percé and the Sioux.* Model by beginning the chart on the board, and then have students copy and complete it. The completed chart might look like this:

Nez Percé	Sioux
In 1877 U.S. soldiers attacked them.	In 1890 U.S. soldiers shot and killed the Sioux leader, Sitting Bull, while trying to arrest him.
Chief Joseph and his tribe fought back.	
They fled to Canada.	The rest of the Sioux fled, but the soldiers chased them.
The soldiers followed them for two months.	
Finally, the soldiers captured the tribe.	At Wounded Knee in South Dakota, soldiers shot and killed more than 200 Sioux.
Many people had died from cold and starvation.	

REACHING ALL STUDENTS: Visual Learners

Bring in photos of Native American art and artifacts, or help students find websites showing these. Alternatively, arrange an excursion to a local museum featuring Native American art. Discuss with students how the art and artifacts show the Native American way of life. Ask students which pieces they like best and why.

Language Tip: Pluperfect

Read the text in the box on page 225, or call on a student to read it. Write *Pluperfect or Past Perfect* on the board. Say, *When you have two past events and you want to say one happened <u>before</u> the other, use the pluperfect, or past perfect, tense. Use* had + *the pluperfect form of the verb to show which happened first.* On the board, write, *Native Americans lived in the United States. The Europeans arrived.* Ask, *How do I make one sentence using* before *and the pluperfect form of* lived? Write the response on the board and have students copy it into their notebooks. (Native Americans <u>had</u> lived in the United States <u>before</u> the Europeans arrived.)

On the board, write, *The soldiers killed more than 200 Sioux. The battle ended. Most of the members died. The tribe was allowed to go back to the Pacific.* Say, *Make two sentences from these four sentences using* before *and the pluperfect form of the verb.* Have students work in pairs. When students have finished, elicit the answers and write them on the board. (The soldiers <u>had</u> killed more than 200 Sioux <u>before</u> the battle ended. Most of the members <u>had</u> died <u>before</u> the tribe was allowed to go back to the Pacific.)

Before You Go On

Have students do the first two questions in pairs. Do the third critical-thinking question as a class.

Answers
1. The U.S. government wanted to put Native Americans on reservations because the government wanted more territory.
2. Chief Joseph and the Nez Percé fled to Canada.
3. Answers will vary. Possible answers: The U.S. government could have let them live freely. The U.S. government could have killed them all. The U.S. government could have left them with more territory.

Working with Timelines

Read the timeline, helping with any new words. Ask comprehension and review questions, and then have students copy the timeline into their notebooks.

Choose World Events that students will find interesting. Bring in pictures and maps to help teach these events.

The Industrial Age, pages 226–227

Preview Pages

Have students <u>preview</u> these pages and <u>predict</u> the topic.

Read the text and captions, or call on students to read them. Help students with any new words. Elicit the key words (railroads, industry), the sentences they're in, and their definitions.

Understand Information Encourage students to compare and contrast, and to draw conclusions as they reread the pages. Have students take turns asking and answering questions about the reading in pairs or small groups. When students have finished, ask the class your own comprehension, picture, and thinking questions. Then ask drawing conclusions questions such as, *Why did new tracks create new jobs for steelworkers, coal miners, and lumberjacks? How did railroads help the economy grow? Why did many people get sick and die? Who made the most money from people working twelve to fourteen hours a day, the workers or the owners?* Say, *Close your books. Tell me about the reading in your own words.* Elicit the main ideas and details.

Organize Information Say, *Let's make a word web about the Industrial Age. Let's find the topic sentences in each paragraph and write them into the word web.* Model by drawing the word web on the board with circles for each sentence. Elicit the first topic sentence for the word web, and then have students copy and complete it. The completed word web might look like this:

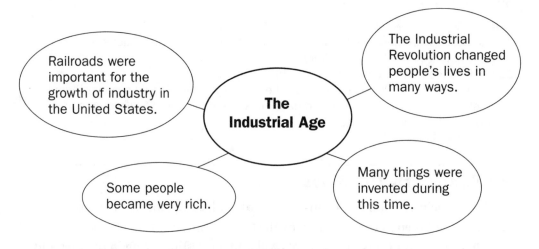

ELSEWHERE IN THE WORLD: Marie and Pierre Curie

After the reading and comprehension check, group students by their native language. Ask them to find a website about Marie Curie in their native language. Let them use this to learn more about Marie and Pierre Curie.

MORE ABOUT IT: The First Cars

After the reading and comprehension check, ask comparing and contrasting questions. Ask, *Do we use the assembly line to make cars today? How much do cars cost now? Why are they more expensive? Do you think it takes fifteen minutes to make a car now?* Ask students to name some other things made on an assembly line.

Have students do the first two questions in pairs. Do the third critical-thinking question as a class.

Answers
1. Railroads were important for the growth of industry in the United States.
2. People moved to the cities to work in factories.
3. Answers will vary. Possible answers: Yes, it was harder because people worked for twelve to fourteen hours a day and conditions were very bad. Many people got sick and died.

Working with Timelines

Read the timeline, helping with any new words. Ask comprehension and review questions, and then have students copy the timeline into their notebooks.

Choose World Events that students will find interesting. Bring in pictures and maps to help teach these events.

Go to www.longmanusa.com/socialstudies for links to interesting websites about America from the Civil War to the Industrial Revolution.

Review and Practice, pages 228–229

Vocabulary

If your students need additional help in reviewing this vocabulary, see the Optional Vocabulary Activities (pages vii–viii). Have students work individually. Check by calling on students to read their sentences. Write the correct answers on the board.

Answers
1. Mason-Dixon Line	**3.** Confederacy	**5.** fort
2. battle	**4.** Union	**6.** Railroads

Check Your Understanding

Have students work individually, in pairs, or in small groups. Let students look back at the text, as needed. Then have students share their answers with the class. Write the answers on the board. Have students correct or add to their answers, if needed.

Answers
1. The Union won the Civil War.
2. The Fourteenth Amendment says that states cannot deny rights to United States citizens. The Fifteenth Amendment says that all men have the right to vote.
3. General Custer and all of his men were killed in a battle against the Sioux and Cheyenne tribes.
4. Some inventions of the Industrial Age were the telephone, the phonograph, the camera, the electric light, the sewing machine, and the car.

Apply Social Studies Skills

 Content Reading Strategy: Draw Conclusions Read the instructions, or call on a student to read them. Pointing to the graphic organizer, review the reading strategy. Ask students, *What do you put together to draw a conclusion?* (clues) Say, *Look at these two clues and draw a new conclusion.* Have students work individually or in pairs to copy the organizer into their notebooks and complete it. To check, elicit one or more responses. (The railroad took the cattle from Texas to markets in Kansas.)

Using Visuals: Read a Graph Read the instructions, or call on a student to read them. Have students work in pairs. Check by eliciting the answers and writing them on the board.

Answers
1. The numbers on the left show miles of track (in thousands).
2. The graph covers twenty years.
3. The building of railroads might help the economy grow.
4. In twenty years, almost 30,000 miles of new railroad track was built in the United States. This probably helped the economy grow.

Discuss

Read the discussion question. Then assign small groups to discuss the question. Circulate to help and comment on students' responses. Allow time for students to share their answers with the class.

 Workbook pages 107–108 may now be assigned.

Evaluation

Self-Assessment Questions

Write the following questions on the board. Have students respond in their notebooks. Then have them share their responses in small groups.
1. How can drawing conclusions help me in reading?
2. How can reading a bar graph help me to learn information?
3. What was difficult for me in this lesson?
4. What was easy for me in this lesson?
5. What was most enjoyable to learn?

Unit Review, pages 230–231

Vocabulary

Have students work individually, in pairs, or in small groups, depending on how much support they need. Check answers as a class, writing the answers on the board.

Timeline Check

Read the instructions, or call on a student to read them. You may want to have students see if they can do this exercise without looking back at dates. Have students work individually, in pairs, or in small groups. Then elicit the answers and write them on the board.

Answers

4	The southern states form the Confederacy.
2	Lewis and Clark explore the land west of the Mississippi River.
5	President Lincoln is assassinated.
1	George Washington becomes the first president of the United States.
7	The Industrial Age begins.
3	Pioneers travel west on the Oregon Trail.
6	Congress passes the Fourteenth and Fifteenth Amendments to the Constitution.

Apply Social Studies Skills

Using Visuals: Read a Graph Read the instructions, or call on a student to read them. Have students work individually or in pairs. Then elicit the answer and write it on the board.

Answer

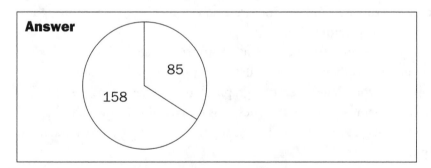

Extension Project

Help students find information on the Internet or in the library, or bring in materials on U.S. presidents. Depending on your resources and student ability, have students work in pairs, in small groups, or as a class. When students have finished, elicit the timeline verbally.

Read More About It

Bring at least one of the suggested books to class. Show the cover and some of the inside pages to students as a preview. Ask students to predict what the book is about.

Read an excerpt to the class. Then ask several comprehension questions. Read the excerpt again before calling on students to answer. Encourage students to find this or another suggested book in their school library or local bookstore.

 Workbook pages 109–110 may now be assigned.

Writing Skills, pages 232–233

Revise a Three-Paragraph Essay

Preview

Have students preview these two pages. Then ask, *What will you practice writing?*

Present the Model

Read the information on page 232, or call on students to read it. Have students reread the introduction. Then ask comprehension questions. Read the model essay, or call on students to read it. Help students with any new words. Then have students reread the essay before having them complete the activity at the bottom of the page in pairs. After students have discussed it, go over each of the questions at the top of the page and elicit any corrections. Have students rewrite the corrected paragraph in their notebooks.

Practice

Note that you may want to choose which essay students write depending on time and student ability. Revising the three-paragraph essay from Unit 5 will be faster and easier for students. Writing a three-paragraph essay from a topic in this unit will require the preparation of a new outline and draft, so this will be a more thorough practice, yet more time consuming.

Choose teaching procedures from Unit 5, as appropriate. Tell students to look at the questions on page 232 as they write. Circulate to monitor and help students.

When students have completed their paragraphs, have them exchange essays with a classmate. Ask the students to look at the questions on page 232 as they check the work. Then have students get together to discuss suggestions. Finally, have students rewrite their work.

 Workbook pages 111–112 may now be assigned.

Unit 7 The Modern World

Unit Overview

Lesson	Content	Social Studies Skills		Writing Skills
		Reading Strategies	Using Visuals	
1	• The Progressive Era • World War I • The Great Depression • World War II	Summarize	Use Print Resources	Edit and Publish a Three-Paragraph Essay
2	• Democracy vs. Communism • The Cold War • The Vietnam Era • The Soviet Union Breaks Up • Central and South America • Asia • Africa • The Gulf Wars and Terrorism	Understand Fact and Opinion	Use Technology Resources	

Objectives

Vocabulary
- Develop new vocabulary related to the modern world in the 20th and 21st centuries
- Use newly acquired vocabulary in context

Concepts
- Acquire knowledge of the world from the Progressive Era to World War II
- Acquire knowledge of the world from the Cold War to the present day

Reading Strategies
- Summarize to understand and remember the main idea and most important details
- Differentiate fact and opinion, and formulate opinions on readings
- Practice previously learned strategies

Building Research Skills
- Understand how to use print resources
- Understand how to use technology resources

Writing Skills
- Practice editing and publishing a three-paragraph essay

Unit Opener, pages 234–235

pages 234–235

Preview Topic

Point to and read the unit title, or call on a student to read it. Say, and write on the board, *In this unit, we'll study about the world in the twentieth and twenty-first centuries.* Point to the photos and ask, *What do you see in these photos? What do you think is happening?* Ask picture, thinking, and background knowledge questions to get students interested in this period. Help with vocabulary, as needed.

Unit Contents

Point to page 235 and say, *These are the people, places, and events we will learn about in this unit.* Help students pronounce the list of names. Ask if students recognize any names. Ask what they know about them. Write this information on the board. Follow the same procedures with place names. Use the world map on pages 22–23 to teach or elicit the locations of these places. For key events, say, *These are the key events we will learn about.* Read the list of key events, or call on a student to read them. Give simple definitions of new words. Have students copy the key events into their notebooks.

Get Ready

Say, *Before we start this unit, let's review some events from Unit 6.* Draw the timeline on the board as students copy it into their notebooks. Elicit the caption for the first date (on page 208) and write it on the board. Have students work in pairs or small groups to find the information and write it on their timelines. The completed timeline might look like this:

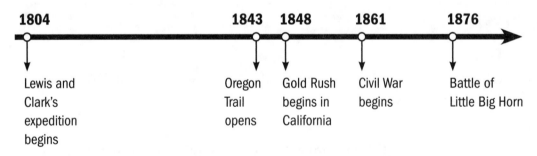

1804	1843	1848	1861	1876
Lewis and Clark's expedition begins	Oregon Trail opens	Gold Rush begins in California	Civil War begins	Battle of Little Big Horn

Lesson ❶

Before You Read, pages 236–239

pages 236–239

Have students <u>preview</u> these pages individually or in pairs. Ask, *What will you learn about in this lesson?*

Vocabulary

Read the captions, or call on students to read them. Help students understand and pronounce any new words. Use pictures, props, maps, and mime. Have students read the captions again silently. Ask picture and comprehension questions for each item to make sure students have understood. Read the key words again and have students say them after you. Then have students close their books. Point to the pictures and ask questions to elicit the key words.

Practice

Have students fill in the blanks. Check by calling on individual students. Write the letters of the correct answers on the board.

> **Answers**
> **1.** b. submarine　　**3.** c. Holocaust　　**5.** b. dictator
> **2.** a. assassination　**4.** c. unemployment　**6.** a. atomic bomb

 Workbook page 113 may now be assigned.

Social Studies Skills

 Content Reading Strategy: Summarize Read the information on the page, or call on students to read it. Help students understand and pronounce any new words. Stop after each section and have students reread, and then ask comprehension questions. Say, *We'll practice summarizing as we read this lesson.*

 Workbook pages 114–115 may now be assigned.

Building Research Skills: Use Print Resources Ask, *What will you practice building in this lesson? What resources will you use? What are some examples of print resources?* Read the information on the page, or call on a student to read it. Help students with any new words. Have an encyclopedia, a dictionary, an atlas, a newspaper, and a news magazine on your desk. Use these to ask comprehension questions such as (holding up the encyclopedia), *What is this? What does it have?* (showing the spine) *How are the subjects arranged? What subjects are in this book?* Have students work in pairs to find the answers to the questions and write them in their notebooks. Check by eliciting the answers and writing them on the board.

> **Answers**
> **1.** You would look in a periodical (to find out what happened in the Middle East last week).
> **2.** You would look in an atlas (to find the capital of Russia).
> **3.** You would look in an encyclopedia (to find information about the Holocaust).
> **4.** You would look in a dictionary (to find the meaning and pronunciation of the word *allies*).

To give students more practice with print resources, arrange a visit to the library. Beforehand, make a list of 10–12 questions that require the use of the four print resources covered here. Make sure the library has the resources to answer the questions. Then have students work individually or in pairs to find the answers to the questions and write them in their notebooks. Set a time deadline, or arrange for a prize for the first student or pair who answers all of the questions correctly.

Workbook page 116 may now be assigned.

Reading ❶

The Progressive Era, pages 240–241

Preview Pages

Have students <u>preview</u> these pages and <u>predict</u> the topic.

Teach Pages

Read the text and captions, or call on students to read them. Help students with any new words.

Understand Information Encourage students to <u>draw conclusions</u> and to <u>compare and contrast</u> as they <u>reread</u> the pages. Write on the board and ask, *What conclusions can you draw about the Spanish-American War? Compare and contrast voting rights for African Americans and for women.* Have students take turns asking and answering questions about the reading in pairs or small groups. When students have finished, ask the class your own comprehension, picture, and thinking questions, including the questions on the board.

Organize Information Model by beginning the timeline on the board, and then have students copy and complete it. The completed timeline might look like this:

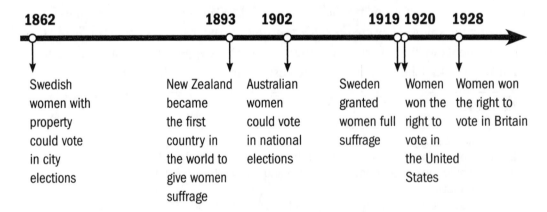

1862	1893	1902	1919	1920	1928
Swedish women with property could vote in city elections	New Zealand became the first country in the world to give women suffrage	Australian women could vote in national elections	Sweden granted women full suffrage	Women won the right to vote in the United States	Women won the right to vote in Britain

> **CONNECT TO TODAY:** The Food and Drug Administration
>
> After the reading and comprehension check, hand out copies of a simple Nutrition Facts label. Help students learn how to read these by eliciting important information such as serving size, calories, fat, cholesterol, sugars, protein, vitamins and minerals, and ingredients. Then ask, *Which contents should you have a lot of every day? Which should you have just a little of?*

As You Read: Summarize

Read the information in the box on page 241, or call on a student to read it. Assign students to pairs. You may want to have each pair flip a coin to see who begins. Say, *You are going to summarize the text on page 240. Remember, you just need to say the main ideas and most important details. If you think your classmate forgot an important piece of information, tell him or her. If you don't think a detail is important, tell your classmate. After the first student has finished summarizing, change roles.* Have students close their books and work in pairs to summarize pages 240–241. Then elicit the main ideas and most important details from several different students.

Before You Go On

Have students work in pairs to answer all three questions. Then elicit the answers and write them on the board.

Answers
1. The United States won the Spanish-American War.
2. Answers will vary. Possible answers: The factories needed reform because people, including children, worked long hours in bad conditions.
3. Women's suffrage was the right of women to vote.

Working with Timelines

Read the timeline, helping with any new words. Ask comprehension and review questions, and then have students copy the timeline into their notebooks.

World War I, pages 242–243

Preview Pages

Have students <u>preview</u> these pages and <u>predict</u> the topic. Ask, *What do you already know about World War I?*

Teach Pages

Read the text and captions, or call on students to read them. Help students with any new words. Help students connect information in the text with the visuals on the map. Elicit the key word (assassination), the sentence it's in, and its definition.

Understand Information Encourage students to <u>compare and contrast</u> as they <u>reread</u> the pages. Write on the board and say, *Compare and contrast the Spanish-American War and World War I as you read.* Have students take turns asking and answering questions about the reading in pairs or small groups. When students have finished, ask the class your own comprehension, picture, and thinking questions, including the statement on the board.

Organize Information Have students organize the information in this reading by making a written summary in their notebooks. Say, *Remember, you just need to write the main ideas and most important details. Keep your books closed unless you need to quickly check spelling.* Have students close their books and work to summarize pages 242–243. Then call on several different students to read their summaries. Comment on each. Compose an "edited" summary on the board. The completed summary might look like this:

> World War I started in 1914 after the assassination of an Archduke of Austria-Hungary. The Central Powers (Germany, the Austro-Hungarian Empire, and Turkey) wanted to expand their control, and the Allies (Great Britain, France, Russia, and Belgium) fought them. The United States joined the Allies after Germany attacked its ships. More than eight million soldiers died. In 1918 the Allies won. President Wilson helped form the League of Nations, but the United States didn't join.

MORE ABOUT IT: Weapons of War

Elicit the key word (submarine), the sentence it's in, and its definition. After the reading and comprehension check, show students photos of the weapons mentioned, or help them find these in the library or on the Internet. Have students compare and contrast these weapons with current military weapons.

CONNECT TO TODAY: United Nations

After students preview, ask them what they already know about the United Nations. After the reading and comprehension check, ask, *Is it important to have the United Nations? Why or why not?*

Optional Activity

This exercise will help personalize and further familiarize students with World War I. Point out the photo of the soldier on page 242. Ask students how old they think he is, if they think he was killed, or if he survived. Then inform students that he was 20 when he fought in the war. On the night of July 19, 1916, on a field in northern France, the Allied forces and the Germans fought a terrible battle on the Western Front (a 475-mile-long battle line between the Germans and the Allied forces). More than 7,000 Allied soldiers were killed or wounded, and 470 were captured by the Germans. The soldier in the photo was shot in the leg, captured, and taken to a hospital in Germany. German doctors operated on him and saved his leg. He then spent about two years in a German prison camp. When the war was over, he was freed. He married and had children, but he never talked about his experience. We know about his life because his granddaughter helped write this book.

Bring in photos of World War I battlefields and trenches, or help students find photos on the Internet. Ask picture and visualizing questions to elicit how difficult and primitive the conditions were, and help students empathize with the soldiers and other people who helped during the war, such as nurses.

Have students work in pairs to answer all three questions. Then elicit the answers and write them on the board.

Answers

1. The assassination of Archduke Franz Ferdinand and his wife, Sophie of Austria-Hungary, sparked World War I.
2. Britain's allies against the Central Powers were France, Russia, Belgium, and the United States.
3. Answers will vary. Possible answers: President Wilson probably didn't want the United States to go to war because he wanted to stay out of Europe's quarrels. Many people die in war, and war is very expensive.

Working with Timelines

Read the timeline, helping with any new words. Ask comprehension and review questions, and then have students copy the timeline into their notebooks.

The Great Depression, page 244
World War II, page 245

Preview Pages

Have students <u>preview</u> these pages and <u>predict</u> the topics. Ask, *What do you already know about World War II?*

Teach Pages

Read the text and captions, or call on students to read them. Teach the More About It box on page 244 before going on to page 245. Help students connect information in the text with the map on page 245. Elicit the key words (unemployment, dictator), the sentences they're in, and their definitions.

Understand Information Encourage students to <u>understand chronological order</u> as they <u>reread</u> the pages. Write on the board and ask, *What are the most important dates in this reading?* Have students take turns asking and answering questions about the reading in pairs or small groups. When students have finished, ask the class your own comprehension, picture, and thinking questions, including the question on the board.

Organize Information Have students make a written summary of the Great Depression on page 244 in their notebooks. (Students will complete a summary of World War II later.) Depending on how much support they need, have them work in pairs or small groups. Say, *Just write the main ideas and most important details. Keep your books closed unless you need to quickly check spelling.* When they have finished, call on several different students to read their summaries. Comment on each. Compose an "edited" summary on the board.

MORE ABOUT IT: The New Deal

After the reading and comprehension check, you may want to show students photos and artwork from the WPA (available on the Internet). Elicit details and ask students to tell you what they think about the photos. Elicit how the creation of the posters and artwork provided jobs, and how the art helped Americans feel better.

MORE ABOUT IT: Internment Camps

After the reading and comprehension check, personalize this reading by asking students to close their eyes. Help students <u>visualize</u> how it would feel to have been Japanese at this time. Say, *Imagine that the government thought all the people from your country might be spies. People from the government come to your house. They say you have to leave your home, neighborhood, and school. You bring some of your things and leave the rest. You go on a bus with others to the camp. There is a wall around the camp and you can't leave. Open your eyes. How do you feel? Is it fair to do this to people from a certain country? Why or why not?*

Before You Go On

Have students work in pairs to answer all three questions. Then elicit the answers and write them on the board.

Answers
1. In 1929 the stock market fell apart and this event started the Great Depression.
2. In 1939 Germany invaded Poland and this event started World War II.
3. Answers will vary. Possible answer: The New Deal programs were called the Alphabet Soup Agencies and Acts because their nicknames were letters of the alphabet.

Working with Timelines

Read the timeline, helping with any new words. Ask comprehension and review questions, and then have students copy the timeline into their notebooks.

Primary Source, page 246

Preview Page

Have students <u>preview</u> this page and <u>predict</u> the topic.

Teach Page

Read the text, or call on students to read it. Help students with any new words.

Understand Information Encourage students to look for the main ideas and most important details as they <u>reread</u> the page.

REACHING ALL STUDENTS: Auditory Learners

Cue and play this excerpt from Franklin Roosevelt's 1941 State of the Union Address for the class (this is available on the Internet). Let students listen to it once with books open, and once or twice with books closed. After students have closed their books, write a few simple content questions on the board. Elicit the answers to the questions after the listening. Ask, *Do you think this is a good speech? Why or why not?*

Have students take turns asking and answering questions about the reading in pairs or small groups. When students have finished, ask the class your own comprehension, picture, and thinking questions. Say, *Close your books. Summarize the reading in your own words.* Call on several different students to complete the summary. Have students open their books and work in pairs or small groups to write the answers to the questions in their notebooks. Elicit the answers and write them on the board. Then discuss with students what they think about these four freedoms, and why.

Answers

1. World War II had begun in Europe when President Roosevelt made his 1941 State of the Union address. France had fallen to the German army. Hitler's planes were also bombing Great Britain.
2. The four freedoms that Roosevelt felt were worth fighting for were freedom of speech, freedom of every person to worship God in his own way, freedom from want, and freedom from fear.

World War II (continued), page 247

Preview Page

Have students <u>preview</u> this page and <u>predict</u> the topic.

Teach Page

Read the text and captions, or call on students to read them. Help students with any new words. Elicit the key words (Holocaust, atomic bombs), the sentences they're in, and their definitions.

Understand Information Encourage students to <u>visualize</u> as they reread the pages. Write on the board and ask, *What did Hiroshima look like before the atomic bomb? When the bomb was dropped? After the bomb?* Have students take turns asking and answering questions about the reading in pairs or small groups. When students have finished, ask the class your own comprehension, picture, and thinking questions, including the question on the board.

Organize Information Have students make a written summary of World War II (pages 245 and 247) in their notebooks. Have students review both of these pages once more before they begin. As there is a lot of information in this reading, let them complete their summaries with books open. Depending on how much support they need, have them work in pairs or small groups. When students have finished, call on several different students to read their summaries. Comment on each. Compose an "edited" summary on the board.

SCIENCE CONNECTION: The Manhattan Project

After the reading and comprehension check, let students view videos of atomic bomb blasts on the Internet. You may also want to let them see a short film taken in Hiroshima after the blast (see the website links below). Discuss the good and bad points of atomic bombs.

Before You Go On

Have students work in pairs to answer all three questions. Then elicit the answers and write them on the board.

Answers
1. Adolf Hitler was Germany's leader. He was a dictator and the head of the Nazi Party.
2. U.S. bombers dropped two atomic bombs on Japan—in Hiroshima and Nagasaki— and Japan surrendered.
3. Answers will vary. Possible answer: People were happy the war was over but thought the atomic bomb was a terrible weapon.

Working with Timelines

Read the timeline, helping with any new words. Ask comprehension and review questions, and then have students copy the timeline into their notebooks.

 Go to www.longmanusa.com/socialstudies for links to interesting websites about the world from the Progressive Era to World War II.

Review and Practice, pages 248–249

Vocabulary

If your students need additional help in reviewing this vocabulary, see the Optional Vocabulary Activities (pages vii–viii). Have students work individually. Check by calling on students to read their sentences. Write the correct answers on the board.

Answers
1. unemployment
2. submarines
3. atomic bomb
4. assassination
5. dictator
6. Holocaust

Check Your Understanding

Have students work individually, in pairs, or in small groups. Let students look back at the text. Then have students share their answers with the class. Write the answers on the board. Have students correct or add to their answers, if needed.

> **Answers**
> 1. During the Progressive Era, industrial production increased and there were many new inventions.
> 2. In 1929 the stock market fell apart (crashed) and many people lost all of their money.
> 3. In 1917 Germany attacked U.S. ships and President Wilson decided to go to war.
> 4. Germany, Italy, and Japan were the Axis Powers; and Great Britain, France, and the United States were the Allies in World War II.

Apply Social Studies Skills

Content Reading Strategy: Summarize Read the instructions, or call on a student to read them. Ask, *What do you write in a summary? What should you make sure your summary has?* Have students do this exercise with books closed. Depending on ability, have them work in pairs or in groups to summarize what they know about World War I. When students have finished, elicit summaries from several different students.

Building Research Skills: Use Print Resources Read the heading. Review print resources by letting students <u>reread</u> page 239, and then asking questions such as, *What print resource is a set of books with articles on many different subjects? How do you spell* encyclopedia? Have students work in pairs or small groups. Say, *You don't need to read or understand every word. Preview each entry and decide where it came from.* Elicit the answer to the first question and write it on the board so students know the answer format. Check by eliciting the answers and writing them on the board.

> **Answers**
> 1. You would find this in a dictionary.
> 2. You would find this in an encyclopedia.
> 3. You would find this in an atlas.
> 4. You would find this in a periodical.

Discuss

Read the discussion question. Then have students discuss the question in small groups. Circulate to help and comment on students' responses. Allow time for students to share their answers with the class.

Workbook pages 117–118 may now be assigned.

Self-Assessment Questions

Write the following questions on the board and have students respond in their notebooks. Then have them share their responses in small groups.

1. How can summarizing help me understand and remember?
2. How can using print resources help me to understand information?
3. What was difficult for me in this lesson?
4. What was easy for me in this lesson?
5. What was most enjoyable to learn?

Lesson ②

Before You Read, pages 250–253

Have students <u>preview</u> these pages individually or in pairs. Then ask, *What are you going to learn about in this lesson?*

Vocabulary

Read the captions, or call on students to read them. Help students with any new words. Have students read the captions again silently. Ask picture and comprehension questions for each item to make sure students have understood. Read the key words again and have students say them after you. Then have students close their books. Point to the pictures and ask questions to elicit the key words.

Practice

Have students fill in the blanks. Check by calling on individual students. Write the letters of the correct answers on the board.

Answers		
1. b. Communism	**3.** a. Democracy	**5.** b. Global
2. c. resources	**4.** b. terrorism	**6.** c. economy

Workbook page 119 may now be assigned.

Social Studies Skills

Content Reading Strategy: Understand Fact and Opinion Write *Draw a Conclusion* on the board. Then write *Fact* on the board and say, *A fact is something you can prove to be true.* Write *Opinion* on the board and say, *An opinion is someone's idea. You can't prove it's true.* Write on the board and say, *The average teenager spends 20 hours a week watching TV. It's terrible that teenagers watch so much TV.* Elicit which is a fact, which is an opinion, and why.

Read the information on the page, or call on students to read it. Help students understand and pronounce any new words. Stop after each section to ask comprehension questions. Then have the students reread the page. Have students work in pairs to write the answers to the questions in their notebooks. When students have finished, elicit the answers and write them on the board.

Answers
1. Possible answers: Before television, many people read magazines and books, and listened to the radio. In 1950 only about 9 percent of households had a TV. By 1960 about 87 percent of households had a TV. The family watched the same program.
2. Possible answers: Television changed American life. Many people believed that watching a TV was something that a family should do together.
3. You can check the facts in an encyclopedia (or on the Internet).
4. Possible answers: The word *believed* shows an opinion in the fifth sentence. The word *perhaps* shows an opinion in the final sentence.

Workbook pages 120–121 may now be assigned.

Building Research Skills: Use Technology Resources Have students preview page 253. Then ask, *What resources did you learn about in Lesson 1? What resources will you learn about in this lesson?* Read the information on the page, or call on a student to read it. Have students reread the page. Then ask comprehension and picture questions.

To help students practice using a computerized catalog, arrange a trip to the school library. Divide the class into groups and give them a list of books to find. The books should be listed by titles, authors, or specific subjects. The group that can find each book first gets a point. To help students search a CD-ROM encyclopedia, create a list of true-false statements that they can research on the CD-ROM. To help students practice searching the Internet, give them a list of questions to answer, such as *What is the name of George Washington's home?* Help them identify key words in the questions to use in their searches.

Workbook page 122 may now be assigned.

Reading ❷

Democracy vs. Communism, page 254
The Cold War, page 255

Preview Pages

Have students <u>preview</u> these pages and <u>predict</u> the topic.

Read the text and captions, or call on students to read them. Help students with any new words, and with the place names on the map. Teach More About It: The Berlin Wall with page 254, and More About It: The Cuban Missile Crisis with page 255. Elicit the key words (democracy/democratic, communism/communist), the sentences they're in, and their definitions.

Understand Information Encourage students to use what they know, to draw conclusions, and to think of their opinion as they reread the pages. Have students take turns asking and answering questions about the reading in pairs or small groups. When students have finished, ask the class your own comprehension, picture, and thinking questions. Ask use what you know, drawing conclusions, and opinion questions such as, *Why do you think the Soviet Union didn't allow its people to visit democratic countries? Why do you think the United States and the Soviet Union didn't fight in a war? Why do you think democratic and communist countries wanted to spread their ideologies? What's your opinion of communism? Why?* Say, *Close your books. Summarize the reading in your own words.*

Organize Information Say, *Make a word web about the Cold War. Use your own words. Keep your book closed unless you need to check spelling.* Model by beginning the word web on the board. Have students work in pairs or small groups. When checking, have students add information they've missed to their word webs. The completed word web may look like this:

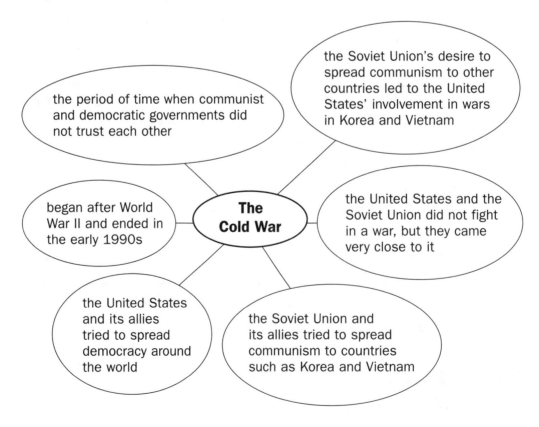

MORE ABOUT IT: The Berlin Wall

After the reading and comprehension check, help students search the Internet for photos of the Berlin Wall and its fall. Then have students close their eyes and visualize being separated from family by the wall. Elicit their feelings.

MORE ABOUT IT: The Cuban Missile Crisis

After previewing, ask, *What do you already know about Cuba?* Have them point out Cuba on the world map on pages 22–23. After the reading and comprehension check, help students visualize the scene. Then have them draw conclusions by asking, *What could have happened?*

Before You Go On

Tell students to look back at page 250 to help answer the first question. Have students work in pairs to answer all three questions. Then elicit the answers and write them on the board.

Answers

1. Democracy is a system of government in which each person can vote to elect a leader. People can own property and practice any religion freely. The government does not have complete control of the economy. Communism is a political system in which the government controls everything in a country, such as factories, farms, and businesses. People can't own property or practice religion freely.
2. The Soviet Union's desire to spread communism to other countries led to the United States' involvement in wars in Korea and Vietnam.
3. Answers will vary. Possible answers: It was probably called the "Iron Curtain" because it went across the land like a curtain, and it was as strong as iron. People couldn't go beyond it.

Working with Timelines

Read the timeline, helping with any new words. Ask comprehension and review questions, and then have students copy the timeline into their notebooks.

The Vietnam Era, page 256
The Soviet Union Breaks Up, page 257

Preview Pages

Have students preview these pages and predict the topics.

Teach Pages

Read the text and captions, or call on students to read them. Help students with any new words. Teach the Science Connection box "The Space Race" and the Profile of

Martin Luther King Jr. with page 256. Elicit the key words (communism/communist, economy), the sentences they're in, and their definitions.

Understand Information Encourage students to <u>use what they know</u>, to <u>draw conclusions</u>, and to think of their <u>opinion</u> as they <u>reread</u> the pages. Have students take turns asking and answering questions about the reading in pairs or small groups. When students have finished, ask the class your own comprehension, picture, and thinking questions. Ask use what you know, drawing conclusions, and opinion questions such as, *Why do you think people thought the Vietnam War was wrong? What do you know about President Reagan? What's your opinion of the Berlin Wall being torn down?* Say, *Close your books. Summarize the reading in your own words.*

SCIENCE CONNECTION: The Space Race

After the reading and comprehension check, ask students to draw a conclusion as to why the United States and the Soviet Union were in a race to space. Ask a use what you know question: *Are the United States and Russia (former Soviet Union) in a space race now?* (Point out that Americans and Russians sometimes travel to space together now.)

PROFILE: Martin Luther King Jr.

After previewing, ask, *What do you already know about Martin Luther King Jr.?* Before the reading, show signs enforcing segregation (available on the Internet), and make sure students understand that African Americans had to sit at the back of the bus so white people could sit at the front.

Organize Information Say, *Let's make a word web about Martin Luther King Jr. Use your own words. Keep your book closed unless you need to check spelling.* Model by beginning the word web on the board. Have students work in pairs or small groups. Check by eliciting the word web, writing it on the board, and having students add information they've missed to their webs in their notebooks. Completed word webs will vary.

Language Tip: Phrasal Verbs

Read the text and examples in the box on page 257, or call on a student to read them. Write *Phrasal Verbs* on the board, and the formula from the box, and then have students copy it. Ask, *What verb does each example use? What particles are in the examples?* Write the phrasal verb examples on the board, elicit or teach their definitions, and have students copy them into their notebooks. Ask, *Do you know of any other phrasal verbs?* Elicit and write several additional phrasal verbs and their definitions on the board, and then have students add them to their lists.

Have students work in pairs to answer all three questions. Then elicit the answers and write them on the board.

Answers

1. There was a war in Vietnam because the North Vietnamese communists and the South Vietnamese rebels (the Viet Cong), wanted to unite the country under one communist system. The United States and its allies didn't want this to happen.
2. President Gorbachev wanted to change the Soviet Union because he wanted to improve his country's economy, which was falling apart when he came to power. He thought it was time for great social changes. He wanted to end the Cold War and to trade with Western countries.
3. Answers will vary. Possible answers: Yes, people fight for workers' rights, minority rights, and animal rights.

Working with Timelines

Read the timeline, helping with any new words. Ask comprehension and review questions, and then have students copy the timeline into their notebooks.

Central and South America, page 258
Asia, page 259

Preview Pages

Have students preview these pages and predict the topic. Ask students what they know about Central America, South America, and Asia. Using the world map on pages 22–23, have students identify which countries are in each of these regions.

Teach Pages

Read the text and captions. Help students with any new words. Elicit the key words (economy, democracy/democratically), the sentences they're in, and their definitions.

Understand Information Encourage students to use what they know, to draw conclusions, and to think of their opinion as they reread the pages. Have students take turns asking and answering questions about the reading in pairs or small groups. When students have finished, ask the class your own comprehension, picture, and thinking questions. Ask use what you know, drawing conclusions, and opinion questions such as, *Does anybody know more information about these civil wars in Latin America? What's your opinion of Pinochet? Why is being in debt not good for an economy?* Say, *Close your books. Summarize the reading in your own words.*

Organize Information Say, *Make a word web about Chile, Japan, or China. Use your own words. Keep your book closed unless you need to check spelling.* Model by beginning one word web on the board. Check the different word webs verbally, and have students add any information they may have missed to their word webs.

ELSEWHERE IN THE WORLD: European Union

After the reading and comprehension check, let students look at a map of the European Union on the EU website. Point out that the name of each country is written in that country's language. Elicit the English names for countries that students are familiar with.

CONNECT TO TODAY: China's Challenges

After the reading and comprehension check, have students write *China* and its population in numbers in their notebooks. Dictate the populations of some other countries (United States = 295 million, Mexico = 106 million, Japan = 128 million, India = 1.1 billion, United Kingdom = 60 million, Iraq = 26 million, Indonesia = 242 million, Australia = 20 million). Make sure students know that 1 billion = 1,000 million. Have students compare these numbers, and then elicit their opinions on the advantages and disadvantages of having a large population.

Optional Activity

Have students use print or technology resources to research and write one or more paragraphs about their native country. Tell them to include both fact and opinion in their writing, and to find pictures and a map to accompany their article. You may want to have students do an outline first. Model by writing part of an outline or paragraph about your native country on the board. After students have finished their paragraphs, have them work with a classmate for feedback, and then do any rewriting. Collect the papers and make any further corrections, and then have students make a final copy. Have each student read his or her paper to the class.

Before You Go On

Have students work in pairs to answer all three questions. Then elicit the answers and write them on the board.

Answers
1. In 1973 in Chile, the democratically elected socialist president Salvador Allende was overthrown in a coup organized by military leader Augusto Pinochet.
2. Japan and China have strong economies.
3. Answers will vary. Possible answers: If I were a leader in Latin America or Asia, I would help the economy grow by trading more. I would help the country become a leader in manufacturing. I would develop any natural resources. And I wouldn't borrow money from the World Bank.

Working with Timelines

Read the timeline, helping with any new words. Ask comprehension and review questions, and then have students copy the timeline into their notebooks.

Africa, page 260
The Gulf Wars and Terrorism, page 261

Preview Pages

Have students <u>preview</u> these pages and <u>predict</u> the topics. Elicit what students <u>already know</u> about Africa, terrorism, and the Gulf Wars. Using the map of Africa on page 21, ask students to find countries they'll encounter in the reading. (Rwanda, Angola, Sierra Leone, Sudan, South Africa) Ask location questions about other major African countries. Then using the world map on pages 22–23, elicit the names of countries in the Middle East.

Teach Pages

Read the text and captions, or call on students to read them. Help students with any new words. Elicit the key words (resources, economy, terrorism, global), the sentences they're in, and their definitions.

Understand Information Encourage students to <u>use what they know</u>, to <u>draw conclusions</u>, and to think of their <u>opinion</u> as they <u>reread</u> the pages. Have students take turns asking and answering questions about the reading in pairs or small groups. When students have finished, ask the class your own comprehension, picture, and thinking questions. Ask use what you know, drawing conclusions, and opinion questions such as, *What other countries do you know that declared themselves independent from their colonial rulers? What do you know about military dictators in Latin America? What's your opinion of dictators?* Say, *Close your books. Summarize the reading in your own words.*

Organize Information Say, *Make a word web about Africa or the Gulf Wars and terrorism. Use your own words. Keep your book closed unless you need to check spelling.* Model by beginning a word web on the board. Have students work in pairs or small groups. Check the word webs verbally. Completed word webs will vary.

MORE ABOUT IT: Apartheid

After the reading and comprehension check, ask <u>comparing and contrasting</u> and <u>opinion</u> questions, such as, *How was apartheid similar to segregation in the United States? How was it different? What's your opinion of apartheid? What's your opinion of Nelson Mandela?*

As You Read: Understand Fact and Opinion

Read the information, or call on a student to read it. Elicit several different answers to the question. (periodicals such as magazines and newspapers, the Internet, the library, CD-ROMs, etc.)

Have students work in pairs to answer all three questions. Then elicit the answers and write them on the board.

Answers

1. Military dictators, who were not elected by the people, ruled most African countries.
2. Reasons for conflict include: Africa is made up of hundreds of ethnic groups. Most African countries are very poor.
3. Answers will vary. Possible answers: Most economies in the world depend on oil for heat, fuel, and industry. Oil is a fairly inexpensive source of energy, and it's easy to get it and to transport it. We use oil in our cars, trucks, and factories.

Working with Timelines

Read the timeline, helping with any new words. Ask comprehension and review questions, and then have students copy the timeline into their notebooks.

Go to www.longmanusa.com/socialstudies for links to interesting websites about the world from the Cold War to the present day.

Review and Practice, pages 262–263

Vocabulary

If your students need additional help in reviewing this vocabulary, see the Optional Vocabulary Activities (pages vii–viii). Have students work individually. Check by calling on students to read their sentences. Write the correct answers on the board.

Answers

1. global	**3.** terrorism	**5.** resources
2. democracy	**4.** Communism	**6.** economy

Check Your Understanding

Have students work individually, in pairs, or in small groups. Let students look back at the text. Then have students share their answers with the class. Write the answers on the board. Have students correct or add to their answers, if needed.

Answers

1. The Cold War started when communist and democratic governments did not trust each other. The United States and its allies tried to spread democracy around the world. The Soviet Union and its allies tried to spread communism. The Cold War ended when communism ended in the Soviet Union.
2. The former Soviet Union fell apart and divided into many smaller countries.
3. Japan and China have strong economies today.
4. Iraq invaded Iran and Kuwait because it wanted to dominate the region.

Apply Social Studies Skills

Content Reading Strategy: Understand Fact and Opinion Elicit facts that students know about September 11, the War on Terror, the war in Afghanistan, and the war in Iraq. Elicit a variety of opinions on these topics. Write *Facts and Opinions* on the board. Do a think-aloud, and write a sample outline and paragraph on the board. Then have students work individually to complete their paragraphs. Have students exchange papers with a classmate for feedback, and then make any corrections before turning their papers in to you. Return the papers with suggestions/corrections, and then have students rewrite them. Call on students to read their papers to the class.

Building Research Skills: Use Technology Resources Have students reread page 253. Then have students work in pairs. You may want to have them do this exercise verbally, or write out the answer structure *I would go to ~ first because . . .* in their notebooks. Check by eliciting the answers and writing them on the board.

Answers
- a book in a library → computerized catalog (easy to search)
- a movie about the life of Martin Luther King Jr. → CD-ROM (stores videos)
- the latest information about your community's government → the Internet (local governments have their own websites)
- a movie clip of the fall of the Berlin Wall → the Internet or a CD-ROM (both have video clips)
- a magazine with an article about the U.S. economy → computerized catalog or the Internet (has online magazine articles)
- the latest pictures taken in space → the Internet (the NASA website)
- sounds and pictures from the 1970s → the Internet or a CD-ROM (both have sounds and pictures)

Discuss

Read the discussion question. Then have students discuss the question in small groups. Circulate to help and comment on students' responses. Allow time for students to share their answers with the class.

Workbook pages 123–124 may now be assigned.

Evaluation

Self-Assessment Questions

Write the following questions on the board. Have students respond in their notebooks. Then have them share their responses in small groups.

1. How can understanding fact and opinion help me in reading?
2. How can using technology resources help me to find information?
3. What was difficult for me in this lesson?
4. What was easy for me in this lesson?
5. What was most enjoyable to learn?

Unit Review, pages 264–265

Vocabulary

Have students work individually, with a partner, or in small groups, depending on how much support they need. Check answers as a class, writing the answers on the board.

Answers

1. assassination
2. dictator
3. economy
4. Submarines
5. global
6. atomic bomb
7. communism
8. resources
9. Holocaust
10. democracy
11. Terrorism
12. unemployment

Timeline Check

Read the instructions, or call on a student to read them. You may want to have students see if they can do this exercise without looking back at dates. Have students work individually, in pairs, or in small groups. Then elicit the answers and write them on the board.

Answers

4	Martin Luther King Jr. wins the Nobel Peace Prize
5	The war in Vietnam ends
2	Women in the United States win the right to vote
3	Hiroshima, Japan, is bombed
7	The Soviet Union breaks up
6	Iraq invades Iran
1	World War I begins

Apply Social Studies Skills

Building Research Skills: Use Technology Resources Read the instructions, or call on a student to read them. Have students work individually or in pairs. Then elicit the answers and write them on the board. Finally, let students practice using a search engine to find and take notes on information on the Internet. Have students work in pairs, small groups, or as a class. Elicit some of the information that students found.

Answers

Students can use these phrases as key words, or they can add other key words to find more specific information (for example, *Archduke Ferdinand, assassination, causes of World War I*).

Extension Project

Elicit key words that students might use to search the Internet to find this information. Have them work online individually, in pairs, or in small groups. Tell them to take notes on what they find. Then elicit the answers verbally.

Read More About It

Bring at least one of the suggested books to class. Show the cover and some of the inside pages to students as a preview. Ask students to predict what the book is about. Read an excerpt to the class. Then ask several comprehension questions. Read the excerpt again before calling on students to answer. Encourage students to find this or another suggested book in their school library or local bookstore.

 Workbook pages 125–126 may now be assigned.

Writing Skills, pages 266–267

Edit and Publish a Three-Paragraph Essay

Preview

Have students preview these two pages. Then ask, *What will you practice doing?*

Present the Model

Read the information on page 266. Have students reread silently, and then ask comprehension questions. Then go over the proofreading marks chart on page 267. To elicit the example correction, ask questions such as *What letter was inserted? What was deleted?*

Read the model essay on page 266, helping with any new words. Then ask, *What's the correction in the second sentence?* Elicit the corrections in the first few sentences, and write the correct sentences on the board.

Have students copy the paragraphs into their notebooks, making corrections as they go. To check, read each sentence in the essay and elicit the corrections verbally.

Practice

Note that you may want to choose which essay students write depending on time and student ability. Revising the three-paragraph essay from Unit 6 will be faster and easier. Writing a three-paragraph essay from a topic in this unit will require the preparation of a new outline and draft, thus more thorough and rewarding, but more time-consuming.

Choose teaching procedures from Unit 5 as appropriate. Tell students to look at the questions on page 232 as they write. Circulate to monitor and help students.

When students have completed their paragraphs, have them exchange essays with a classmate. Ask the students to look at the proofreading marks on page 267 as they check the work. Then have students get together to discuss suggestions. Finally, have students rewrite their work and hand it in to you. Mark any suggestions for corrections, and then have students rewrite, as needed. Have some students read their essays to the class in a presentation. Check that they read slowly and clearly.

 Workbook pages 127–128 may now be assigned.

Understanding the Past Tense

Teach these pages after Getting Started if your students need help with the past tense.

For each section, read the introduction and examples, or call on students to read them. Help students understand any new words. Then follow the teaching procedures outlined below for each section.

Tell students they don't need to understand every word in the practice section—they just need to understand how to use the past tense. Depending on student level and ability, have students work individually, in pairs, in small groups, or as a class to write the practice answers into their notebooks. Be sure they understand that they must write complete sentences. Elicit answers and write them on the board.

 Workbook pages 130–134 may be assigned for homework or done in class after each section. Elicit the first few answers for each exercise.

Simple Past Tense of Regular Verbs, pages 279–280

After reading each point, elicit the rule and help students with more examples.

- Elicit the rule that verbs ending in -e just take -d. Write other examples of words taking -d or -ed on the board and elicit past tense forms. (lie, follow, trade, plant, use)
- Elicit or teach the rule that -y at the end of a word usually changes to -i before -ed. Also, teach students that the final consonant often doubles before -ed in one-syllable words ending in a vowel and a consonant. Write other examples of each of these types of words on the board and elicit their past tense forms. (fry, carry, plan, hop, dry, ram)
- Ask a student to tell you three things that he or she did yesterday. Write this on the board as three sentences, and then show students how to form a compound sentence. (He went to school, ate dinner, and watched TV.)

Practice

> **Answers**
> 1. asked
> 2. started
> 3. planted
> 4. needed
> 5. designed, sewed
> 6. learned
> 7. rained, hailed, snowed
> 8. moved
> 9. discovered
> 10. signed

Negative Statements About the Past, page 281

After reading the introduction, elicit the rule. Write these sentences on the board: *We sailed on the ocean. Sacagawea cried out for help.* For each sentence, ask, *How do we make this sentence negative? Where does* didn't *go?* (add *didn't* before the verb) Show the transformations on the board by adding *didn't*.

Practice

Answers

1. They didn't add an amendment.
2. He didn't start a new political party.
3. They didn't want to settle in the West.
4. It didn't arrive on time.
5. She didn't thank them for their help.
6. They didn't believe in many different gods.
7. The law didn't end slavery.
8. They didn't develop a calendar.
9. They didn't try to grow a new kind of wheat.
10. I didn't like the way the story ended.

Simple Past Tense of Irregular Verbs, pages 282–283

After reading each point, elicit the rule. Help students with more examples, and help them learn the boxed irregular verbs.

For points with sentence examples, write one or more new sentences on the board and elicit the transformation. For example (in order of presentation):

- The soldier falls. ⟶ The soldier fell.
- He cuts his finger. ⟶ He cut his finger.
- He cut his finger. ⟶ He didn't cut his finger.
- She is a general. ⟶ She was a general.
- Was she a general? ⟶ Yes, she was.
- Was he a slave? ⟶ No, he was not. / No, he wasn't.
- His name was Washington. ⟶ What was his name?

For points with boxed irregular verbs, have students say each verb after you in present and past form. Then have students copy the verbs into their notebooks. When students have finished, say the verbs in the present tense at random, eliciting the past tense forms. When students are ready, do this with books closed.

Practice

Answers

1. wrote   2. didn't find   3. fought   4. tried   5. didn't keep   6. told

1. What did they choose?
2. What did he bring?
3. Why did they need help?
4. Where did she want to live?
5. When did the stock market crash?
6. What did they want?

1. traveled   3. paid   5. wanted   7. got   9. followed
2. saw   4. had   6. organized   8. taught   10. helped

Workbook Answer Key

GETTING STARTED: INTRODUCTION (pages 1–16)

What Is Social Studies?
(pages 1–2)

Vocabulary

A.

1. f 3. d 5. a
2. e 4. b 6. c

B.

1. Geography
2. government
3. Economics
4. History
5. social studies

C.

1. voters 4. buy
2. weather 5. weather
3. oceans 6. science

D.

1. goods 4. Trade
2. services 5. weather
3. past

E.

1. F 3. F 5. T
2. T 4. F

F.

Economics: 1. money 2. goods
Geography: 1. weather
　　　　　　 2. mountains
History: 1. past
Government: 1. leaders 2. vote
　　　　　　　 3. democracy

What Is Social Studies?
(page 3)

Vocabulary

History　　　　 Economics
Geography　　　 Government

The Five Themes of Geography (page 4)

A.

1. Location 4. Interaction
2. Place 5. Region
3. Movement
Secret word: **ocean**

B.

Location ⟷ a place
Region ⟷ common features
Geography ⟷ five themes
Place ⟷ different climate, landforms, or plants
Movement ⟷ from one place to another
Interaction ⟷ affects the world

Answers may vary. Possible answers:

1. A region has common features.
2. Geography has five themes.
3. A place has different climate, landforms, or plants.
4. Movement is going from one place to another.
5. Interaction affects the world.

Geographic Terms (pages 5–6)

A.

1. c 5. h 9. b
2. j 6. d 10. e
3. g 7. i
4. a 8. f

B.

1. i 5. g 9. f
2. j 6. h 10. c
3. d 7. a
4. b 8. e

C.

1. island 4. coast
2. sea 5. peninsula
3. gulf

Globes and Maps (pages 7–12)

A.

1. globe
2. map

B.

1. map 6. globe or map
2. globe 7. map, map
3. map 8. globe
4. map 9. map, map
5. map, globe 10. globe

C.

1. This is a political map because it shows countries, states, and cities.
2. London is the capital of the United Kingdom.
3. Portugal and France share a border with Spain.
4. Russia is north of Romania.
5. Portugal, Spain, France, and the United Kingdom have coasts on the Atlantic Ocean.

Maps (pages 9–10)

A.

1. key
2. scale
3. compass rose

B.

1. Papua New Guinea is north of Australia.
2. New Zealand is southeast of Australia.

C.

1. Australia is the largest country on the map.
2. The Indian Ocean is west of Australia.
3. Cook Strait is in New Zealand.
4. Tasmania is an island.
5. Answers will vary. Possible answer: The Great Sandy Desert is a desert in Australia.

D.

1. F 3. T 5. T
2. T 4. F

E.

1. Australia
2. New Zealand
3. Australia
4. Australia
5. New Zealand
6. Australia
7. New Zealand
8. Australia
9. New Zealand
10. Australia
11. New Zealand

Maps (pages 11–12)

A.

1. b 5. c 9. b
2. c 6. a 10. c
3. b 7. b
4. a 8. c

B.

1. Answers will vary. Possible answer: China, Japan, and North Korea are three countries in Asia.
2. The capital of Canada is Ottawa.
3. Chile, Bolivia, Brazil, Colombia, and Ecuador border Peru.
4. Yemen is south of Saudi Arabia.
5. Nigeria is on the African continent.

C.

1. T	5. F	9. T
2. T	6. F	10. T
3. T	7. T	
4. T	8. F	

Using Timelines, Charts, and Graphs (pages 13–15)

Timelines and Charts (pages 13–14)

A.

1. The first successful climb to the summit of Mount Everest was in 1953.
2. The first woman to climb to the summit was Junko Tabei in 1975.
3. The oldest climber reached the summit in 2003.
4. Two British men disappeared on Mount Everest in 1924.
5. Mount Everest was named for Sir George Everest in 1865.

B.

1. T	3. F	5. T
2. F	4. F	

C.

1. The title of this chart is "Major Events in World War II."
2. The chart shows the years 1940–1945.
3. Japan bombed Pearl Harbor on December 7, 1941.
4. The Germans surrendered on May 7, 1945.
5. The Japanese surrendered on September 2, 1945.

Graphs (page 15)

1. This graph is a bar graph.
2. This graph shows the year 1860.
3. Large planters and medium planters were less than 10 percent of the white population.
4. The nonslaveholding whites were 76 percent of the white population.
5. The small slaveholders were 20 percent of the white population.

Using Primary Sources
(page 16)

Answers may vary. Possible answers:
1. People wrote the U.S. Constitution about 200 years ago.
2. They used ink and paper.
3. Answers will vary.
4. "We the People" are the citizens of the United States.

UNIT 1: LESSON 1
(pages 17–22)

Before You Read (pages 17–20)

Vocabulary (page 17)

A.

1. e	3. f	5. d
2. a	4. b	

B.

Sentences will vary.

C.

1. irrigation
2. Archaeologists
3. crops
4. Agriculture
5. hunter-gatherers
6. glaciers

Social Studies Skills
(pages 18–20)

Content Reading Strategy: Preview (page 18)

A.

1. "Early Farmers" and "The Bronze Age"
2. Answers will vary. Possible answers: Farmers, settled, canals, irrigation, Bronze Age, traded, and goods. These words stand out on the page.
3. Farmers, a farm, Bronze Age tools, pins, and a razor
4. Answers will vary. Possible answers: I will learn about some of the first farmers, irrigation, and what the Bronze Age is.

B.

1. The Stone Age
2. The Ice Age
3. Early Farmers
4. The Bronze Age
5. Mesopotamia
6. Primary source: Cuneiform
7. The Phoenicians

Using Visuals: Use a Timeline (page 19)

1. People make bronze is the first event on the timeline.
2. First libraries in Egypt is the last event on the timeline.
3. The wheel was invented in 3500 B.C.E.
4. This timeline covers 4,100 years.
5. They grew rice in southeast Asia in 5000 B.C.E.

Using Visuals: Use a Timeline (page 20)

A.

Students should fill in the timeline as follows (starting with the entry on the far left):

8000 B.C.E.	Towns develop in Middle East
7000 B.C.E.	Farming begins in Mesopotamia
6600 B.C.E.	People begin to make bronze tools
6000 B.C.E.	Wheat farming spreads in the Nile Valley and Africa
4000 B.C.E.	Farming begins in central Europe

B.

1. Farming begins in central Europe. The date is 4000 B.C.E.
2. There are 1,000 years between the first event and the second event.
3. Farming begins in Mesopotamia and people begin to make bronze tools.
4. People begin to make bronze tools and wheat farming spreads in the Nile Valley and Africa.
5. Farming began in Mesopotamia in 7000 B.C.E.

Lesson 1: More Review and Practice (pages 21–22)

Vocabulary

1. agriculture	4. glaciers
2. irrigation	5. crops
3. archaeologist	

Secret word: **tools**

Vocabulary in Context

1. irrigation
2. archaeologist
3. Glaciers
4. crops
5. Hunter-gatherers

Timeline Check

1. Hammurabi built a new empire in 1792 B.C.E.
2. In 1500 B.C.E. Ethiopia became an independent power and the earliest known settlement was established in Mexico.
3. The first dictionary was written in China in 1100 B.C.E.

Check Your Understanding

1. c   3. a   5. c
2. b   4. b

Apply Social Studies Skills

Content Reading Strategy: Preview

1. The Mediterranean Sea and the Red Sea
2. The Eastern Desert
3. Lower Egypt, Upper Egypt, Lower Nubia, and Upper Nubia
4. This is a map of Egypt a long time ago.

UNIT 1: LESSON 2
(pages 23–28)

Before You Read (pages 23–26)

Vocabulary (page 23)

A.

1. Pyramids   4. invaders
2. classes   5. ruler
3. ancient   6. society

B.

ruler ⟷ pharaoh
pyramid ⟷ slaves
society ⟷ classes
invaders ⟷ walls

Sentences will vary.

C.

1. F   3. T   5. T
2. T   4. F   6. F

Social Studies Skills
(pages 24–26)

Content Reading Strategy: Predict (page 24)

Answers will vary. Possible written answers:
Prediction 1: The hunter-gatherers will eat the mammoth meat.
Prediction 2: They will use the mammoth's bones to make tools.
Prediction 3: They will use the mammoth's hide (skin) to make clothes.

Content Reading Strategy: Predict (page 25)

1. This person is an archaeologist.
2. She is looking for ancient objects.
3. Answers will vary. Possible answers:
   · She will find ancient tools.
   · She will find ancient pottery.
   · She will find human bones.

Using Visuals: Use a Timeline (page 26)

A.

Students should fill in the timeline as follows (starting with the entry on the far left):

3000 B.C.E.	Sumerians create first writing system
2500 B.C.E.	Ink first used in Egypt and China
1300 B.C.E.	Chinese make and use simple books
1000 B.C.E.	Earliest samples of Phoenician writing
750 B.C.E.	Development of first Indian writing system
550 B.C.E.	Appearance of writing from left to right

B.

1. Sumerians create first writing system is the first event on the timeline.
2. There are 1,200 years between the second event and the third event.
3. People began to write from left to right in 550 B.C.E.
4. Around 1300 B.C.E. the Chinese made and used simple books.
5. Ink was first used in Egypt and China.

Lesson 2: More Review and Practice (pages 27–28)

Vocabulary

1. d   3. e   5. f
2. a   4. c   6. b

Vocabulary in Context

1. Ancient   3. ruler
2. society   4. class

Timeline Check

1. The Middle Kingdom began in Egypt in 1991 B.C.E.
2. In 700 B.C.E., the Celts moved into England, and Nubia gained independence from Egypt.
3. Confucius was born in 551 B.C.E.

Check Your Understanding

1. T   3. F   5. F
2. F   4. T

Apply Social Studies Skills

Content Reading Strategy: Predict

Answers will vary.

Using Visuals: Use a Timeline

1. The Nubians push into Egypt is the event that happened first.
2. After Nubia gained independence from Egypt, the Nubians moved their capital to Meroë.
3. Meroë fell in the year 250 C.E.

Unit 1: Unit Review
(pages 29–30)

Vocabulary

1. invaders   5. archaeologists
2. ruler   6. pyramids
3. ancient   7. glaciers
4. society   8. irrigation

Vocabulary in Context

1. F. Early farmers grew crops and raised animals.
2. F. Pharaohs were buried in pyramids.
3. T.
4. F. In ancient China the family was very important to the society.

Timeline Check

2
3
5
6
1
4

Apply Social Studies Skills

Content Reading Strategies: Preview and Predict

Predictions will vary.

Unit 1: Writing Skills
(pages 31–32)

A.

Details will vary.

B.

Paragraphs will vary.

C.

Word webs will vary.

D.

Paragraphs will vary.

UNIT 2: LESSON 1
(pages 33–38)

Before You Read (pages 33–36)

Vocabulary (page 33)

A.

1. b   3. f   5. d
2. e   4. c   6. a

B.

Sentences will vary.

C.

1. monuments   4. amphitheater
2. Pottery   5. sculptures
3. Drama

D.

1. monuments   4. drama
2. marble   5. pottery
3. pottery

Social Studies Skills
(pages 34–36)

Content Reading Strategy: Visualize
(page 34)

A.

Pictures will vary.

B.

Sentences will vary.

Using Visuals: Use a Map Key
(page 35)

1. Mesopotamia is the large region shown on the map.
2. Sumer is located in the south of Mesopotamia.
3. The name of the mountain range is the Zagros Mountains.
4. The names of the cities are Kish, Erech, and Ur.
5. The cities are located in Sumer.

Using Visuals: Use a Map Key
(page 36)

1. This is a map of the Persian Empire.
2. The cities on the map are Athens, Sparta, Babylon, and Persepolis.
3. Babylon and Persepolis are capitals.
4. The Mediterranean Sea and the Black Sea are the bodies of water.
5. You could add a symbol for mountains.

Lesson 1: More Review and Practice (pages 37–38)

Vocabulary

1. amphitheater   4. festivals
2. monuments   5. drama
3. sculptures   6. pottery

Vocabulary in Context

1. sculptures   4. festivals
2. pottery   5. amphitheaters
3. Drama

Timeline Check

1. The Parthenon was completed in Athens in 432 B.C.E.
2. Hippocrates founded the science of medicine in 430 B.C.E.
3. The Chinese began to use a crossbow in 360 B.C.E.
4. Alexander invaded India in 327 B.C.E.

Check Your Understanding

1. b   3. b   5. a
2. c   4. c

Apply Social Studies Skills

Content Reading Strategy: Visualize
Pictures will vary.

Using Visuals: Use a Map Key

1. capital   3. mountain
2. city   4. river

UNIT 2: LESSON 2
(pages 39–44)

Before You Read (pages 39–42)

Vocabulary (page 39)

A.

1. prison   4. aqueducts
2. senate   5. structures
3. Colosseum   6. government

B.

senate ⟷ laws
prison ⟷ punishment
Colosseum ⟷ gladiators
aqueduct ⟷ water

Sentences will vary.

C.

1. F   3. T   5. F
2. T   4. F

Social Studies Skills
(pages 40–42)

Content Reading Strategy: Ask Questions (page 40)

A.

Questions will vary.

B.

Questions will vary.

C.

Questions will vary.

D.

Answers will vary.

Using Visuals: Use a Compass Rose
(page 41)

1. Olympia, Mycenae, Athens, Corinth, Marathon, and Delphi are north of Sparta.
2. Mount Olympus is south of Macedonia.
3. The Aegean Sea is east of Greece.
4. Greece is west of Asia Minor.
5. The island of Crete is southeast of Sparta.

Using Visuals: Use a Compass Rose
(page 42)

1. The Mediterranean Sea is directly north of Egypt.
2. Babylon and Persepolis are east of Alexandria.
3. Sparta, Athens, and Troy are north of Alexandria.
4. Yes, Persia is west of India.
5. No, Babylon is west of Persepolis.

Lesson 2: More Review and Practice (pages 43–44)

Vocabulary

1. e   3. b   5. d
2. f   4. a   6. c

Vocabulary in Context

1. F   3. T   5. F
2. T   4. F

Timeline Check

1. Copper was first used in East Africa in 680 B.C.E.
2. In 14 C.E. the Roman emperor Augustus died.
3. Mayan city-states flourished in 350 C.E.
4. In 632 C.E. the prophet Muhammad died.

Check Your Understanding

1. b   3. a   5. b
2. c   4. c

Apply Social Studies Skills

Content Reading Strategy: Ask Questions

Questions will vary.

Using Visuals: Use a Compass Rose

1. T   3. F   5. F
2. F   4. T

Unit 2: Unit Review
(pages 45–46)

Vocabulary

1. Colosseum   6. senate
2. pottery   7. amphitheater
3. structures   8. sculptures
4. festivals   9. prison
5. aqueducts   10. drama

Vocabulary in Context

1. pottery   4. prison
2. monument   5. government
3. sculptures

Timeline Check

5
2
3
4
6
1

Apply Social Studies Skills

Using Visuals: Use a Map Key and Compass Rose

1. The map key includes the dates 1000 C.E. and 120 C.E.
2. Yes, the area of the Roman Empire is from an earlier time.
3. The red line shows the border of the Roman Empire in 120 C.E.
4. The city of Kiev is farthest north on the map.
5. The city of Mecca is farthest south on the map.

Unit 2: Writing Skills
(pages 47–48)

A.

The lives of rich and poor people in Rome were very different.

B.

Chariot races were a popular form of entertainment in Greece and Rome.

C.

Answers will vary. Possible answer: Spartan boys were taught about war from a very early age.

D.

Paragraphs will vary.

UNIT 3: LESSON 1
(pages 49–54)

Before You Read (pages 49–52)

Vocabulary (page 49)

A.

1. c   3. d   5. f
2. a   4. e   6. b

B.

Sentences will vary.

C.

1. knight   4. cathedrals
2. crusade   5. peasant
3. manor   6. Feudalism

D.

1. farmer   3. manor
2. cathedral   4. armor

Social Studies Skills
(pages 50–52)

Content Reading Strategy: Monitor Comprehension (page 50)

Answers will vary. Possible answers:
1. Armor was important to a knight because it protected him in battle. His armor was made of large pieces of metal and of small rings of metal. This armor was used to protect parts of the body. A helmet was used to protect the knight's head.
2. Chainmail was armor used to protect the parts of a knight's body that were not protected by metal plates. It was made of tiny rings of metal attached tightly together.
3. I see hard plates and a helmet.
4. The armor in the photograph is from the fifteenth century.
5. Answers will vary. Possible answer: Armor could not protect knights against more powerful weapons such as gunpowder weapons.

Content Reading Strategy: Monitor Comprehension (page 51)

Answers will vary. Possible answers:
1. Kings, lords, and knights were part of the ruling class. The ruling class owned most of the land. Lords protected land for the kings. The lords gave land to knights if they promised to fight in battle.
2. I see a king, noblewomen, and noblemen.
3. The noblewomen were the wives and daughters of kings, lords, and knights.

Using Visuals: Read a Map
(page 52)

1. The lines of latitude go horizontally on the map.
2. The lines of longitude go up and down on the map.
3. The line 40°N latitude goes through Castile and Aragon.
4. The city of Paris is located on 2°E longitude and 48°N latitude.
5. The lines 10°E longitude and 50°N latitude go through the Holy Roman Empire.

Lesson 1: More Review and Practice (pages 53–54)

Vocabulary

1. c   3. d   5. a
2. e   4. b

Vocabulary in Context

1. feudalism   4. Peasants
2. knight   5. manor
3. Crusades

Timeline Check

1. The Crusaders captured Jerusalem and put it under Christian rule.
2. The Turks defeated the Byzantine emperor Romanus IV in 1071.
3. Charlemagne died before the Holy Roman Empire was divided.
4. The Mongols under Genghis Kahn captured the Chinese capital of Beijing.
5. Muhammad was born in 570 C.E.

Check Your Understanding

1. b   3. b   5. a
2. a   4. c

Apply Social Studies Skills

Content Reading Strategy: Monitor Comprehension

Answers will vary. Possible answers:
1. Peasants did all of the work on a manor. They lived very poorly.
2. Peasants were poor because they had very little land. They had to pay taxes to the lord and give him part of their harvest.

Using Visuals: Read a Map

1. 5°E longitude, 44°N latitude
2. 6°E longitude, 49°N latitude
3. 38°E longitude, 37°N latitude

UNIT 3: LESSON 2

(pages 55–60)

Before You Read (pages 55–58)

Vocabulary (page 55)

A.

1. cliff dwellers
2. samurai
3. silk
4. dynasty
5. trade
6. canal

B.

dynasty ←——→ China
canals ←——→ cliff dwellers
samurai ←——→ warrior
trade ←——→ silk

Sentences will vary.

C.

1. F Dynasties ruled in China and Japan.
2. T
3. F Cliff dwellers were a group of people who lived under cliffs.
4. T
5. F China traded silk with other parts of the world.

Social Studies Skills

(pages 56–58)

Content Reading Strategy: Understand Chronological Order (page 56)

A.

Possible underlined answers:

400	Ghanaian empire, controlled all trade routes, Sahara Desert
800	Ghana, reached its height, major trading kingdom
1100	Soso people, took over, Kingdom of Ghana

B.

Students should fill in the timeline as follows (starting with the entry on the left):

400	Ghanaian empire controls all trade routes across the Sahara Desert
800	Ghana reaches its height as a major trading kingdom
1100	Soso people take over the Kingdom of Ghana

Content Reading Strategy: Understand Chronological Order (page 57)

A.

Possible answers:

1167	Genghis Khan, born
1206	Genghis Khan, first great khan, Mongol Empire
1207	Genghis Khan, led the Mongols, first invasion
1227	Genghis Kahn, died
1260	Kublai Khan, became the ruler, Mongol Empire
1294	Kublai Khan, died

B.

Students should fill in the timeline as follows (starting with the entry on the left):

1167	Genghis Khan is born
1206	Genghis Khan becomes the first great khan of the Mongol Empire
1207	Genghis Khan leads the Mongols on their first invasion
1227	Genghis Khan dies
1260	Kublai Khan becomes the ruler of the Mongol Empire
1294	Kublai Khan dies

Using Visuals: Use a Map Scale (page 58)

1. It is about 800 miles from Surat to Madurai in India.
2. The Bay of Bengal is about 1,250 miles across at its widest part.
3. It is about 600 miles from Xi'an to Yangzhou.
4. It is about 1,800 miles from Patna to Guangzhou.
5. A mile is longer than a kilometer.

Lesson 2: More Review and Practice (pages 59–60)

Vocabulary

1. cliff dwellers
2. trade
3. dynasty
4. samurai
5. silk

Secret word: **canal**

Vocabulary in Context

1. F The Song dynasty was a government in China.
2. T
3. F The civilizations in Mesoamerica did not have samurai warriors.
4. F The Silk Road was a land route used by traders.
5. T

Timeline Check

1. The Black Death killed many people in 1348.
2. The city of Delhi was founded in India after the Huns invaded.
3. The Aztecs began living in Tenochtitlán in 1325.
4. In 1192 Minamoto Yoritomo was made the first shogun.
5. In 1294 Kublai Khan died.

Check Your Understanding

1. a
2. b
3. b
4. c
5. a

Apply Social Studies Skills

Content Reading Strategy: Understand Chronological Order

Date	Event
250	Mayas live in Mesoamerica
900	Mayas abandon their cities
1100s	Aztecs live in the area of present-day Mexico
1470s	Aztecs spread to areas surrounding present-day Mexico
1519	Spanish invade Aztecs

Using Visuals: Use a Map Scale

1. T
2. F
3. T
4. F

Unit 3: Unit Review

(pages 61–62)

Vocabulary

1. canals
2. samurai
3. manor
4. silk
5. Crusades
6. Feudalism
7. cliff dwellers
8. cathedrals
9. Trade
10. dynasty

Vocabulary in Context

1. feudalism
2. Peasants
3. manor
4. knights
5. samurai

Timeline Check

618	The Tang dynasty starts.
1100	Aztecs begin living in Tenochtitlán.
1348	The Black Death sweeps across Europe.
1368	Mongols overthrown in China.

Apply Social Studies Skills

Using Visuals: Read a Map and Use a Map Scale

1. The city of Cuzco is near 70°W and 15°S.
2. Middle America is north of the equator.
3. The Gulf of Mexico is between 100°W and 80°W longitude.
4. It is about 3,000 miles across the middle of North America.
5. It is about 1,600 miles from the equator to the Tropic of Capricorn.

Unit 3: Writing Skills

(pages 63–64)

Answers will vary. Possible answers:
1. The emperor was the head of the government.
2. The emperor appointed a shogun.
3. The shogun had the power to make laws, collect taxes, and protect the land from foreign invaders.
1. The warlords controlled large armies.
2. Samurai warriors were special soldiers in these armies.
3. The samurai swore to die for the warlords.

UNIT 4: LESSON 1

(pages 65–70)

Before You Read (pages 65–68)

Vocabulary (page 65)

A.

1. c	3. f	5. b
2. d	4. e	6. a

B.

Sentences will vary.

C.

1. printing press
2. manuscript
3. movable type
4. clergy
5. explorer
6. protests

D.

1. printing press
2. protests
3. soldier
4. explorer

Social Studies Skills

(pages 66–68)

Content Reading Strategy: Reread (page 66)

A.

Answers will vary. Possible answer:
Main idea: Ferdinand Magellan was a Portuguese explorer who traveled to many places and made many discoveries.

B.

1. Ferdinand Magellan was an explorer.
2. Ferdinand Magellan was from Portugal.
3. Magellan sailed to Asia and South America.
4. A strait is a narrow waterway.
5. Ferdinand Magellan found the llama in South America.

Content Reading Strategy: Reread (page 67)

A.

Answers will vary. Possible answer:
Main idea: Christians and Muslims fought over the city of Jerusalem for a long time.

B.

1. The Christians and the Muslims fought to control Jerusalem.
2. The first Crusade took control of Jerusalem in 1099.
3. A Muslim leader named Salah al-Din conquered Jerusalem in 1187.
4. In 1247 the Muslims were driven out of Jerusalem by the Egyptians.
5. The city of Jerusalem enjoyed religious harmony under the Ottoman Empire until the mid-nineteenth century.

Using Visuals: Use Physical Maps (page 68)

1. The continent of Africa is south of Europe.
2. The Balkan Mountains, the Transylvanian Alps, and the Carpathian Mountains are north of the Balkan Peninsula.
3. The English Channel is to the south of Great Britain.
4. The islands of Corsica and Sardinia, and the Balearic Islands are west of the Italian Peninsula.
5. The Danube River is in central Europe.

Lesson 1: More Review and Practice (pages 69–70)

Vocabulary

1. d	3. b	5. a
2. f	4. e	6. c

Vocabulary in Context

1. printing press
2. movable type
3. manuscripts
4. protests

Timeline Check

1. Leonardo da Vinci was born in 1452.
2. In 1385 Portugal became independent from Spain.
3. The Muslims recaptured Jerusalem in 1244.
4. The peasant revolt in China happened before the peasant revolt in Germany.
5. Martin Luther nailed his list of protests onto a church door in 1517.

Check Your Understanding

1. c	3. c	5. b
2. a	4. b	

Apply Social Studies Skills

Content Reading Strategy: Reread

1. The Roman Catholic Church felt very angry with Martin Luther.
2. The Roman Catholic Church eventually made some reforms.

Using Visuals: Physical Maps

1. The names of the states in northern Italy were the Republic of Genoa, the Duchy of Milan, the Republic of Venice, and the Republic of Florence.
2. The islands of Sardinia and Corsica are west of Naples.
3. Sicily is located in the south.
4. Italy is a peninsula.

UNIT 4: LESSON 2

(pages 71–76)

Before You Read (pages 71–74)

Vocabulary (page 71)

A.

1. f	3. a	5. b
2. c	4. e	6. d

B.

Sentences will vary.

C.

1. F Voyages were trips made in a ship.
2. T
3. T
4. F The explorers conquered many peoples (or lands).

5. F   The Spanish explorers brought diseases to the indigenous people.

D.

1. Aztecs
2. smallpox
3. compass
4. smallpox
5. Atlantic

Social Studies Skills
(pages 72–74)

Content Reading Strategy: Use Selective Attention (page 72)

A.

Possible answer: The Renaissance was an important period of scientific discoveries and artistic changes.

B.

Name
Leonardo da Vinci
Michelangelo
Johannes Gutenberg

Artist or Inventor?
Artist
Artist
Inventor

Painting or Invention?
Painting
Painting
Invention

C.

Answers will vary. Possible answers:
1. The key words *important* and *Renaissance*
2. Selective attention
3. By looking for key words and sentences

Content Reading Strategy: Use Selective Attention (page 73)

A.

Possible answer: The scientific method is a way of performing experiments.

B.

1. read
2. reread
3. words, sentences
4. answered

C.

1. The Age of Enlightenment was a period of new scientific discoveries during the 1600s that encouraged new ways of thinking.
2. Galileo used the scientific method to prove his theory.
3. Sir Isaac Newton proved the theory that gravity controls the movement of the earth around the sun.

Using Visuals: Use Different Types of Maps (page 74)

1. The map of Europe is a political map because it shows the names of countries, regions, and cities.
2. The map of Italy is a physical map because it shows physical features, such as mountains and seas.
3. The map of Europe shows country borders.
4. These maps both show Italy.
5. The map of Europe shows a larger area.

Lesson 2: More Review and Practice (pages 75–76)

Vocabulary

1. **I**ndigenous
2. **n**avigation
3. **c**onquered
4. dise**a**ses
5. voyage**s**

Secret word: **Incas**

Vocabulary in Context

1. T
2. F   A Portuguese explorer sailed around the Cape of Good Hope.
3. T
4. F   The Spanish army conquered the Incas.
5. T

Timeline Check

1. In 1682 Sir Isaac Newton discovered the law of universal gravitation.
2. Francisco Pizarro killed the Incan emperor in 1533.
3. Joan of Arc fought the Battle of Orléans in 1429.
4. In 1507 German mapmakers named the New World "America" after the explorer Amerigo Vespucci.
5. Hernán Cortés arrived in Mexico in 1519.

Check Your Understanding

1. b
2. c
3. b
4. a
5. c

Apply Social Studies Skills

Content Reading Strategy: Use Selective Attention

The Aztecs lived in Mexico.
Possible answer: The Aztecs lived in the area of present-day Mexico. The Incas lived in the area of present-day Peru.

Using Visuals: Use Different Types of Maps

1. F
2. T
3. T
4. T
5. F

Unit 4: Unit Review
(pages 77–78)

Vocabulary

1. indigenous
2. explorer
3. routes
4. manuscript
5. conquered
6. protests
7. Movable type
8. navigation

Vocabulary in Context

1. explorers
2. voyages
3. navigation
4. routes
5. conquered

Timeline Check

1. 1682
2. 1632
3. 1532
4. 1452

Apply Social Studies Skills

Using Visuals: Use Different Types of Maps

Completed maps should be similar to the map in the Student Book.

Unit 4: Writing Skills
(pages 79–80)

A.

Paragraphs will vary.

B.

Outlines and paragraphs will vary.

UNIT 5: LESSON 1
(pages 81–86)

Before You Read (pages 81–84)

Vocabulary (page 81)

A.

People	Places
indentured servant	colony
settlers	plantation
slaves	territory

B.

1. plantation
2. Settlers
3. Slaves
4. colony
5. territory
6. Indentured servants

C.

Jamestown	←→	colony
indentured servants	←→	freedom
slaves	←→	work hard
settlers	←→	plantations

Sentences will vary.

Social Studies Skills
(pages 82–84)

Content Reading Strategy: Use What You Know (page 82)

A.

Word webs will vary.

B.

Additions will vary.

C.

Corrected webs will vary.

Using Visuals: Read a Chart (page 83)

1. Christopher Columbus sailed the earliest.
2. Three explorers explored for Spain. They were Christopher Columbus, Hernán Cortés, and Francisco Pizarro.
3. John Cabot explored from 1497 to 1498. England sent him.
4. Hernán Cortés went to Mexico.
5. Answers will vary.

Using Visuals: Read a Chart (page 84)

Students fill in the underlined material.

Columbus's Voyages	Dates of Voyages
First voyage	1492–1493
Second voyage	1493–1496
Third voyage	1498–1500
Fourth voyage	1502–1504

Areas Visited

(first voyage) Cuba, Hispañola
(second voyage) Dominica, Leeward Islands, Virgin Islands, Puerto Rico, Hispañola, Cuba
(third voyage) Trinidad, Margarita, Hispañola
(fourth voyage) Honduras, coast of Central America to Panama, Jamaica

Lesson 1: More Review and Practice (pages 85–86)

Vocabulary

1. colony
2. plantation
3. slaves
4. territory
5. indentured servants

Vocabulary in Context

1. settlers
2. plantations
3. colony
4. Slaves
5. territory

Timeline Check

1. British rule in India began after the French and Indian War started.
2. An earthquake killed 30,000 in Lisbon, Portugal, in 1755.

Check Your Understanding

1. b	3. c	5. a
2. a	4. c	

Apply Social Studies Skills

Content Reading Strategy: Use What You Know

Answers will vary.

Using Visuals: Read a Chart

1. A shoemaker
2. A silversmith
3. A wheelwright
4. A printer
5. A blacksmith

UNIT 5: LESSON 2
(pages 87–92)

Before You Read (pages 87–90)

Vocabulary (page 87)

A.

1. document
2. treaty
3. representatives
4. tax
5. revolt
6. independence

B.

Sentences will vary.

C.

1. T
2. F If a country wants independence, it wants to be free.
3. F A tax is money you give to the government.
4. T
5. F Representatives in the government are elected.

Social Studies Skills
(pages 88–90)

Content Reading Strategy: Look for Cause and Effect (page 88)

Cause: Puritans did not have religious freedom in England. **Effect:** Puritans settled in Massachusetts.

Cause: Settlers in Jamestown did not have enough food during the first winter. **Effect:** Many settlers died.

Cause: Columbus returned from his first voyage to tell about new lands and peoples. **Effect:** Europe became interested in the New World.

Content Reading Strategy: Look for Cause and Effect (page 89)

Answers will vary. Possible answers:

1. Columbus wanted to find a quicker route to Asia.
2. Many colonists died.
3. Farmers in the South needed more workers.
4. They fought in the French and Indian War.
5. Colonists arrived in the New World.

Using Visuals: Read a Chart (page 90)

1. The chart is about the estimated colonial population from 1630 to 1770.
2. The years on the chart increase by twenty years for each row.
3. This chart covers 140 years.
4. The total increase in population from 1630 to 1770 was 2,143,500.
5. Possible answer: Because more and more settlers and slaves arrived.

Lesson 2: More Review and Practice (pages 91–92)

Vocabulary

1. revolt
2. document
3. independence
4. treaty
5. representatives

Vocabulary in Context

1. tax
2. document
3. representatives
4. revolt
5. Independence

Timeline Check

1. In 1750 Spain and Portugal divided South American colonies, and the first coal mine opened in the colonies.
2. The Russians were exploring Alaska in 1764.
3. Los Angeles was founded after the Boston Tea Party.
4. The first successful hot air balloon was in 1783.

Check Your Understanding

1. b	3. a	5. c
2. d	4. e	

Apply Social Studies Skills

Content Reading Strategy: Look for Cause and Effect

1. The people in this picture are colonists.

2. The colonists were angry that they had to pay taxes.

3. Possible answer: The British were very angry. The British passed more laws.

Using Visuals: Read a Chart

1. The British and the colonists are represented in this chart.

2. Yes, this chart shows cause and effect.

Unit 5: Unit Review
(pages 93–94)

Vocabulary

treaty ⟷ document

president ⟷ government

tax ⟷ protest

independence ⟷ colony

tobacco ⟷ plantations

Sentences will vary.

Vocabulary in Context

Students fill in the underlined material.

Singular Noun

1. <u>settler</u>
2. <u>tax</u>
3. representative
4. colony
5. <u>revolt</u>

Plural Noun

1. settlers
2. <u>taxes</u>
3. <u>representatives</u>
4. <u>colonies</u>
5. revolts

Verb

1. <u>to settle</u>
2. to tax
3. <u>to represent</u>
4. <u>to colonize</u>
5. <u>to revolt</u>

Sentences will vary.

Timeline Check

<u>2</u>

<u>1</u>

<u>4</u>

<u>3</u>

<u>5</u>

Apply Social Studies Skills

Using Visuals: Read a Chart

1. I learned about the printer, wheelwright, and blacksmith in my Student Book.

2. The wigmaker, miller, and apothecary jobs are new to me.

3. Answers will vary.

Unit 5: Writing Skills
(pages 95–96)
Essays will vary.

UNIT 6: LESSON 1
(pages 97–102)

Before You Read (pages 97–100)

Vocabulary (page 97)

A.

1. c   3. d   5. b

2. f   4. a   6. e

B.

Sentences will vary.

C.

1. F   The gold rush was a time period.

2. T

3. F   A wagon train is a long line of wagons.

4. T

5. T

D.

1. Native Americans
2. tribe
3. factory
4. gold rush
5. industry

Social Studies Skills
(pages 98–100)

Content Reading Strategy: Compare and Contrast (page 98)

A.

Venn diagrams will vary. Completed diagrams may include the following information:

Washington

· commander of Continental Army
· helped write U.S. Constitution
· first president of U.S.

Both

· helped set up new government
· helped write U.S. Constitution
· landowner and farmer
· owned slaves
· great leader

Jefferson

· wrote Declaration of Independence
· third president of U.S.

Content Reading Strategy: Compare and Contrast (page 99)

A.

Venn diagrams will vary. Completed diagrams may include the following information:

Native American Tribe

· already living in New World
· knew how to survive in New World

Both

· had system of government to make laws
· had leaders to run government
· were communities

Colony of Settlers

· immigrants
· did not know how to survive in New World

Using Visuals: Read a Graph
(page 100)

1. Germany
2. Ireland
3. 2% of immigrants came from China.
4. Canadians
5. Possible answer: These groups came to the United States in search of new opportunities.

Lesson 1: More Review and Practice (pages 101–102)

Vocabulary

1. pioneers   4. Immigrants
2. **w**agon train   5. gold ru**s**h
3. trib**e**   6. indus**t**ry

Secret word: **west**

Vocabulary In Context

1. pioneers   3. tribes
2. wagon trains   4. immigrants

Timeline Check

1. F   3. T   5. F
2. T   4. F

Check Your Understanding

1. b   3. b   5. c
2. a   4. c

Apply Social Studies Skills

Content Reading Strategy: Compare and Contrast

Venn diagrams will vary. Completed diagrams may include the following information:

Great Plains Indians

· lived in tents
· moved around

Both

· needed food, water, and shelter
· made laws
· used the land

Settlers

· lived in houses made of stone and wood
· stayed in one place

Using Visuals: Read a Graph

1. Most of the slaves went to the non-Spanish Caribbean islands.
2. The fewest slaves went to Europe and Asia.
3. Portugal bought more slaves than Spain.
4. 15% of slaves went to Spanish America.
5. The total slave population that was sent to different parts of the world.

UNIT 6: LESSON 2
(pages 103–108)

Before You Read
(pages 103–106)

Vocabulary (page 103)

A.

1. fort	4. Union
2. Mason-Dixon Line	5. Confederacy
3. battle	6. railroads

B.

Sentences will vary.

Content Reading Strategy: Draw Conclusions (page 104)

Conclusions will vary. Possible conclusion:
Pioneers used the transcontinental railroad instead of wagon trains to travel west.

Content Reading Strategy: Draw Conclusions (page 105)

Conclusions will vary. Possible conclusion:
The U.S. government was able to use gold as its currency.

Using Visuals: Read a Graph (page 106)

1. New York had more factories in 1860.
2. Georgia had fewer factories in 1890.
3. Yes, Georgia increased the amount of factories from 1860 to 1890 by 2,395.
4. Yes, New York increased the amount of factories from 1860 to 1890 by 43,216.
5. There were more factories in New York than in Georgia because New York was industrial. Georgia had more plantations than factories.

Lesson 2: More Review and Practice (pages 107–108)
Vocabulary

1. battles	4. Confederacy
2. Mason-Dixon Line	5. Union
3. fort	

Vocabulary in Context

1. F   The Union won the Civil War.
2. T
3. T
4. F   The southern states wanted to be called the Confederacy.
5. F   The Mason-Dixon Line was an imaginary line.

Timeline Check

1. In 1876 Korea became an independent nation.
2. The Spanish-American War began in 1898.
3. The Franco-Prussian War began in 1870.
4. The first typewriters were made in 1873.
5. In 1890 Sitting Bull was shot and killed, and the Battle of Wounded Knee took place.

Check Your Understanding

1. b	3. b	5. c
2. c	4. a	

Apply Social Studies Skills

Content Reading Strategy: Draw Conclusions

Conclusions will vary. Possible conclusion: Cities grew.

Using Visuals: Read a Graph

1. F
2. F
3. T

Unit 6: Unit Review
(pages 109–110)

Vocabulary

1. h	5. c	9. b
2. a	6. i	10. g
3. f	7. j	
4. e	8. d	

Sentences will vary.

Vocabulary in Context

1. Railroads	4. Immigrants
2. industry	5. pioneers
3. tribes	

Timeline Check

5
6
1
2
3
4

Apply Social Studies Skills

Content Reading Strategy: Compare and Contrast

Venn diagrams will vary. Completed diagrams may include the following information:

North
- industrial
- had many factories
- opposed slavery

Both
- under same federal government
- had cities and ports
- economy depended on trade
- used new inventions to expand economy

South
- agricultural
- had many plantations
- supported slavery

Unit 6: Writing Skills
(pages 111–112)

A.

1. Yes
2. Yes
3. No
4. The migration of Europeans to the Americas began in the 1500s. Lewis and Clark traveled west across the United States to find a water route to the Pacific Ocean.
5. No

B.

Revised essays will vary.

C.

Answers will vary.

UNIT 7: LESSON 1
(pages 113–118)

Before You Read
(pages 113–116)

Vocabulary (page 113)

A.

1. c	3. d	5. b
2. e	4. f	6. a

B.

Sentences will vary.

C.

1. assassination
2. Holocaust
3. Submarines
4. Unemployment
5. dictator

D.

1. jobs
2. submarines
3. dictator
4. unemployment
5. submarines

Social Studies Skills
(pages 114–116)

Content Reading Strategy: Summarize (page 114)

Possible summary:

The German submarines, or U-boats, were important weapons in World War I. They were designed not to make noise while underwater. They did a lot of damage to British ships.

Content Reading Strategy: Summarize (page 115)

Possible summary:

The Holocaust in Nazi Germany killed many people between 1941 and 1945. These people, mostly Jewish, were put in concentration camps. Around 12 million people were killed in the Holocaust.

Building Research Skills: Use Print Resources (page 116)

1. Print resources are used to do research, or to find more information about something.
2. I would look for the political borders of Asian countries in an atlas.
3. If I wanted to find out about the life of Adolf Hitler or Archduke Franz Ferdinand, I would use an encyclopedia.
4. I would look in periodicals for information about what is happening in my home country today.
5. If I wanted to find out whether a word is an adjective, a noun, or a verb, I would look in a dictionary.

Lesson 1: More Review and Practice (pages 117–118)
Vocabulary

1. dictator
2. Holocaust
3. unemployment
4. atomic bomb
5. submarines
6. assassination

Secret word: **allies**

Vocabulary in Context

1. assassination
2. dictator
3. submarine
4. atomic bomb
5. Holocaust

Timeline Check

1. In 1918 World War I ended and Wilson created the 14 Point Plan for Peace.
2. In 1929 the stock market collapsed and the Great Depression began.

Check Your Understanding

1. b 3. c 5. c
2. c 4. a

Apply Social Studies Skills

Content Reading Strategy: Summarize

Possible summary:

The stock market crash in 1929 started the Great Depression. Banks lost money and many people lost their jobs. When Roosevelt became president in 1932, he created the New Deal programs to end the Great Depression.

Building Research Skills: Use Print Resources

1. a dictionary
2. an encyclopedia
3. periodicals
4. an atlas

UNIT 7: LESSON 2
(pages 119–124)

Before You Read
(pages 119–122)

Vocabulary (page 119)

A.

1. Communism
2. resources
3. Economy
4. democracy
5. Terrorism
6. global

B.

terrorism ←→ hijacking
resources ←→ oil and gold
economy ←→ money and business
democracy ←→ free elections

Sentences will vary.

C.

1. F Diamonds and oil are resources from the earth.
2. F Communism is a system in which you cannot have free elections.

---

3. T
4. T
5. F Terrorism is a political action.

Social Studies Skills
(pages 120–122)

Content Reading Strategy: Understand Fact and Opinion (page 120)

Answers will vary. Possible answers:

1. Fact: Franklin Delano Roosevelt was the only U.S. president elected to four terms of office.
   Fact: Roosevelt became president in 1933 during the Great Depression.
2. Opinion: The New Deal programs were successful.
   Opinion: Roosevelt did not want to go to war.
3. Facts can be checked in an encyclopedia or on the Internet.
4. The word "perhaps" helped me identify the opinions. The phrases "some people believe" and "might have" also helped.
5. Answers will vary.

Content Reading Strategy: Understand Fact and Opinion (page 121)

Answers will vary. Possible answers:

1. Fact: Home computers and cellular phones have changed the way most people communicate.
   Fact: The Internet started in 1969 as a U.S. government project to help researchers communicate with each other.
2. Opinion: People never imagined they would be so popular.
   Opinion: Many people believe the Internet is the best invention ever.
3. Facts can be checked in periodicals or on the Internet.
4. The word "perhaps" helped me identify the opinions. The phrases "many people believe" and "there might be" also helped.
5. Answers will vary.

Building Research Skills: Use Technology Resources (page 122)

1. You can find photographs, videos, text, and sound on a CD-ROM. You can also find many print resources on a CD-ROM.
2. You can find information about books in a library in a computerized catalog.
3. I would use a computerized catalog to find a book about the Internet.

4. I would use a CD-ROM or the Internet to find information on Nelson Mandela.
5. Answers will vary.

Lesson 2: More Review and Practice (pages 123–124)

Vocabulary

1. d	3. b	5. f
2. a	4. c	6. e

Vocabulary in Context

1. T
2. T
3. F   Natural resources are very important to a country.
4. T
5. F   Communism is a political system.

Timeline Check

1. In 1948 Israel became a nation.
2. President John F. Kennedy was assassinated in 1963.
3. The My Lai massacre in Vietnam occurred in 1969.
4. The nuclear disaster in Chernobyl, Ukraine, occurred in 1986.

Check Your Understanding

1. a	3. b	5. c
2. c	4. a	

Apply Social Studies Skills

Content Reading Strategy: Understand Fact and Opinion

1. F	3. F	5. F
2. O	4. O	

Building Research Skills: Use Technology Resources

1. CD-ROMs or the Internet
2. a computerized catalog
3. CD-ROMs or the Internet
4. the Internet
5. CD-ROMs or the Internet

Unit 7: Unit Review
(pages 125–126)
Vocabulary

resources ←→ oil and diamonds
World War I ←→ submarines
global ←→ terrorism
Cuba ←→ communism
unemployment ←→ the Great Depression
atomic bomb ←→ World War II

Sentences will vary.

Vocabulary in Context

1. Assassinations
2. Dictators
3. global
4. resources

Timeline Check

5,	1966
1,	1903
6,	1994
2,	1929
3,	1940
4,	1941

Apply Social Studies Skills

Content Reading Strategy: Understand Fact and Opinion

1. F	3. F	5. F
2. O	4. O	

Unit 7: Writing Skills
(pages 127–128)
A.

Students should find multiple spelling, capitalization, and punctuation errors.

UNDERSTANDING THE PAST TENSE (pages 129–134)

Simple Past Tense of Regular Verbs (page 129)
A.

1. voted	6. asked
2. helped	7. needed
3. died	8. compared
4. showed	9. arrived
5. studied	10. carried

B.

1. elected	6. traveled
2. helped	7. explored
3. dried	8. delivered
4. learned	9. listed
5. watched	10. wanted

C.

1. The map key helped us find mountains, rivers, and cities.
2. I used a globe to find the distance.
3. We studied how people, things, and ideas move.
4. Students located the pyramid on a map of Mexico.

Negative Statements about the Past (Regular Verbs)
(page 130)
A.

1. didn't advise
2. didn't warn
3. didn't order
4. didn't force
5. didn't sign
6. didn't create
7. didn't hurry
8. didn't return
9. didn't live
10. didn't decide

B.

1. The southern colonies didn't want to end slavery.
2. The Germans didn't invent the submarine.
3. The fighter planes didn't destroy Tokyo.
4. Columbus didn't explore the New World for Portugal.
5. Lewis and Clark didn't travel across Colombia and Peru.

C.

1. didn't visit
2. didn't happent
3. didn't end
4. didn't work
5. didn't export

Simple Past Tense of Irregular Verbs (pages 131–132)
A.

1. came	6. won
2. went	7. got
3. drew	8. gave
4. had	9. fell
5. fought	10. began

B.

1. People in Japan didn't choose their emperor.
2. The Spanish explorers didn't give gold to the Aztecs.
3. The Egyptians didn't buy the pyramids.
4. Most countries didn't keep their colonies.
5. Juan Ponce de León didn't find the Fountain of Youth.

C.

1. was	3. was	5. were
2. were	4. were	

D.

1. Did you draw a map of Asia?
2. Did the South and the North fight in the American Civil War?
3. Did the Roman Empire have an emperor named Julius Caesar?
4. Did she think geography was difficult?
5. Did the Portuguese bring the first slaves from Africa?

E.

1. What did the Mayas leave?
2. When did the Great Depression begin?
3. Where was the Berlin Wall?
4. Why did the Pilgrims leave England?
5. Why did many native people die?

Simple Past Tense: Regular and Irregular Verbs
(pages 133–134)

A.

1. went	Sentences will vary.
2. stopped	Sentences will vary.
3. lived	Sentences will vary.
4. told	Sentences will vary.
5. needed	Sentences will vary.
6. took	Sentences will vary.
7. saw	Sentences will vary.
8. said	Sentences will vary.
9. left	Sentences will vary.
10. found	Sentences will vary.

B.

1. didn't agree	6. came
2. landed	7. broke
3. painted	8. happened
4. had	9. learned
5. was	10. didn't build

C.

1. was	8. helped
2. experienced	9. wanted
3. didn't go	10. won
4. attended	11. continued
5. went	12. died
6. graduated	13. was
7. moved	14. became

Introduction to the Tests

Each unit has three tests: two Lesson Tests and an overall Unit Test. The tests cover key vocabulary, content, social studies skills, and include a writing section. The writing section should be scored holistically, using the four-point writing rubric below. Each response should receive a score from 0 to 4 points, with 4 points being the highest score. The Getting Started unit is an exception in that it has one test for the entire unit and no writing section. To calculate the scores, follow this procedure:

- The Lesson Tests have 11 items, each worth 1 point. The writing section is worth a maximum of 4 points. So the maximum score for a Lesson Test is 15 points.
- The Unit Tests have 21 items, each worth 1 point. The writing section is worth a maximum of 4 points. So the maximum score for a Unit Test is 25 points.

Scoring the Writing Sections	
Score	**Description**
4 points	The paragraph is focused, well organized, and complete. There is a logical beginning, middle, and end. The paragraph begins with a main idea and gives details and/or examples that relate to the main idea. There is a demonstrated understanding of the content of the lesson or unit. There is a demonstrated command of spelling, capitalization, punctuation, grammar, usage, and sentence structure. The paragraph may contain some errors in writing conventions, but these errors do not detract from the overall fluency.
3 points	The paragraph as a whole is focused and mostly complete, but is not as well focused, well organized, and complete. There is a logical beginning, middle, and end. The paragraph begins with a main idea and gives details and/or examples that relate to the main idea. There is a demonstrated understanding of the content of the lesson or unit. There is a demonstrated command of spelling, capitalization, punctuation, grammar, usage, and sentence structure. The paragraph may contain some errors in writing conventions, but these errors do not detract from the overall fluency.
2 points	The paragraph shows some sense of focus in that it may have a main idea, but no details, or details, but no main idea. The student may shift from idea to idea without a logical transition. The paragraph may also include irrelevant information, repetition, and gaps in ideas, or simply list ideas with little development. There is only a vague understanding of the content. There is a limited command of writing conventions, and there are errors in spelling, capitalization, punctuation, grammar, usage, and sentence structure throughout the paragraph. These errors may weaken the overall fluency of the paragraph.
1 point	The paragraph as a whole is not focused and has little or no sense of completeness. There is no main idea and few details. The details that exist may be randomly presented or repeated. The paragraph may also include irrelevant ideas. There is little understanding of content or writing conventions. The errors that exist weaken the paragraph by causing an overall lack of fluency.
0 points	The paragraph is completely incorrect, irrelevant, or incoherent, or the student does not attempt to respond to the writing prompt at all.

Name _____ Date _____

Getting Started: Introduction Test

What Is Social Studies?

Choose the best answer. Circle the letter.

1. The study of countries, oceans, mountains, and weather is _____.

   a. economics

   b. history

   c. geography

   d. government

2. The study of things that happened in the past is _____.

   a. history

   b. government

   c. economics

   d. geography

3. The study of the people who control what happens in a country is _____.

   a. geography

   b. economics

   c. history

   d. government

4. The study of money, goods, and services is _____.

   a. government

   b. geography

   c. economics

   d. history

5. Location, region, place, movement, and interaction are _____.

   a. the five themes of economics

   b. the five themes of geography

   c. the five themes of government

   d. the five themes of history

Name _____ Date _____

Geographic Terms

Look at the numbers on the picture. Choose the best answer. Circle the letter.

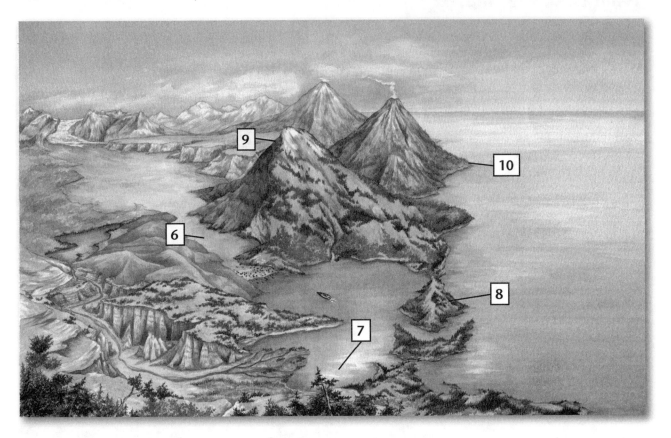

6. This _____ flows from a lake.

   a. hill

   b. plain

   c. river

   d. peninsula

7. This _____ is part of the ocean.

   a. bay

   b. valley

   c. desert

   d. canyon

8. This _____ has water on three sides.

   a. hill

   b. delta

   c. canyon

   d. peninsula

9. This _____ is very high.

   a. hill

   b. continent

   c. mountain

   d. island

10. This volcano is on the _____.

   a. river

   b. coast

   c. valley

   d. desert

Maps

Look at the map. Choose the best answer. Circle the letter.

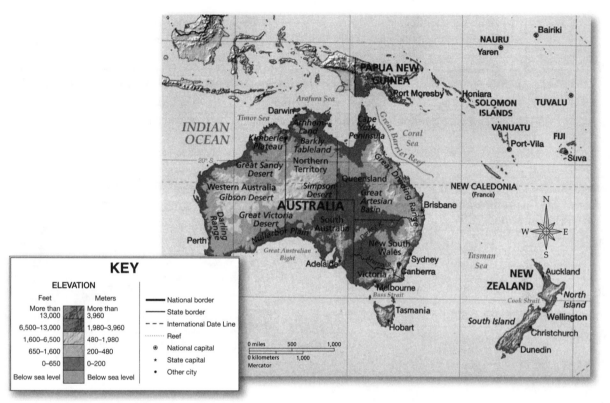

11. What is New Caledonia?

   a. A continent

   b. A peninsula

   c. A canyon

   d. An island

12. Look at the scale. About how far is New Caledonia from Brisbane, Australia?

   a. About 100 miles

   b. About 1,000 miles

   c. About 5,000 miles

   d. About 10,000 miles

13. Look at the compass rose. Which direction is New Caledonia from Australia?

   a. North

   b. South

   c. East

   d. West

14. Which country is north of Australia?

   a. Fiji

   b. Vanuatu

   c. New Zealand

   d. Papua New Guinea

15. Look at the key. What is the capital of Vanuatu?

   a. Port-Vila

   b. Yaren

   c. Wellington

   d. Canberra

Name _____ Date _____

Using Visuals

Look at the visuals. Choose the best answer. Circle the letter.

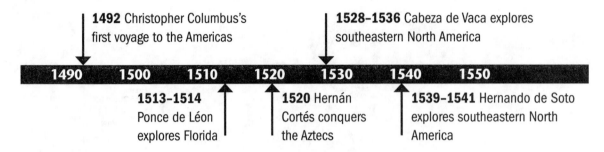

1492 Christopher Columbus's first voyage to the Americas

1528–1536 Cabeza de Vaca explores southeastern North America

| 1490 | 1500 | 1510 | 1520 | 1530 | 1540 | 1550 |

1513–1514 Ponce de Léon explores Florida

1520 Hernán Cortés conquers the Aztecs

1539–1541 Hernando de Soto explores southeastern North America

Immigration to the U.S. from Latin America and the Caribbean, 2004	
Mexico	114,984
Central America	53,435
South America	54,155
The Caribbean	67,660
All Areas	290,234

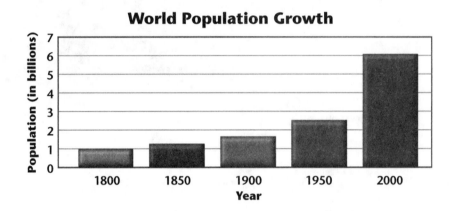

World Population Growth

16. Look at the timeline. What is the first event?

  a. Cabeza de Vaca explores

  b. Christopher Columbus's first voyage

  c. Ponce de León explores

  d. Hernando de Soto explores

17. What is the last event on the timeline?

  a. Cabeza de Vaca explores

  b. Christopher Columbus's first voyage

  c. Ponce de León explores

  d. Hernando de Soto explores

18. Look at the chart. Which region had the most immigrants in 2004?

  a. Mexico

  b. The Caribbean

  c. Central America

  d. South America

19. How many people came from all Latin American and Caribbean areas?

  a. 114,984

  b. 54,435

  c. 67,660

  d. 290,234

20. Look at the bar graph. What was the world population in 1800?

  a. About 1 person

  b. About 100,000 people

  c. About 1,000,000,000 people

  d. About 1,000,000,000,000,000,000 people

Unit 1: Lesson 1 Test

Key Words

Choose the best answer. Circle the letter.

1. Scientists who study how early humans lived are _____.

   a. warriors

   b. farmers

   c. archaeologists

   d. hunter-gatherers

2. Glaciers covered much of the earth during the _____.

   a. Stone Age

   b. Ice Age

   c. Bronze Age

   d. time of Mesopotamia

3. Early humans were not farmers, they were _____.

   a. hunter-gatherers

   b. archaeologists

   c. warriors

   d. rulers

4. Growing crops and raising animals for food is _____.

   a. trade

   b. irrigation

   c. agriculture

   d. archaeology

Using Visuals

Look at the timeline. Choose the **true** statement. Circle the letter.

2,500,000 B.C.E.   **2,000,000 B.C.E.**   **10,000 B.C.E.**

Stone Age begins   Ice Age begins   Ice Age ends

5. **a.** The Ice Age lasted almost 10,000 years.

   b. The Ice Age lasted almost 500,000 years.

   c. The Ice Age lasted almost 2,000,000 years.

   d. The Ice Age lasted almost 2,500,000 years.

Name _____ Date _____

Choose the best answer. Circle the letter.

6. What happened in the Stone Age?

   a. Hunter-gathers made tools from stone.

   b. Hunter-gathers made weapons from stone.

   c. Hunter-gatherers learned how to make fire.

   d. All of the above.

7. Why did early farmers settle near large rivers?

   a. They used the rivers to irrigate their crops.

   b. They liked to swim in the rivers.

   c. There were no glaciers near rivers.

   d. There were many animals near rivers.

8. What happened in the Bronze Age?

   a. The earth was very cold and people adapted.

   b. The first people came to North America.

   c. People made a new metal and began trading.

   d. People learned how to make fire.

9. Where did an early civilization begin?

   a. Mesopotamia

   b. Babylon

   c. Assyria

   d. All of the above

10. Look at the picture of cuneiform below. Who created this first system of writing?

   a. The Babylonians

   b. The Sumerians

   c. The Phoenicians

   d. None of the above

11. Which alphabet is the basis of many languages, including English?

   a. The Sumerian alphabet

   b. The Phoenician alphabet

   c. The Babylonian alphabet

   d. The Assyrian alphabet

Writing

Write a paragraph in your notebook about early humans. Make sure your paragraph has a beginning, a middle, and an end.

Name _____ Date _____

Unit 1: Lesson 2 Test

Key Words

Choose the best answer. Circle the letter.

1. The ancient Egyptian civilization is _____.

   a. about 1,000 years old

   b. about 2,000 years old

   c. about 3,000 years old

   d. about 5,000 years old

2. Egyptian society had upper, middle, and lower _____.

   a. kingdoms

   b. classes

   c. rulers

   d. invaders

3. The rulers of ancient Egypt were called _____.

   a. pharaohs

   b. emperors

   c. mummies

   d. invaders

4. For the mummies of pharaohs, the Egyptians built large tombs called _____.

   a. coffins

   b. palaces

   c. pyramids

   d. temples

Using Visuals

Look at the timeline. Choose the **true** statement. Circle the letter.

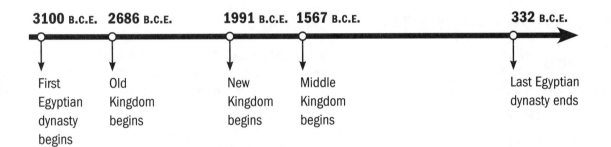

3100 B.C.E.   **2686** B.C.E.   **1991** B.C.E.   **1567** B.C.E.   **332** B.C.E.

First Egyptian dynasty begins   Old Kingdom begins   New Kingdom begins   Middle Kingdom begins   Last Egyptian dynasty ends

5. **a.** Egyptian dynasties ruled Egypt for about 1,567 years.

    b. Egyptian dynasties ruled Egypt for about 2,332 years.

    c. Egyptian dynasties ruled Egypt for about 2,768 years.

    d. Egyptian dynasties ruled Egypt for about 3,100 years.

Content

Choose the best answer. Circle the letter.

6. Who was the first woman to rule Egypt alone?

   a. Khufu

   b. Cyrus

   c. Darius

   d. Hatshepsut

7. Look at the picture. What is it?

   a. Nubian art

   b. Persian wall carvings

   c. Egyptian hieroglyphics

   d. Chinese writing with symbols and pictures

8. What land did Egypt rule for about 1,000 years?

   a. Nubia

   b. Persia

   c. China

   d. Persepolis

9. Which famous teachers did many Chinese follow?

   a. Qin and Zhou

   b. Confucius and Lao Tzu

   c. Khufu and Hatshepsut

   d. Cyrus and Darius

10. Why did the emperor Shi Huangdi build the Great Wall of China?

    a. He built it for a tomb.

    b. He built it for the gods.

    c. He built it to irrigate crops.

    d. He built it to keep his kingdom safe from invaders.

11. Who ruled over most of the Middle East?

    a. The ancient Nubians

    b. The ancient Egyptians

    c. The ancient Persians

    d. The ancient Chinese

Writing

Write a paragraph in your notebook about Egyptian mummies, pyramids, and pharaohs. Make sure your paragraph has a beginning, a middle, and an end.

Unit 1: Unit Test

Key Words

Choose the best answer. Circle the letter.

1. A scientist who looks for early tools, pottery, and bones is _____.

    a. a mummy

    b. a hunter-gatherer

    c. an archaeologist

    d. an invader

2. Look at the picture below. During the Stone Age, early humans were _____.

    a. traders

    b. farmers

    c. archaeologists

    d. hunter-gatherers

3. Farmers in Mesopotamia used irrigation to water their _____.

    a. classes

    b. crops

    c. glaciers

    d. archaeologists

4. The civilizations of Mesopotamia, Egypt, and Persia are _____.

    a. rulers

    b. invaders

    c. ancient

    d. hunter-gatherers

5. The pharaohs of Egypt and kings of Persia were _____.

    a. rulers

    b. invaders

    c. archaeologists

    d. hunter-gatherers

6. Slaves were at the lowest level of Egyptian society's _____.

    a. invaders

    b. classes

    c. rulers

    d. pyramids

Content

Choose the best answer. Circle the letter.

7. When did people first start using tools and weapons made of stone?

a. About 400,000 years ago, in Mesopotamia

b. About 700,000 years ago, in the Bronze Age

c. About 2,000,000 years ago, in the Ice Age

d. About 2,500,000 years ago, in the Stone Age

8. Where were the first cities about 4,000 years ago? Why?

a. They were near the ocean because of trade.

b. They were near glaciers because they covered the earth.

c. They were near rivers because farmers needed water.

d. They were in the mountains because it was cool.

9. Look at the pictures. When were these early tools made?

a. During the Stone Age

b. During the Ice Age

c. During the Bronze Age

d. During the Egyptian dynasties

10. What did people begin doing after these tools were invented?

a. They began hunting.

b. They began traveling and trading.

c. They began gathering.

d. They began using fire.

11. What happened in Mesopotamia?

a. The wheel was invented.

b. The first system of writing, cuneiform, was created.

c. The great civilizations of Babylon and Assyria began.

d. All of the above.

12. Which ancient civilization had an Old, Middle, and New Kingdom?

a. Babylon

b. Egypt

c. China

d. Persia

13. How were the pharaohs of Egypt buried?

    a. They were mummified.

    b. They were placed in three or four coffins.

    c. They were buried in tombs inside pyramids.

    d. All of the above.

14. Why was Hatshepsut famous?

    a. He built the largest pyramid in Egypt.

    b. She rebuilt many old temples.

    c. She was the first woman to rule Egypt alone.

    d. Both b and c.

15. Look at the picture below. Who built this wall to keep invaders out?

    a. Darius, the king of Persia

    b. Khufu, the Egyptian pharaoh

    c. Shi Huangdi, the Chinese emperor

    d. Hatshepsut, the Egyptian pharaoh

16. Where was the Persian civilization located?

    a. In modern-day Iran

    b. In modern-day Egypt

    c. In modern-day China

    d. In modern-day Lebanon

Reading Strategies

Choose the best answer. Circle the letter.

17. What do you look at to **preview**?

    a. The headings

    b. The pictures and captions

    c. The vocabulary words and their meanings

    d. All of the above

18. What do you do when you **predict**?

    a. Look at a page before you read.

    b. Think about your own life.

    c. Guess what will happen next.

    d. Write answers to all the questions.

Using Visuals

Look at the timeline. Choose the best answer. Circle the letter.

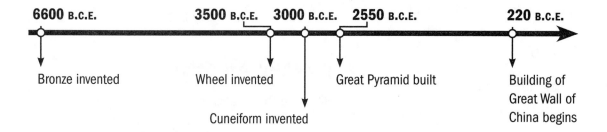

6600 B.C.E.   **3500** B.C.E.   **3000** B.C.E.   **2550** B.C.E.   **220** B.C.E.

Bronze invented   Wheel invented   Great Pyramid built   Building of Great Wall of China begins

Cuneiform invented

19. What's the first event on the timeline?

   a. Bronze was invented.

   b. The building of the Great Wall of China began.

   c. The wheel was invented.

   d. Cuneiform was invented.

20. What happened in 3500 B.C.E.?

   a. Bronze was invented.

   b. The wheel was invented.

   c. Cuneiform was invented.

   d. The Great Pyramid was built.

21. Which two events have about 2,000 years between them?

   a. The invention of bronze and the invention of the wheel.

   b. The invention of the wheel and the building of the Great Pyramid.

   c. The creation of cuneiform and the building of the Great Wall of China.

   d. The building of the Great Pyramid and the building of the Great Wall of China.

Writing

Write about an early civilization in your notebook. Choose the Stone Age, the Ice Age, the Bronze Age, Mesopotamia, Egypt, Nubia, China, or Persia. Make sure your paragraph has a beginning, a middle, and an end.

Unit 2: Lesson 1 Test

Key Words

Choose the best answer. Circle the letter.

1. The Greeks made beautiful _____.

   a. marble sculptures

   b. clay pottery

   c. monuments and amphitheaters

   d. All of the above

2. The Parthenon is a large temple, or _____.

   a. sculpture

   b. monument

   c. amphitheater

   d. marketplace

3. The ancient Greeks liked to watch dramas in _____.

   a. sculptures

   b. monuments

   c. amphitheaters

   d. marketplaces

4. The Olympic Games began as a _____.

   a. drama

   b. festival

   c. sculpture

   d. All of the above

Using Visuals

Look at the map and key. Choose the best answer. Circle the letter.

5. What is Marathon?

   a. A sea

   b. A city

   c. A river

   d. A mountain

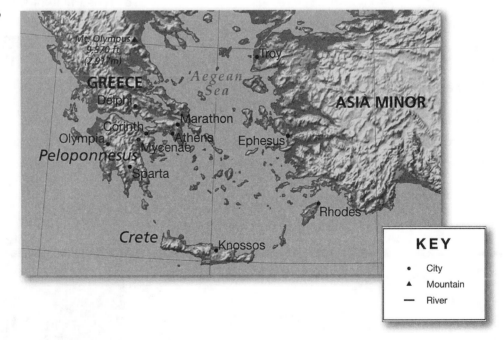

Name _____   Date _____

Content

Choose the best answer. Circle the letter.

6. Who was the ruler of Egypt when the Romans conquered it?

   a. King Khufu

   b. Queen Cleopatra

   c. Queen Hatshepsut

   d. King Tutankhamen

7. What important idea did the Greeks create?

   a. Cities

   b. Slavery

   c. Democracy

   d. Agriculture

8. Who was allowed to vote in Athens?

   a. Men

   b. Women

   c. Slaves

   d. All of the above

9. What Greek city-state fought Athens in the Peloponnesian War?

   a. Sparta

   b. Marathon

   c. Macedonia

   d. Persia

10. Who were Socrates and Plato?

   a. They were actors.

   b. They were philosophers.

   c. They were rulers of Greece.

   d. They were famous commanders.

11. Look at the picture below. Who became the ruler of most of the ancient world?

   a. Plato

   b. Socrates

   c. Alexander the Great

   d. King Philip of Macedonia

Writing

Write a paragraph in your notebook about life during the Golden Age of Greece. Write about the government, people, entertainment, and arts. Make sure your paragraph has a beginning, a middle, and an end.

Unit 2: Lesson 2 Test

Key Words

Choose the best answer. Circle the letter.

1. The senate advised the leaders of Rome's _____.

   a. villas

   b. Barbarians

   c. government

   d. All of the above

2. The Romans built structures such as _____.

   a. aqueducts

   b. the Colosseum

   c. Hadrian's Villa

   d. All of the above

3. Many gladiator fights were held at the _____.

   a. Colosseum

   b. aqueduct

   c. senate

   d. prison

4. To bring water to the cities, the Romans built _____.

   a. prisons

   b. aqueducts

   c. villas

   d. republics

Using Visuals

Look at the map of Constantinople and the compass rose. Choose the best answer. Circle the letter.

5. Where is the Forum of Arcadius?

   a. South of the palace

   b. East of the aqueduct

   c. West of the Forum Bovi

   d. North of the Golden Horn

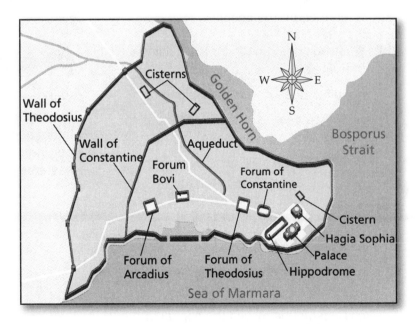

Content

Choose the best answer. Circle the letter.

6. Look at the picture. Who was Julius Caesar?

   a. He made himself dictator of Rome and was assassinated.

   b. He was the first emperor of Rome.

   c. He was one of the best emperors of Rome.

   d. He was the last emperor of Rome.

7. How many years did emperors rule Rome?

   a. For 50 years

   b. For 100 years

   c. For 500 years

   d. For 1,500 years

8. Which was **not** a reason for Rome's decline?

   a. It was too large to defend.

   b. It was invaded by Greece.

   c. The government didn't have enough money to pay its soldiers.

   d. The emperors were corrupt and didn't care about the people.

9. What was one reason for the decline of Rome?

   a. Julius Caesar was assassinated.

   b. The emperors were corrupt and didn't care about the people.

   c. Rome had a civil war.

   d. Cleopatra conquered Rome.

10. How did the Byzantine Empire begin?

    a. Rulers from Greece began a new empire.

    b. Barbarians conquered Rome and created a new empire.

    c. Constantine moved the capital of the Roman Empire to Byzantium.

    d. All of the above.

11. How far did the Muslim Empire spread?

    a. From Rome to Greece

    b. From Greece to Persia

    c. From Constantinople to China

    d. From Baghdad to Persia, North Africa, and present-day Spain

Writing

Write a paragraph in your notebook about the history of the Roman Empire. Include information about Caesar, the emperors, and the decline of the empire. Make sure your paragraph has a beginning, a middle, and an end.

Name _____ Date _____

Unit 2: Unit Test

Key Words

Choose the best answer. Circle the letter.

1. Greeks used marble to make beautiful
_____.

   a. pottery

   b. sculptures

   c. festivals

   d. aqueducts

2. Greeks watched both sad and funny dramas
in the _____.

   a. Colosseum

   b. amphitheaters

   c. monuments

   d. prisons

3. For entertainment, Romans watched
gladiators in _____.

   a. prisons

   b. the government

   c. Hadrian's Villa

   d. the Colosseum

4. The Roman republic was a type of _____.

   a. villa

   b. criminal

   c. monument

   d. government

5. Look at the picture below. These are Roman
_____.

   a. monuments

   b. prisons

   c. aqueducts

   d. sculptures

6. The group that made laws in Rome was
_____.

   a. the senate

   b. the *agora*

   c. the city-state

   d. the philosophers

Content

Choose the best answer. Circle the letter.

7. Why did Cleopatra poison herself?

   a. A snake bit her in the Parthenon.

   b. King Tutankhamen died at the age of 18.

   c. Alexander the Great conquered Egypt.

   d. Roman soldiers invaded her city.

8. What kind of government did Athens have?

   a. A republic

   b. A democracy

   c. A senate

   d. A king

9. Who were two famous Greek philosophers?

   a. Cato and Cicero

   b. Socrates and Plato

   c. Philip and Alexander

   d. Carter and Carnarvon

10. Look at the picture. Who are these people? Who did they fight?

    a. They are Spartan soldiers. Sparta fought Athens.

    b. They are Spartan soldiers. Sparta fought Macedonia.

    c. They are Macedonian soldiers. Macedonia fought Egypt.

    d. They are Macedonian soldiers. Macedonia fought Rome.

11. What did Alexander the Great do?

    a. He conquered many nations.

    b. He built many new cities.

    c. He became the ruler of most of the ancient world.

    d. All of the above.

12. Which statement is **not** true?

    a. Cato was the last Roman emperor.

    b. Octavian was the first Roman emperor.

    c. Hadrian was one of the best Roman emperors.

    d. Julius Caesar was a dictator.

13. What happened when the Roman government didn't pay its soldiers?

    a. The soldiers got jobs as gladiators.

    b. The soldiers assassinated Julius Caesar.

    c. The Roman empire declined and Barbarians conquered Rome.

    d. All of the above.

14. What was Justinian's Code?

    a. An important book that Byzantine scholars copied

    b. A fair system of laws established by a Byzantine emperor

    c. A type of government established by the emperor Hadrian

    d. A kind of mathematics introduced during the Byzantine Empire's Golden Age

15. What is a Golden Age?

    a. A time when gold is discovered

    b. A time when an empire is very large

    c. A time when people have a lot of money

    d. A time when life is very good

16. Look at the picture. What is this?

    a. The Colosseum in Rome

    b. Hadrian's Villa in Tivoli

    c. The Hagia Sophia in Constantinople

    d. The Abbasid Palace in Baghdad

Reading Strategies

Choose the best answer. Circle the letter.

17. What do you when you **visualize**?

    a. Create a picture in your mind.

    b. Guess what will happen next.

    c. Look carefully at the pictures on the page.

    d. All of the above.

18. What questions do you ask yourself when you **ask questions**?

    a. Do I already know something about this?

    b. What do I think about this?

    c. What do I remember about what I read?

    d. All of the above.

Name _____ Date _____

Using Visuals

Look at the map of the Roman Empire. Use the map and key to choose the best answer. Circle the letter.

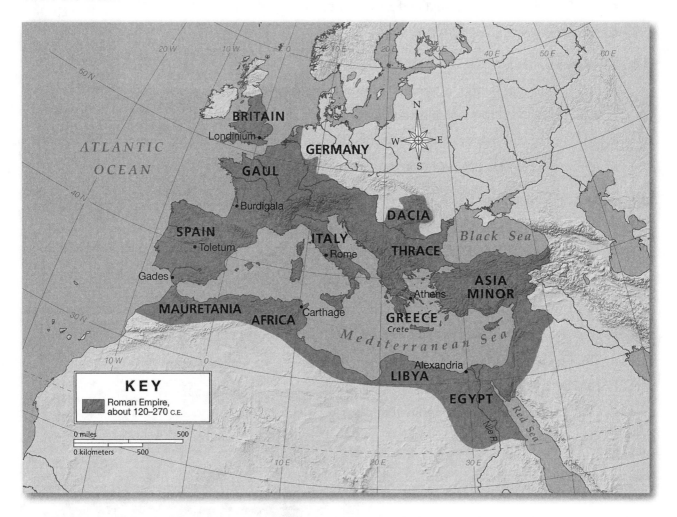

KEY

Roman Empire, about 120–270 C.E.

0 miles 500
0 kilometers 500

19. Which country was not part of the Roman Empire at this time?

a. Spain

b. Britain

c. Germany

d. Egypt

20. Which country is east of Rome?

a. Spain

b. Asia Minor

c. Mauretania

d. Britain

21. Which direction is Alexandria from Athens?

a. North

b. East

c. South

d. West

Writing

Write a paragraph in your notebook comparing life in ancient Greece and Rome to life today. How was it similar? How was it different? Make sure your paragraph has a beginning, a middle, and an end.

Name _____ Date _____

Unit 3: Lesson 1 Test

Key Words

Choose the best answer. Circle the letter.

1. The lowest class in Europe during the Middle Ages was the serfs, or _____.

   a. peasants

   b. knights

   c. nobles

   d. pastures

2. The system where a serf served a lord and a lord served the king is _____.

   a. vassals

   b. knights

   c. expedition

   d. feudalism

3. The soldiers who served the lords and wore armor were called _____.

   a. peasants

   b. manors

   c. knights

   d. nobles

4. European Christians fought Muslim Turks for control of Jerusalem in wars called the _____.

   a. Black Death

   b. cathedrals

   c. Crusades

   d. feudalism

Using Visuals

Look at the map. What is the longitude and latitude of Jerusalem? Circle the letter of the best answer.

5. **a.** 32°E longitude, 35°N latitude

   b. 35°E longitude, 32°N latitude

   c. 42°E longitude, 45°N latitude

   d. 45°E longitude, 42°N latitude

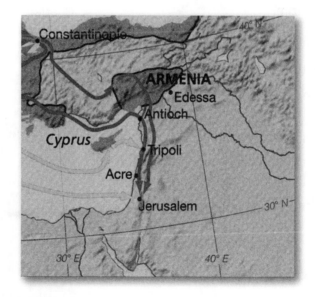

Content

Choose the best answer. Circle the letter.

6. When were the Middle Ages?

   a. From about 500 to 700

   b. From about 500 to 1000

   c. From about 500 to 1500

   d. From about 500 to 1800

7. What happened to Christianity as the Byzantine Empire lost power?

   a. It spread across the Arabian Peninsula, North Africa, and Spain.

   b. It divided into the Eastern Orthodox Church and the Roman Catholic Church.

   c. It became the main religion in Bihar and Bengal, India.

   d. All of the above.

8. Whose teachings became the basis of Islam?

   a. Mecca

   b. Muhammad

   c. Medina

   d. Al-Khawarizimi

9. Look at the picture. Who was Charlemagne?

   a. He was the King of the Pala dynasty.

   b. He was a Pope who became an emperor in 800.

   c. He was a Viking who sailed the North Sea and attacked Europe.

   d. He was a ruler who united Europe for the first time since the Roman Empire.

10. What happened after Charlemagne died?

   a. Europe was again divided into many small kingdoms.

   b. The Vikings attacked Europe for the next 300 years.

   c. His empire declined and feudalism developed.

   d. All of the above.

11. Which statement is **not** a reason many towns grew into cities by about 1300?

   a. Europe was unified under the King of the Franks.

   b. Trade grew with other countries.

   c. People moved near trade routes.

   d. Manors couldn't feed everyone who lived on them.

Writing

Write a paragraph in your notebook about Europe in the Middle Ages. Include Charlemagne, feudalism, and the Crusades. Make sure your paragraph has a beginning, a middle, and an end.

Name _____   Date _____

Unit 3: Lesson 2 Test

Key Words

Choose the best answer. Circle the letter.

1. To connect two rivers, the Chinese built a 1,000-mile long _____.

  a. cliff

  b. canal

  c. road

  d. mound

2. The Chinese invented gunpowder and the compass during the Tang and Song _____.

  a. clans

  b. daimyo

  c. samurai

  d. dynasties

3. Marco Polo's *The Book of Travels* helped increase _____.

  a. trade

  b. canals

  c. martial arts

  d. small wars

4. Between 1000 and 1867 in Japan, there were skilled warriors called _____.

  a. kendo

  b. cliff dwellers

  c. samurai

  d. Mongols

Using Visuals

Look at the map. Estimate the distance across South America at its widest point. Circle the letter of the best answer.

5. a. It's about 1,500 miles across.

  b. It's about 2,000 miles across.

  c. It's about 3,000 miles across.

  d. It's about 4,000 miles across.

Content

Choose the best answer. Circle the letter.

6. How long did the Tang dynasty rule China?

   a. For 50 years

   b. For 200 years

   c. For 300 years

   d. For 500 years

7. Who conquered Russia, Eastern Europe, Korea, and China?

   a. Marco Polo

   b. Genghis Kahn and the Mongols

   c. Yoritomo and his son

   d. The Minamoto clan

8. Look at the picture below. What does it show?

   a. Tang Taizong visiting Europeans in his palace.

   b. Minamoto Yoritomo visiting a samurai warrior.

   c. Marco Polo visiting Kublai Khan.

   d. Marco Polo visiting Ghengis Khan.

9. What was the trade route between China and Europe called?

   a. The Silk Road

   b. The Jade Road

   c. The Gunpowder Road

   d. The Porcelain Road

10. Which statement is **not** true about Japan during the shogun system?

   a. A shogun ruled Japan.

   b. Samurai warriors were loyal to a powerful warlord called a *daimyo*.

   c. Samurai warriors were members of clans.

   d. A samurai warrior had to surrender to an enemy.

11. What are three ancient civilizations of the Americas?

   a. The Mayas, the Aztecs, and the Anasazi

   b. The Mayas, the Haab, and the Aztecs

   c. The Tzolkin, the Haab, and the Anasazi

   d. The Haab, the Anasazi, and the Mayas

Writing

Write a paragraph in your notebook about Marco Polo and China. Make sure your paragraph has a beginning, a middle, and an end.

Unit 3: Unit Test

Key Words

Choose the best answer. Circle the letter.

1. In the Middle Ages, both Europe and Japan had a system of government called _____.

   a. feudalism

   b. Christianity

   c. a crusade

   d. a republic

2. Workers on a lord's manor were poor serfs, or _____.

   a. nobles

   b. princes

   c. peasants

   d. samurai

3. Look at the picture below. It shows _____.

   a. a manor

   b. a cathedral

   c. a mound

   d. a cliff dwelling

4. Muslims and Christians fought to control Jerusalem in the _____.

   a. cathedrals

   b. plague

   c. dynasties

   d. Crusades

5. The Chinese built a 1,000-mile canal during the Tang _____.

   a. shogun

   b. dynasty

   c. manor

   d. daimyo

6. The trade route between China and Europe was named after _____.

   a. Marco Polo

   b. a knight

   c. silk

   d. porcelain

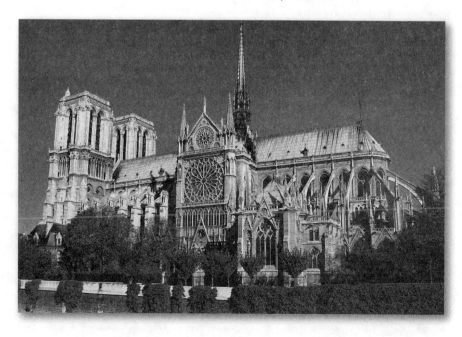

Content

Choose the best answer. Circle the letter.

7. Who united Europe for the first time since the Roman Empire?

   a. The emperor of Constantinople

   b. The pope of the Roman Catholic Church

   c. The King of the Franks, Charlemagne

   d. The Italian trader, Marco Polo

8. Why did Europe divide into small kingdoms again after this?

   a. The government declined and Vikings attacked.

   b. The Mongols invaded Europe and many people died.

   c. The Bubonic plague, or Black Death, killed many people.

   d. The Church divided into Roman Catholic and Eastern Orthodox.

9. Which statement is **not** true about feudalism in Europe?

   a. Lords, vassals, and serfs lived on manors.

   b. Serfs farmed and gave most of the harvest to the lord.

   c. Most people were lords or knights.

   d. Armies were made up of knights.

10. What grew after the Crusades?

   a. Trade, cities, and technology

   b. Small battles between clans

   c. Viking attacks from northern Europe

   d. Fights between Christians and Muslims

11. Look at the picture below. What killed 25 million people in 1340?

   a. The Crusades

   b. The Bubonic plague, or Black Death

   c. The Mongols invaded Europe

   d. None of the above

12. What did the Chinese invent while the Song and Tang dynasties ruled?

   a. The compass

   b. Gunpowder

   c. Feudalism

   d. Both a and b.

13. Who was Genghis Khan?

    a. He invented gunpowder.

    b. He traded with Europe and met Marco Polo.

    c. He conquered Russia, Eastern Europe, Korea, and northern China.

    d. He built a canal to connect the Huang and Chiang rivers.

14. Why was Marco Polo's book about China important?

    a. Europeans learned about China.

    b. It was the first book printed on the Chinese printing press.

    c. Trade increased between China and Europe.

    d. Both a and c.

15. Look at the picture. Who is it?

    a. The leader of the Pala dynasty

    b. The shogun Minamoto Yoritomo

    c. The warrior Wulfstan

    d. A Muslim Turk

16. Who were the samurai?

    a. The "knights" of Japan

    b. The "peasants" of Japan

    c. The "lords" of Japan

    d. The "kings" of Japan

Reading Strategies

Choose the best answer. Circle the letter.

17. What do you do when you **monitor comprehension**?

    a. Check your understanding as you read.

    b. After you read, tell yourself what the text means.

    c. Look for clues on the page to help you understand.

    d. All of the above.

18. What do you do to **understand chronological order**?

    a. Look at the headings, pictures, and captions.

    b. Ask yourself, Did I understand this?

    c. Create a picture in your mind.

    d. Look for dates and words like *first, then,* and *finally.*

Using Visuals

Look at the map of China during the Tang and Song dynasties. Choose the best answer. Circle the letter.

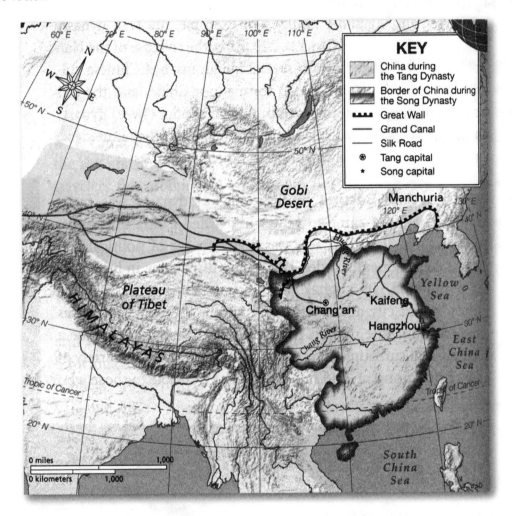

KEY

China during the Tang Dynasty

Border of China during the Song Dynasty

Great Wall

Grand Canal

Silk Road

⊛ Tang capital

★ Song capital

19. Which line of latitude crosses both the Great Wall of China and the Silk Road?

a. 30°N

b. 40°N

c. 100°E

d. 110°E

20. What city is closest to 120°E longitude, 30°N latitude?

a. Hangzhou

b. Kaifeng

c. Chang'an

d. None of the above

21. About how many miles apart are Chang'an and Hongzhou?

a. About 100 miles

b. About 200 miles

c. About 600 miles

d. About 1,500 miles

Writing

Write a paragraph in your notebook about feudalism in either Europe or Japan. Include your opinion of feudalism. Make sure your paragraph has a beginning, a middle, and an end.

Unit 4: Lesson 1 Test

Key Words

Choose the best answer. Circle the letter.

1. During the Renaissance, Lorenzo de Medici got things from all over the world from _____.

   a. clergy

   b. explorers

   c. Lutherans

   d. humanists

2. Johannes Gutenberg invented the printing press in Europe with _____.

   a. clergy

   b. manuscripts

   c. movable type

   d. All of the above

3. Before the printing press, books were handwritten _____.

   a. deeds

   b. patrons

   c. reforms

   d. manuscripts

4. Martin Luther made a list of protests against the teachings of the Roman Catholic _____.

   a. Jesuits

   b. clergy

   c. explorers

   d. humanists

Using Visuals

Look at the map. Choose the **true** statement about the Iberian Peninsula. Circle the letter of the answer.

5. **a.** There are seven rivers.

   b. There are no mountains.

   c. Most of the land is below sea level.

   d. The elevation is mostly 1,600–6,500 feet.

KEY

ELEVATION

Feet		Meters
More than 13,000		More than 3,960
6,500–13,000		1,980–3,960
1,600–6,500		480–1,980
650–1,600		200–480
0–650		0–200
Below sea level		Below sea level

Content

Choose the best answer. Circle the letter.

6. Which statement is **not** true about the Crusades?

   a. It lasted for 200 years.

   b. Many people were killed.

   c. The Crusaders were Muslim Turks.

   d. Arabs and Europeans learned about each other.

7. What does the word *renaissance* mean? How long did the period last?

   a. Renaissance means revival or rebirth. It lasted from the 1300s through the 1600s.

   b. Renaissance means trade. It lasted from the 1400s through the 1700s.

   c. Renaissance means art. It lasted from the 1200s through the 1800s.

   d. Renaissance means exploration. It lasted from the 1100s through the 1300s.

8. Which statement is **not** true about the Renaissance?

   a. It began in Germany and spread all over Europe.

   b. Humanists studied the classics of Greece and Rome.

   c. It was a time of important inventions, art, and literature.

   d. Artists used perspective and proportion.

9. Look at the picture. Who painted it?

   a. Michelangelo

   b. Francesco Petrarch

   c. Leonardo da Vinci

   d. Lorenzo de Medici

10. What new idea did the artist use in this painting?

   a. Colored paint

   b. Shadow and light

   c. The perspective of the room

   d. Texts of the ancient Greeks

11. What did Martin Luther do during the Reformation?

   a. He helped create the first Protestant Church.

   b. He helped force the Roman Catholic Church to make reforms.

   c. He led a movement called Lutheranism.

   d. All of the above.

Writing

Write a paragraph in your notebook about the Italian Renaissance. Include your opinion of this period. Make sure your paragraph has a beginning, a middle, and an end.

Name _____ Date _____

Unit 4: Lesson 2 Test

Key Words

Choose the best answer. Circle the letter.

1. Prince Henry of Portugal made voyages to Africa and became an expert on _____.

   a. diseases

   b. conquering

   c. navigation

   d. indigenous peoples

2. Christopher Columbus wanted to sail to India and thought the Atlantic Ocean was the most direct _____.

   a. route

   b. circulation

   c. continent

   d. navigation

3. Columbus landed in present-day Bahamas and met the Tainos, the _____.

   a. people of India

   b. cartographers

   c. indigenous people

   d. explorers

4. The islands became a Spanish colony and many Tainos died of European _____.

   a. wars

   b. diseases

   c. cartographers

   d. navigation

Using Visuals

Look at the map. What kind of map is it? Circle the letter of the best answer.

5. **a.** A physical map

   b. A political map

   c. A national map

   d. A navigational map

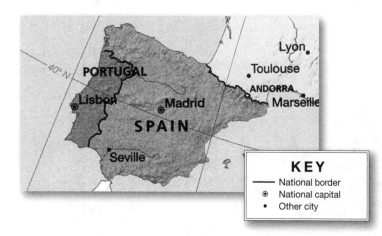

Name _____ Date _____

Content

Choose the best answer. Circle the letter.

6. Which Europeans started the African slave trade?

   a. The Italians

   b. The Spanish

   c. The French

   d. The Portuguese

7. Who gave Columbus money for three ships in 1492?

   a. Queen Isabella of Spain

   b. Henry the Navigator

   c. King Ferdinand of Portugal

   d. Queen Isabella of Italy

8. Look at the picture below. What does it show?

   a. Machu Picchu, built by the Incas in about 1470

   b. Tenochtitlán, the center of the Aztec Empire

   c. The African Kingdom of Mali, a center for learning

   d. Cuzco, built by the Incas in Peru

9. Which statement is **not** true about this city?

   a. It was ruled by an emperor named Moctezuma.

   b. A Spanish explorer named Hernán Cortés conquered it in 1521.

   c. There were no warriors in the city, so it was easily conquered.

   d. Mexico City was later built on top of it.

10. Who was Francisco Pizarro?

   a. An Italian explorer who conquered the Aztecs and stole their treasures

   b. A Spanish explorer who conquered the Aztecs and stole their treasures

   c. A Portuguese explorer who conquered the Incas and stole their treasures

   d. A Spanish explorer who conquered the Incas and stole their treasures

11. What did Galileo Galilei do during the Enlightenment?

   a. He defined the idea of gravity.

   b. He discovered the basics of modern chemistry.

   c. He observed that the earth revolved around the sun.

   d. He figured out how the heart and circulation of the blood works.

Writing

Write a paragraph in your notebook about European explorers in the Americas. Make sure your paragraph has a beginning, a middle, and an end.

Unit 4: Unit Test

Key Words

Choose the best answer. Circle the letter.

1. Look at the picture below. It shows Gutenberg's _____.

   a. navigation tools

   b. cartographers with manuscripts

   c. telescope that magnified objects

   d. printing press with movable type

2. Before this, Europeans used handwritten _____.

   a. telescopes

   b. cartographers

   c. manuscripts

   d. perspective drawings

3. Martin Luther helped create the first Protestant Church with his list of _____.

   a. protests

   b. routes

   c. clergy

   d. deeds

4. Prince Henry of Portugal used maps and navigation tools to go on _____.

   a. explorers

   b. voyages

   c. helicopters

   d. wars

5. Spanish explorers crossed the Atlantic and conquered the kingdoms of _____.

   a. the reformed clergy

   b. the Silk Road

   c. indigenous peoples

   d. Portuguese colonies

6. Many Incas and Aztecs died from smallpox and other European _____.

   a. diseases

   b. protests

   c. reforms

   d. inventions

Name _____ Date _____

Choose the best answer. Circle the letter.

7. What began in Italy in the 1300s and continued to the 1600s?

    a. The Middle Ages, a time of cathedrals and feudalism

    b. The Crusades, a battle for control of Jerusalem

    c. The Renaissance, or rebirth of the ideas, literature, and art of ancient Greece and Rome

    d. The Enlightenment, a period of new discoveries in science

8. What did the humanists study?

    a. They studied astronomy and mathematics.

    b. They studied the trade route called the Silk Road.

    c. They studied how the heart and circulation of blood works.

    d. They studied the ideas, literature, and art of ancient Greece and Rome.

9. Look at the picture. What new ideas did the artist use?

    a. Proportion

    b. Perspective

    c. Light and shadow

    d. All of the above

10. Who was a ruler and patron of the arts in Florence?

    a. Lorenzo de Medici

    b. Francesco Petrarch

    c. Leonardo da Vinci

    d. Michelangelo

11. What happened during the Reformation in the 1500s?

    a. Scientists made many important discoveries.

    b. Jesuit clergy helped reform the Lutheran Church.

    c. Jesuit clergy helped reform the Roman Catholic Church.

    d. All of the above.

12. What were the Portuguese the first to do?

    a. Sail around Africa's Cape of Good Hope to India

    b. Sail to parts of Africa that Europeans had never been to before

    c. Bring people from Africa to be sold as slaves

    d. All of the above

13. How did Columbus discover the Americas?

    a. The Italian government wanted to explore the Atlantic.

    b. King Ferdinand and Queen Isabella of Spain wanted gold from the new lands.

    c. Queen Isabella gave him money to sail across the Atlantic to India.

    d. He sailed around Africa's Cape of Good Hope and discovered the Bahamas.

14. Look at the picture. What is it?

    a. The Incan city of Machu Picchu in Peru

    b. The Incan city of Cuzco in Peru

    c. The Aztec city of Tenochtitlán in Mexico

    d. The African kingdom of Mali

15. Which Spanish explorers conquered the Aztecs and the Incas?

    a. Vasco da Gama and Francisco Pizarro

    b. Hernán Cortés and Francisco Pizarro

    c. Christopher Columbus and Hernán Cortés

    d. Vasco da Gama and Christopher Columbus

16. What happened during the Enlightenment of the 1600s?

    a. Galileo Galilei discovered the earth revolved around the sun.

    b. Isaac Newton defined the ideas of gravity.

    c. William Harvey discovered how the heart works.

    d. All of the above.

Reading Strategies

Choose the best answer. Circle the letter.

17. What do you do when you **reread**?

    a. After you read, tell yourself what the text means.

    b. Read a text again to understand the main idea and some details.

    c. Write notes about the topic as you read.

    d. All of the above.

18. What do you do when you **use selective attention**?

    a. Look for words like *in, at, on,* and *by* in the text.

    b. Take time to read each word and sentence very carefully.

    c. Look for key words to answer a question or write about a topic.

    d. All of the above.

Name _____ Date _____

Using Visuals

Look at the maps below. Choose the best answer. Circle the letter.

19. Which map shows the names of countries and cities?

    a. The political map on the right

    b. The political map on the left

    c. The physical map on the right

    d. The physical map on the left

20. Which map shows the names of mountains and peninsulas?

    a. The political map on the right

    b. The political map on the left

    c. The physical map on the right

    d. The physical map on the left

21. What's a mountain range that's located in both the United States and Canada?

    a. Mount McKinley

    b. The Sierra Madres

    c. The Rocky Mountains

    d. The Appalachian Mountains

Writing

Write a paragraph in your notebook about one of the major periods after the Middle Ages: the Renaissance, the Reformation, the voyages of exploration, or the Enlightenment. Briefly describe the period and why it was important. Make sure your paragraph has a beginning, a middle, and an end.

Unit 5: Lesson 1 Test

Key Words

Choose the best answer. Circle the letter.

1. In 1607 in Virginia, English settlers formed the Jamestown _____.

    a. colony

    b. territory

    c. fields

    d. city

2. The settlers who had to work for 4–7 years without pay were _____.

    a. slaves

    b. carpenters

    c. blacksmiths

    d. indentured servants

3. In the South, slaves worked to grow cotton, tobacco, and rice on large _____.

    a. tribes

    b. territories

    c. plantations

    d. slave ships

4. In the French and Indian War, the British and French fought over _____.

    a. slavery

    b. territory

    c. religious freedom

    d. the Jamestown colony

Using Visuals

Look at the chart. What animals did Columbus bring back to Europe? Circle the letter of the answer.

5. a. Horses and cows

    b. Sheep and pigs

    c. Turkeys

    d. Both a and b.

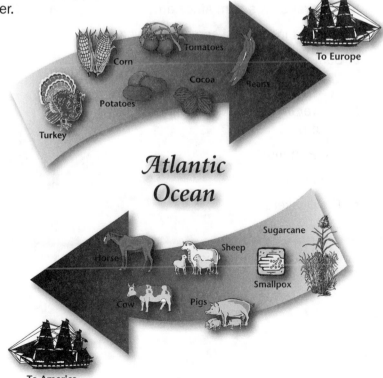

Content

Choose the best answer. Circle the letter.

6. What was **not** a reason people came to the colonies?

    a. They wanted to own land.

    b. They wanted religious freedom.

    c. They came to take gold from the Native Americans.

    d. They came to work for other people as slaves or servants.

7. What happened during the first winter in Jamestown?

    a. Many people got sick and died.

    b. Jamestown started its own government.

    c. The Jamestown government made laws.

    d. The settlers celebrated the first Thanksgiving.

8. What happened the same year Jamestown started its own government?

    a. The French and Indian War started.

    b. The first slaves from Africa arrived.

    c. The first indentured servants arrived.

    d. Both a and b.

9. Look at the picture. Who came on the *Mayflower* in 1620 and named their colony Plymouth?

    a. The Pilgrims

    b. The Puritans

    c. The Quakers

    d. All of the above

10. Which settlers came to America because they wanted religious freedom?

    a. The Pilgrims

    b. The Puritans

    c. The Quakers

    d. All of the above

11. What did African slaves do in the southern colonies?

    a. They worked in the fields.

    b. They were blacksmiths and carpenters.

    c. They were servants, cooks, and housekeepers.

    d. All of the above.

Writing

Write a paragraph in your notebook about southern plantations. Include your opinion. Make sure your paragraph has a beginning, a middle, and an end.

Unit 5: Lesson 2 Test

Key Words

Choose the best answer. Circle the letter.

1. When they bought molasses, newspapers, and tea, colonists had to pay Britain a _____.

   a. tax

   b. treaty

   c. revolt

   d. boycott

2. In Philadelphia, representatives from twelve colonies decided to _____.

   a. revolt

   b. obey

   c. tax

   d. punish

3. After the War for Independence, Britain and the colonies signed a _____.

   a. tax

   b. revolt

   c. treaty

   d. constitution

4. Later, representatives wrote the U.S. Constitution, an important _____.

   a. treaty

   b. document

   c. declaration

   d. boycott

Using Visuals

Look at the cause and effect chart. Why did the colonists boycott British goods? Circle the letter of the best answer.

5. **a.** Because of the tax laws

   b. Because they were angry

   c. Because goods were more expensive

   d. All of the above

Cause	Effect
British goods became more expensive. The colonists were angry because they thought the tax laws were unfair.	The colonists decided to boycott British good.

Content

Choose the best answer. Circle the letter.

6. Look at the picture. Which statement is **not** true about the Boston Tea Party?

   a. It was a protest against British taxes.

   b. Colonists threw tea into the water.

   c. Colonists used fire to destroy the ships.

   d. Colonists dressed up as Native Americans.

7. How did the British punish the colonists?

   a. They closed Boston Harbor.

   b. They made the colonists feed the British soldiers.

   c. They made the colonists house the British soldiers.

   d. All of the above.

8. What happened when British troops marched on Lexington and Concord to take colonists' guns in 1775?

   a. The boycott of British goods began.

   b. They signed the Treaty of Paris.

   c. The War for Independence began.

   d. The British army lost and surrendered.

9. What document did Jefferson write about liberty, equality, and justice in 1776?

   a. The Treaty of Paris

   b. The Declaration of Independence

   c. The United States Constitution

   d. The Intolerable Acts

10. Which statement is **not** true about George Washington?

   a. He led the colonial army in many battles.

   b. He became the first president of the United States.

   c. He trapped the British at Yorktown and they surrendered.

   d. He was an architect and helped create the U.S. money system.

11. What is the U.S. Constitution?

   a. A plan for government that united the states

   b. An explanation of why the colonists wanted to be independent from Britain

   c. A treaty that ended the War for Independence

   d. An important document signed on July 4, 1776

Writing

Write a paragraph in your notebook about the reasons the colonists wanted to be independent from Britain. Make sure your paragraph has a beginning, a middle, and an end.

Name _____ Date _____

Unit 5: Unit Test

Key Words

Choose the best answer. Circle the letter.

1. The first lasting English settlement in North America was _____.

   a. the Mayflower

   b. Plymouth Plantation

   c. the Jamestown colony

   d. territory west of the Appalachian Mountains

2. Thousands of English settlers came as _____.

   a. slaves

   b. minutemen

   c. representatives

   d. indentured servants

3. Look at the picture below. It shows _____.

   a. settlers in a colony

   b. slaves on a plantation

   c. indentured servants in a field

   d. Native Americans in a territory

4. The Boston Tea Party of 1773 was a protest against _____.

   a. British taxes

   b. a British treaty

   c. independence

   d. American representatives

5. After the Treaty of Paris was signed, colonists had _____.

   a. a tax revolt

   b. independence

   c. a boycott of British goods

   d. the first African slaves

6. George Washington and Thomas Jefferson were early colonial _____.

   a. settlers

   b. tax collectors

   c. representatives

   d. indentured servants

Content

Choose the best answer. Circle the letter.

7. Which statement is **not** true about Jamestown?

   a. Jamestown was near the Atlantic Ocean.

   b. Life was very easy and relaxed in Jamestown.

   c. It started its own government in 1619 and made laws.

   d. Many people died during the first winter in Jamestown.

8. Who were the Puritans and the Pilgrims?

   a. They owned large plantations in the southern colonies.

   b. They were the first English people to settle in Jamestown.

   c. They were religious groups who spoke out against slavery and prisons.

   d. They were English people who settled in Massachusetts to have religious freedom.

9. What was the French and Indian War?

   a. The British fought the Native Americans for the Appalachian Mountains.

   b. The French fought the Native Americans for the Appalachian Mountains.

   c. The British fought the French for territory west of the Appalachian Mountains. Some Native American tribes fought on both sides.

   d. Both a and b.

10. Why did Britain decide to tax the colonists?

   a. To help pay for the French and Indian War

   b. To punish them for the Boston Tea Party

   c. Tea and molasses were difficult to find

   d. All of the above

11. Look at the picture above. What does it show?

   a. The Boston Tea Party

   b. A slave ship arriving in North America

   c. Colonists arriving in Jamestown

   d. The *Mayflower* arriving in Plymouth

12. Why did the colonists fight the War for Independence?

   a. The colonists thought the British would never give them freedom.

   b. The British told the colonists to house and feed British troops.

   c. British troops wanted to take weapons away from the colonists.

   d. All of the above.

13. How did the War for Independence end?

    a. About 250 British were killed in Lexington on April 19, 1775.

    b. The Declaration of Independence was written on July 4, 1776.

    c. George Washington trapped the British army in Yorktown in 1781.

    d. The states sent representatives to a meeting in Philadelphia in 1787.

14. Look at the picture. Who is this?

    a. George Washington, the first president

    b. Thomas Jefferson, the third president

    c. Valentin Haüy, founder of a school for the blind

    d. None of the above

15. Which statement is **not** true about Thomas Jefferson?

    a. He was an architect and designed buildings.

    b. He helped make the U.S. money system.

    c. He wrote all of the U.S. Constitution.

    d. He wrote the Declaration of Independence.

16. Which document was a plan for government that united the states under one government?

    a. The Treaty of Paris

    b. The Intolerable Acts

    c. The Declaration of Independence

    d. The U.S. Constitution

Reading Strategies

Choose the best answer. Circle the letter.

17. What do you do when you **use what you know**?

    a. After you read, tell yourself what the text means.

    b. Think about what you already know about a topic.

    c. Look for key words to help you answer a question or write about a topic.

    d. All of the above.

18. What do you do when you **look for cause and effect**?

    a. Look for why something happens.

    b. Look for what made an event happen.

    c. Look for what happens because of an event.

    d. All of the above.

Using Visuals

Look at the chart below. Choose the best answer. Circle the letter.

The Thirteen Original Colonies		
Colony Name	**Year Founded**	**Year It Became a Royal Colony**
Virginia	1607	1624
Massachusetts	1620	1691
New York	1624	1685
New Hampshire	1629	1679
Maryland	1632	*
Rhode Island	1636	*
Delaware	1638	*
Connecticut	1639	*
North Carolina	1653	1729
New Jersey	1664	1702
South Carolina	1670	1719
Pennsylvania	1681	*
Georgia	1733	1752

* privately owned

19. How long after it was founded did Virginia become a royal colony?

    a. 10 years

    b. 17 years

    c. 24 years

    d. 56 years

20. How long after it was founded did Massachusetts become a royal colony?

    a. 11 years

    b. 21 years

    c. 71 years

    d. 91 years

21. What was the last colony to become a royal colony?

    a. Georgia

    b. Pennsylvania

    c. New Hampshire

    d. New York

Writing

Write a paragraph about the War for Independence. Write about how it started and ended, and what happened in North America after the war. Make sure your paragraph has a beginning, a middle, and an end.

Unit 6: Lesson 1 Test

Key Words

Choose the best answer. Circle the letter.

1. In the early 1800s, Lewis and Clark explored the West and met many Native American _____.

    a. wagon trains

    b. immigrants

    c. pioneers

    d. tribes

2. In the 1840s, pioneers traveled west on the Oregon Trail _____.

    a. on buffalo

    b. in wagon trains

    c. on transcontinental railroads

    d. on the Underground Railroad

3. After gold was discovered in 1848, more people moved west during a time called the _____.

    a. pioneer rush

    b. wagon rush

    c. cattle rush

    d. gold rush

4. In the 1860s, two transcontinental railroads were built by Irish and Chinese _____.

    a. tribes

    b. translators

    c. immigrants

    d. abolitionists

Using Visuals

Look at the circle graph. What percent of colonists did English and Africans make up? Circle the letter of the answer.

5. **a.** 48.7%

    b. 20%

    c. 68.7%

    d. 31.3%

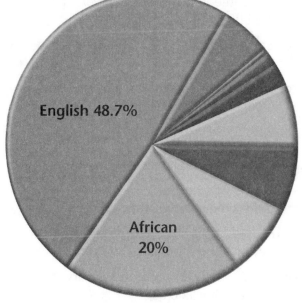

Colonial Population, 1775: English and African

English 48.7%

African 20%

Name _____ Date _____

Choose the best answer. Circle the letter.

6. Why were the ten amendments to the U.S. Constitution called the Bill of Rights?

   a. They were added right after the Constitution was written.

   b. They helped the government pay its bills and established a bank.

   c. They were bills that people had to pay if they were accused of a crime.

   d. They were rights that no one could take away, such as freedom of religion and speech.

7. Who helped Lewis and Clark as they explored the territory west of the Mississippi River?

   a. A large tribe of nomadic translators

   b. A Shoshone woman named Sacagawea

   c. A young Shoshone-French boy named Jean Baptiste

   d. The young riders of the Pony Express

8. What is a reason many buffalo died in the West?

   a. The cattle in the west took over land that the buffalo used for food.

   b. Smog from factories in the North killed them.

   c. They died of smallpox and other diseases brought by European cattle.

   d. Both a and b.

9. Who were the abolitionists?

   a. People who helped build the transcontinental railways

   b. People who did not want to change their way of life in the South

   c. People who wanted to end slavery because it was cruel

   d. People who started the first factories in the North

10. How had the nation become more divided by the 1860s?

   a. There were free states in the North.

   b. There were slave states in the South.

   c. It was divided into eastern and western states.

   d. Both a and b.

11. Look at the picture below. Which statement is **not** true about Harriet Tubman?

   a. She was born a slave.

   b. She was a spy for the plantation owners.

   c. She escaped to freedom on the Underground Railroad.

   d. She helped 300 slaves run away to freedom.

Writing

Write a paragraph in your notebook about the exploration and settling of the West. Make sure your paragraph has a beginning, a middle, and an end.

Unit 6: Lesson 2 Test

Key Words

Choose the best answer. Circle the letter.

1. In the early 1860s, the southern states wanted to create their own country south of the _____.

   a. railroads

   b. Confederacy

   c. Mason-Dixon Line

   d. Underground Railroad

2. The Civil War began at Fort Sumter in 1861 with a terrible _____.

   a. battle

   b. fort

   c. assassination

   d. segregation

3. In 1865 the Civil War ended with the surrender of General Lee, the commander of the army of the _____.

   a. fort

   b. Union

   c. Confederacy

   d. Mason-Dixon Line

4. During the Reconstruction of 1865–1877, the government worked to help the southern states rejoin the _____.

   a. Mason-Dixon Line

   b. Union

   c. Gettysburg

   d. Confederacy

Using Visuals

Look at the bar graph. About how many bales of cotton were grown in the United States in 1850? Circle the letter of the best answer.

5. a. 2,000

   b. 20,000

   c. 200,000

   d. 2,000,000

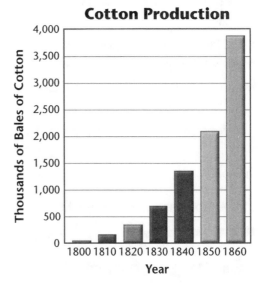

Cotton Production

Content

Choose the best answer. Circle the letter.

6. What happened five days after the end of the Civil War?

　a. President Lincoln gave a speech called the Gettysburg Address.

　b. John Wilkes Booth assassinated President Lincoln at Ford's Theater.

　c. Congress passed the Voting Rights Act.

　d. Alexander Graham Bell invented the first telephone.

7. Why did the U.S. Congress pass the Fourteenth and Fifteenth Amendments?

　a. Congress wanted the southern states to feel better about the war.

　b. Congress did not want African Americans to have too many rights.

　c. Congress wanted African Americans to be able to work and vote.

　d. None of the above.

8. Look at the picture. What did Chief Joseph say the Nez Percé promised Lewis and Clark?

　a. The Nez Percé agreed to give Lewis and Clark all their land.

　b. They agreed to let Lewis and Clark pass through their country.

　c. They agreed never to make war on white men.

　d. Both b and c.

9. Why did the Sioux and Cheyenne fight General Custer and his men at Little Big Horn?

　a. They wanted to keep their land.

　b. They didn't want to move to a reservation.

　c. The U.S. government wanted to take their territory.

　d. All of the above.

10. When were the telephone, camera, and lightbulb invented?

　a. During the Railroad Age

　b. During the Industrial Age

　c. During the Reconstruction

　d. During the Civil Rights Movement

11. How were conditions for workers at this time?

　a. Good. Railroads became safer and faster.

　b. Bad. Many people moved to small towns or farms.

　c. Very bad. Many people got sick and died.

　d. Very good. Many people made fortunes.

Writing

Write a paragraph in your notebook about the Civil War. Include reasons for the war and dates of key events. Make sure your paragraph has a beginning, a middle, and an end.

Unit 6: Unit Test

Key Words

Choose the best answer. Circle the letter.

1. The Lewis and Clark expedition helped lead to the settling of the West by _____.

   a. pioneers

   b. tribes

   c. industrialists

   d. abolitionists

2. The U.S. government wanted more territory, so it created reservations for Native American _____.

   a. forts

   b. tribes

   c. immigrants

   d. wagon trains

3. Look at the picture below of Little Big Horn. General Custer and his men were killed by the Sioux and Cheyenne during this _____.

   a. gold rush

   b. fort

   c. battle

   d. discovery

4. Some people, such as John D. Rockefeller, made a fortune in the oil _____.

   a. battle

   b. forts

   c. Union

   d. industry

5. Many slaves tried to escape to free states in the North on the Underground _____.

   a. Union

   b. Confederacy

   c. Railroad

   d. Mason-Dixon Line

6. The Civil War started when the southern states seceded and became the _____.

   a. Confederacy

   b. Union

   c. Mason-Dixon Line

   d. Reconstruction

Content

Choose the best answer. Circle the letter.

7. Which was **not** a reason that settlers moved west in the 1800s?

    a. Gold was discovered near San Francisco in 1848.

    b. Most of the factories were built in the West.

    c. The government funded two transcontinental railways in the 1860s.

    d. The West was a good place to raise cattle.

8. Who was Sacagawea?

    a. She was George Washington's wife.

    b. She was a translator and guide who helped Louis and Clark explore the West.

    c. She was an African-American woman who helped many slaves escape.

    d. She was a woman who worked to help the poor in New York.

9. How did life change for the Native Americans after 1860?

    a. They couldn't travel freely anymore.

    b. Many were killed trying to fight the U.S. government.

    c. They lost most of the buffalos they used for food.

    d. All of the above.

10. Look at the picture. What was **not** a reason for the decline of the buffalo?

    a. Farmers and ranchers fenced in the land and shot the buffalo.

    b. Native Americans hunted them for food and to make clothes from their skins.

    c. The U.S. government put the buffalo on a reservation.

    d. Cattle ate the grass that the buffalo needed.

11. What did the abolitionist Frederick Douglass do?

    a. He supported the Confederacy.

    b. He made a fortune in the Industrial Age.

    c. He fought at the Battle of Wounded Knee.

    d. He published an antislavery newspaper.

12. Where and when did the Civil War start?

    a. It started with a battle in Washington in November, 1860.

    b. It started with a battle at Fort Sumter in April, 1861.

    c. It started with a battle at Gettysburg in July, 1863.

    d. It started with a battle at Wounded Knee in December, 1890.

13. What event ended the Civil War?

    a. In April 1862, the Union commander-in-chief General Grant surrendered.

    b. In April 1865, the Confederate commander-in-chief General Lee surrendered.

    c. In April 1865, President Lincoln was assassinated at Ford's Theater.

    d. In April 1877, Reconstruction of the South ended.

14. Who was John Wilkes Booth?

    a. He assassinated President Lincoln.

    b. He was the commander-in-chief of the Union army.

    c. He was a general who fought the Native Americans.

    d. He was the chief of the Nez Percé tribe.

15. Look at the picture below. Why was the period after the Civil War called the Reconstruction?

    a. The government wanted to reconstruct, or rebuild, the United States.

    b. The government wanted to reconstruct slavery.

    c. The government wanted to reconstruct reservations for Native Americans.

    d. All of the above.

16. What happened during the Industrial Age?

    a. Some people became very rich.

    b. Many people moved to the cities to work.

    c. The telephone and lightbulb were invented.

    d. All of the above.

Reading Strategies

Choose the best answer. Circle the letter.

17. What do you do when you **compare and contrast**?

    a. Think about how two things are the same and different.

    b. Use a timeline to see when events happened.

    c. Draw a bar graph.

    d. All of the above.

18. What do you do when you **draw conclusions**?

    a. Draw a Venn diagram.

    b. Put together clues, use what you know, and figure something out.

    c. Close your eyes and imagine a picture.

    d. All of the above.

Name _____   Date _____

Look at the bar graph. Choose the best answer. Circle the letter.

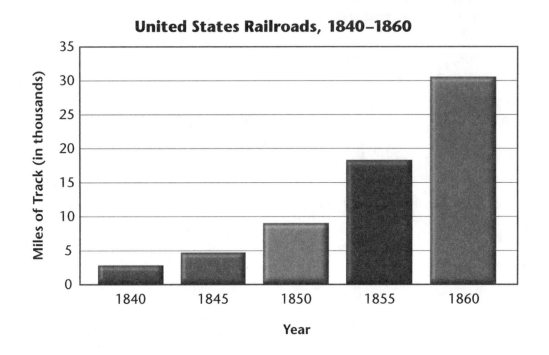

United States Railroads, 1840–1860

19. About how many miles of railroad track were there in 1840?

    a. About 2.5 miles of track

    b. About 250 miles of track

    c. About 2,500 miles of track

    d. About 25,000 miles of track

20. About how many **more** miles of track were there twenty years later?

    a. About 2,750 more miles

    b. About 3,000 more miles

    c. About 27,500 more miles

    d. About 30,000 more miles

21. When did the amount of track grow the fastest?

    a. Between 1840 and 1845

    b. Between 1845 and 1850

    c. Between 1850 and 1855

    d. Between 1855 and 1860

Writing

Write a paragraph in your notebook about the exploration and settling of the West and the decline of the Native Americans' way of life in the 1800s. Include your opinion. Make sure your paragraph has a beginning, a middle, and an end.

Name _____ Date _____

Unit 7: Lesson 1 Test

Key Words

Choose the best answer. Circle the letter.

1. World War I began in Europe in 1914 after _____.

   a. a submarine attack

   b. an assassination

   c. the Holocaust

   d. the Treaty of Versailles

2. In 1929 the fall of the stock market led to the Great Depression and _____.

   a. the Holocaust

   b. the suffrage movement

   c. high unemployment

   d. the invention of the submarine

3. Under dictator Adolf Hitler, the Nazis killed 12 million people during the _____.

   a. Holocaust

   b. assassination

   c. unemployment

   d. atomic bomb attacks

4. World War II ended in 1945 when Hiroshima and Nagasaki were destroyed by _____.

   a. submarines

   b. unemployment

   c. atomic bombs

   d. the Holocaust

Using Visuals

Look at the picture. Which print resource is this boy using? Circle the letter of the answer.

5. a. An atlas

   b. A periodical

   c. A dictionary

   d. An encyclopedia

Content

Choose the best answer. Circle the letter.

6. Look at the picture. Who is Emmeline Pankhurst?

    a. A leader of the women's suffrage movement

    b. A nurse during World War I

    c. A leader of the fight against women voting

    d. Both a and c

7. Who did the Allies (Britain, France, Russia, the United States, and others) fight in World War I?

    a. The Central Powers (Germany, Austria-Hungary, and Turkey)

    b. The Central Powers (Germany and Norway)

    c. The Central Powers (Germany, Greece, and Italy)

    d. The League of Nations

8. How did World War I end?

    a. After more than 8 million soldiers were killed

    b. In November 1918, when Germany agreed to stop fighting

    c. With the peace treaty called the Treaty of Versailles

    d. All of the above

9. Which statement is **not** true about Franklin D. Roosevelt?

    a. He declared war on Germany in 1917.

    b. He was president of the United States during the Great Depression.

    c. He created a set of programs called the New Deal to help with unemployment.

    d. He was president of the United States when World War II started in Germany.

10. When did the United States join the Allies to fight the Axis Powers in World War II?

    a. When Germany invaded Poland in 1939

    b. When Italy and Japan joined Germany in 1940

    c. When Japan bombed Pearl Harbor in Hawaii in 1941

    d. When Great Britain and France declared war on Germany in 1939

11. What organizations were formed to prevent future wars after World Wars I and II?

    a. The League of Nations, then the Manhattan Project

    b. The League of Nations, then the United Nations

    c. The Manhattan Project, then the United Nations

    d. The United Nations, then the League of Nations

Writing

Write a paragraph in your notebook about the major events in the world after World War I. Include information about the Great Depression and World War II. Make sure your paragraph has a beginning, a middle, and an end.

Name _____ Date _____

Unit 7: Lesson 2 Test

Key Words

Choose the best answer. Circle the letter.

1. The Cold War was about the spread of democracy and _____.

   a. global economies

   b. torture

   c. terrorism

   d. communism

2. China is a large country of 1.3 billion with a strong and growing _____.

   a. democracy

   b. terrorism

   c. economy

   d. genocide

3. In the Persian Gulf, oil is the most important _____.

   a. genocide

   b. resource

   c. terrorism

   d. economy

4. Look at the picture. Today, a major global threat is the spread of _____.

   a. terrorism

   b. resources

   c. democracy

   d. apartheid

Using Visuals

Which resource is **not** a technology resource? Circle the letter of the best answer.

5. a. CD-ROMs

   b. The Internet

   c. Computerized catalogs

   d. Encyclopedias

Name _____ Date _____

Content

Choose the best answer. Circle the letter.

6. After World War II, what did the Soviet Union create to divide it from the West?

   a. The Iron Curtain

   b. The Berlin Wall

   c. The Great Wall of China

   d. Both a and b

7. Who did the United States fight in Asia in the 1960s and 1970s?

   a. Vietnamese communists

   b. Soviet communists

   c. Rwandans who were causing genocide

   d. Chilean torturers

8. Look at the picture below. What did Martin Luther King Jr. do?

   a. He fought for civil rights for African Americans.

   b. He led a boycott against segregated buses.

   c. He won the Nobel Peace Prize in 1964.

   d. All of the above.

9. What happened in the Soviet Union in 1991?

   a. A military leader assassinated President Gorbachev.

   b. Many protesters who wanted democracy were killed.

   c. Communism ended and the Berlin Wall was torn down.

   d. All of the above.

10. What happened in the ten years after military leader Pinochet took power in Chile?

   a. Chile fought wars with Brazil and Guatemala.

   b. At least 3,000 people were murdered and over 100,000 were tortured in Chile.

   c. Pinochet fought against apartheid in Chile.

   d. Pinochet fought against genocide in Chile.

11. What did Iraq do to try to dominate the Middle East?

   a. It invaded Iran in 1980 and Kuwait in 1990.

   b. It became a leader in manufacturing automobiles and electronics.

   c. It helped with attacks in New York and Washington on September 11, 2001.

   d. All of the above.

Writing

Write a paragraph in your notebook about the beginning and end of the Cold War. Include reasons for the war and key events. Make sure your paragraph has a beginning, a middle, and an end.

Unit 7: Unit Test

Key Words

Choose the best answer. Circle the letter.

1. During the Great Depression, the United States had high unemployment and a depressed _____.

   a. resources

   b. economy

   c. democracy

   d. dictator

2. Look at the picture below. It shows people in a concentration camp during _____.

   a. the Cold War

   b. World War I

   c. the Vietnam War

   d. the Holocaust

3. At the end of World War II, Japan surrendered when the United States used _____.

   a. coalitions

   b. resources

   c. atomic bombs

   d. submarines

4. After independence, many African countries were ruled by military _____

   a. dictators

   b. terrorists

   c. genocides

   d. demonstrations

5. The United States fought the Korean and Vietnam wars to stop the spread of _____.

   a. unemployment

   b. democracy

   c. terrorism

   d. communism

6. In 1968 in Tennessee, the civil rights leader Martin Luther King Jr. was _____.

   a. assassinated

   b. hijacked

   c. tortured

   d. rounded up

Content

Choose the best answer. Circle the letter.

7. What helped women get the right to vote in the early 1900s?

    a. The women's suffrage movement

    b. Protests where women demanded the right to vote

    c. Great leaders like Susan B. Anthony and Emmeline Pankhurst

    d. All of the above

8. What started World War I in Europe?

    a. An archduke and his wife were assassinated in 1914.

    b. Germany attacked U.S. ships in 1917.

    c. The Allies signed the Treaty of Versailles in 1919.

    d. The Great Depression began in 1929.

9. Which side did the United States join in World War I?

    a. The Central Powers, including Germany and the Austro-Hungarian Empire

    b. The Allies, including Britain, France, and Russia

    c. The Axis Powers, including Germany, Italy, and Japan

    d. Both a and b

10. What event started World War II in Europe?

    a. Germany attacked U.S. submarines in 1929.

    b. Germany invaded Poland in 1939.

    c. Japan bombed Pearl Harbor in 1941.

    d. The Nazis bombed Pearl Harbor in 1941.

11. Look at the picture above. When did World War II end?

    a. In 1941, soon after the United States joined the war

    b. In 1945, when the Germans surrendered

    c. In 1945, soon after the United States bombed Hiroshima and Nagasaki

    d. In 1961, when the British dropped an atomic bomb

12. What was the Iron Curtain?

    a. It was a crisis between Cuba, the Soviet Union, and the United States.

    b. It was a tunnel under the Berlin Wall in Germany.

    c. It was an invisible line that divided the Soviet Union from the West.

    d. It was a top-secret project to create an atomic bomb.

13. What happened when the Berlin Wall was torn down in 1991?

   a. Communism ended in the Soviet Union.

   b. The Cold War was over.

   c. The Soviet Union divided into many countries.

   d. All of the above.

14. Look at the picture above. What happened in Tiananmen Square in 1989?

   a. Protesters who wanted democracy were killed.

   b. Communism ended in China.

   c. Protesters won the right to vote.

   d. Bill Clinton visited China.

15. Why did Saddam Hussein invade Iran and Kuwait?

   a. He wanted to improve relations with them.

   b. He wanted Iraq to dominate the region.

   c. He wanted to stop the spread of democracy.

   d. All of the above.

16. What is a major global threat in the modern world?

   a. The spread of communism

   b. The spread of acts of terrorism

   c. The power of military dictators

   d. The spread of the apartheid system

Reading Strategies

Choose the best answer. Circle the letter.

17. What do you do when you **summarize** information?

   a. Say how two things are the same and different.

   b. Ask yourself questions as you read the information.

   c. Say or write it in a shorter form.

   d. All of the above.

18. What do you do when you **understand fact** and **opinion**?

   a. Ask yourself which statements are facts and can be proved.

   b. Ask yourself which statements are opinions and can't be proved.

   c. Look for words such as *believe, think,* and *feel* to find opinions.

   d. All of the above.

Using Visuals

Look at the pictures of print and technology resources. Choose the best answer.
Circle the letter.

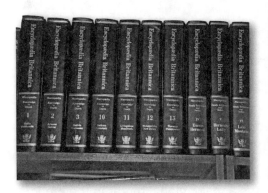

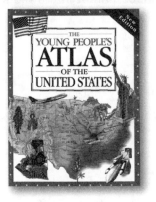

19. Where would you look to find the latest news?

    a. On the Internet

    b. In a periodical

    c. In an encyclopedia

    d. Both a and b

20. Where would you look to find a map of Europe?

    a. In an atlas

    b. In a periodical

    c. In a dictionary

    d. All of the above

21. Where would you look to find out the meaning of the word *apartheid*?

    a. In a periodical

    b. In an atlas

    c. On a CD-ROM

    d. In a dictionary

Writing

Write a paragraph in your notebook about a country you know well. Write about its recent history, its current situation, and what you think its future will be like. Include facts and opinions. Make sure your paragraph has a beginning, a middle, and an end.

Tests Answer Key

Getting Started: Introduction Test

1. c	11. d
2. a	12. b
3. d	13. c
4. c	14. d
5. b	15. a
6. c	16. b
7. a	17. d
8. d	18. a
9. c	19. d
10. b	20. c

Unit 1: Lesson 1 Test

1. c	7. a
2. b	8. c
3. a	9. d
4. c	10. b
5. c	11. b
6. d	

Writing
See Scoring the Writing Sections on page 218.

Unit 1: Lesson 2 Test

1. d	7. c
2. b	8. a
3. a	9. b
4. c	10. d
5. c	11. c
6. d	

Writing
See Scoring the Writing Sections on page 218.

Unit 1: Unit Test

1. c	12. B
2. d	13. D
3. b	14. d
4. c	15. C
5. a	16. A
6. b	17. D
7. d	18. c
8. c	19. a
9. c	20. b
10. b	21. d
11. d	

Writing
See Scoring the Writing Sections on page 218.

Unit 2: Lesson 1 Test

1. d	7. C
2. b	8. A
3. c	9. a
4. b	10. b
5. b	11. c
6. b	

Writing
See Scoring the Writing Sections on page 218.

Unit 2: Lesson 2 Test

1. c	7. c
2. d	8. b
3. a	9. b
4. b	10. c
5. c	11. d
6. a	

Writing
See Scoring the Writing Sections on page 218.

Unit 2: Unit Test

1. b	12. a
2. b	13. c
3. d	14. b
4. d	15. d
5. c	16. c
6. a	17. a
7. d	18. d
8. b	19. c
9. b	20. b
10. a	21. c
11. d	

Writing
See Scoring the Writing Sections on page 218.

Unit 3: Lesson 1 Test

1. a	7. b
2. d	8. b
3. c	9. d
4. c	10. d
5. b	11. a
6. c	

Writing
See Scoring the Writing Sections on page 218.

Unit 3: Lesson 2 Test

1. b	7. b
2. d	8. c
3. a	9. a
4. c	10. d
5. c	11. a
6. c	

Writing
See Scoring the Writing Sections on page 218.

Unit 3: Unit Test

1. a	12. d
2. c	13. c
3. b	14. a
4. d	15. b
5. b	16. a
6. c	17. d
7. c	18. d
8. a	19. b
9. c	20. a
10. a	21. c
11. b	

Writing
See Scoring the Writing Sections on page 218.

Unit 4: Lesson 1 Test

1. b	7. a
2. c	8. a
3. d	9. c
4. b	10. b
5. d	11. d
6. c	

Writing
See Scoring the Writing Sections on page 218.

Unit 4: Lesson 2 Test

1. c	7. a
2. a	8. b
3. c	9. c
4. b	10. d
5. b	11. c
6. d	

Writing
See Scoring the Writing Sections on page 218.

Unit 4: Unit Test

1. d	12. d
2. c	13. c
3. a	14. a
4. b	15. b
5. c	16. d
6. a	17. b
7. c	18. c
8. d	19. a
9. d	20. d
10. a	21. c
11. c	

Writing

See Scoring the Writing Sections on page 218.

Unit 5: Lesson 1 Test

1. a	7. a
2. d	8. b
3. c	9. a
4. b	10. d
5. c	11. d
6. c	

Writing

See Scoring the Writing Sections on page 218.

Unit 5: Lesson 2 Test

1. a	7. d
2. a	8. c
3. c	9. b
4. b	10. d
5. d	11. a
6. c	

Writing

See Scoring the Writing Sections on page 218.

Unit 5: Unit Test

1. c	12. d
2. d	13. c
3. b	14. a
4. a	15. c
5. b	16. d
6. c	17. b
7. b	18. d
8. d	19. b
9. c	20. c
10. a	21. a
11. a	

Writing

See Scoring the Writing Sections on page 218.

Unit 6: Lesson 1 Test

1. d	7. b
2. b	8. a
3. d	9. c
4. c	10. d
5. c	11. b
6. d	

Writing

See Scoring the Writing Sections on page 218.

Unit 6: Lesson 2 Test

1. c	7. c
2. a	8. d
3. c	9. d
4. b	10. b
5. d	11. c
6. b	

Writing

See Scoring the Writing Sections on page 218.

Unit 6: Unit Test

1. a	12. b
2. b	13. b
3. c	14. a
4. d	15. a
5. c	16. d
6. a	17. a
7. b	18. b
8. b	19. c
9. d	20. c
10. c	21. d
11. d	

Writing

See Scoring the Writing Sections on page 218.

Unit 7: Lesson 1 Test

1. b	7. a
2. c	8. d
3. a	9. a
4. c	10. c
5. b	11. b
6. a	

Writing

See Scoring the Writing Sections on page 218.

Unit 7: Lesson 2 Test

1. d	7. a
2. c	8. d
3. b	9. c
4. a	10. b
5. d	11. a
6. d	

Writing

See Scoring the Writing Sections on page 218.

Unit 7: Unit Test

1. b	12. c
2. d	13. d
3. c	14. a
4. a	15. b
5. d	16. b
6. a	17. c
7. d	18. d
8. a	19. d
9. b	20. a
10. b	21. d
11. c	

Writing

See Scoring the Writing Sections on page 218.